FREEDOM UNDER FIRE

Freedom Under Fire

U.S. Civil Liberties in Times of War

by

Michael Linfield

South End Press   Boston, MA

Cover by Jane Carey
Back cover photo of Michael Linfield by Tess Steinkolk
Typesetting, design and layout by the South End Press collective
Printed on acid-free recycled paper

Library of Congress Cataloging-in-Publication Data
Linfield, Michael.
    Freedom under fire : U.S. civil liberties in times of war / by Michael Linfield
        p. cm.
    Includes bibliographical references.
    ISBN 0-89608-375-6 : $40.00. -- ISBN 0-89608-374-8 (pbk.) : $14.00
    1. Civil rights--United States--History. 2. War and emergency legislation--United States--History. 3. War and emergency powers--United States--History. 4. Freedom of the press--United States--History. I. Title.
    KF4749.L56 1990
    342.73'085--dc20   90-9411
    [347.30285]   CIP

ISBN 0-89608-374-8 paper
ISBN 0-89608-375-6 cloth

South End Press, 116 Saint Botolph Street, Boston, MA 02115
9 8 7 6 5 4 3 2 1   90 91 92 93 94 95 96 97 98 99

Dedication

To my parents —

who, by their example,
have taught me to fight for justice.

Acknowledgements

I wish to thank the following people:

At Harvard Law School: Professors Abram Chayes and Anthony Lewis for their advice and critique of the manuscript, and Professor Henry Steiner and Jack Tobin of the Harvard Law School Human Rights Program who provided support, encouragement and funding for my investigations in Nicaragua;

In Washington, D.C.: Judith Appelbaum of Reichler, Appelbaum & Wippman who helped arrange for my internship with the Chief Justice of the Nicaraguan Supreme Court;

In Nicaragua: Dr. Alejandro Serrano Caldera, Chief Justice of the Supreme Court of Nicaragua; Fernando Perez Peña, who gave up a law practice in the United States to volunteer his services in Nicaragua; and journalist Mark Cook, whose article "Human Rights in Times of War" gave me the original idea for this book;

In New York: Tess Steinkolk;

In Los Angeles: Millie Loeb and Miriam Ludwig for their encouragement, love and editorial advice; and the lawyers and staff at Alschuler, Grossman & Pines for allowing me the time to complete this manuscript;

In Boston: Todd Jailer and the entire staff at South End Press.

Table of Contents

About the Author

Michael Linfield graduated *magna cum laude* from Harvard Law School in 1989. While at Harvard, he received a Ferguson Fellowship to study human rights in Nicaragua. He made two trips to Nicaragua in 1987 and 1988, serving as the intern to the Chief Justice of the Nicaraguan Supreme Court during the summer of 1987. Both trips were funded by the Harvard Law School Human Rights Program.

Prior to entering Harvard, Michael Linfield was elected to the Los Angeles County and California State Democratic Central Committees. He served as chief lobbyist for the United Farm Workers Union, West Coast Director of the J.P. Stevens Boycott, liaison to the Governor of California on pension investment issues, Deputy to the Mayor of West Hollywood, and Vice-President of the American Civil Liberties Union of Southern California. Michael Linfield is currently associated with the law firm of Alschuler, Grossman & Pines in Los Angeles.

War-Time Violations of Civil Liberties in the United States

	Revolutionary War Era	Civil War Era	World War I Era	World War II and Korean War Era	Vietnam War Era
Fundamental Human Rights	Blacks enslaved. Genocide of Indians.	Blacks enslaved. Genocide of Indians.	No government policy of murder, torture, or disappearances. Governmental toleration of, and complicity in, attacks upon minorities.	No government policy of murder, torture, or disappearances. Governmental toleration of, and complicity in, attacks upon minorities.	Evidence of government participation in murder of minority activists. Governmental toleration of, and complicity in, attacks upon minorities.
Press Censorship	Publication of Royalist materials prohibited. Major opposition editors arrested and their papers closed.	Papers closed, presses confiscated and editors jailed for printing anti-Union articles.	Federal censorship board established. All war news censored. Subversive papers banned from mails. Pre-approval of foreign language papers required.	Voluntary press code for war news and economic information. Political censorship. All reporting from Korea cleared by military censors.	Anti-war press infiltrated, harassed and bombed; editors and vendors jailed. Prior restraint imposed on one writer. Sporadic attempts to censor establishment press.

	Revolutionary War	Civil War	World War I	World War II	Vietnam War
Censorship of Other Media		All wireless communications censored.	Telegraphs seized and censored. Movies showing unpatriotic subjects censored.	Voluntary wartime radio code including censorship of war news. Political propaganda excluded from mails during Korean War.	Occasional attempts to pressure establishment media to present the administration line.
Freedom of Speech	People arrested for speech criticizing administration.	Illegal to speak against the war effort or conscription. Former U.S. Congressman banished.	Public meetings banned. Arrests for statements critical of war. State laws prohibited public speech by radicals.	Hundreds of state laws prohibiting speech by subversives.	Conspiracy trials of anti-War leaders. 40 Prisoners of Conscience, longest jailed for 12 years.
Seditious Libel	Two dozen people arrested under Sedition Act, serving terms of up to 18 months.		2,000 arrests under Sedition Act; 900 sentenced to up to 20 years; thousands convicted under state sedition, red flag and criminal syndicalism laws.	150 Smith Act prosecutions, 90% convicted. Mail and travel restricted by McCarran Act. Communist Party outlawed. Other sedition prosecutions.	

	Revolutionary War	Civil War	World War I	World War II	Vietnam War
Suspension of Habeas Corpus		*Habeas corpus* unconstitutionally suspended by Lincoln, ignoring ruling of Chief Justice. Confederate leaders jailed for two years after war without charges.	2,700 arrested during Palmer raids denied *habeas corpus*. Aliens summarily deported.	*Habeas corpus* suspended in Hawaii after Pearl Harbor. 120,000 Japanese-Americans interned in concentration camps. Aleuts interned.	McCarran Act allowed for mass internment of U.S. citizens during times of emergency. Post-war plans to suspend *habeas corpus* and impose military government.
Special Tribunals and Military Tribunals	Local Committees for Safety tried suspected Loyalists.	10-30,000 civilians tried by military tribunals during War. Eight people charged with assassination of Lincoln tried by military tribunal. Two years after end of war, state legislatures dissolved and replaced by military authorities.	State and local citizens committees established numerous "slacker" courts to try those whose support for war was suspect.	Military tribunals used to try civilians in Hawaii. Suspected Nazi infiltrators tried and executed by military tribunal. Hundreds tried before House Un-American Activities Committee.	

	Revolutionary War	Civil War	World War I	World War II	Vietnam War
Freedom to Travel	Restrictions on travel into war zone. Relocation, exile and banishment of Loyalists.	Passports instituted during war. Two people exiled from Union.	Aliens prohibited from entering the country on ideological grounds. Several thousand aliens deported.	Curfew and travel restrictions. Thousands of aliens deported. Passports denied to U.S. citizens for ideological reasons. Aliens denied visas on ideological grounds.	Aliens denied visas on ideological grounds. Five countries off-limits to travel by U.S. citizens. One citizen currently being denied passport.
Domestic spying and treatment of internal opposition	Harassment of Loyalists by citizen groups including economic boycotts, tar-and-feathering, and physical violence.	Thousands killed in anti-draft riots.	Pacifists and socialists arrested. Elected socialists denied seats in Legislature.	Citizen committees to counteract subversion. FBI kept files on subversives, including elected officials and political parties.	CIA mail-opening program. 500,000 secret investigations by FBI's COINTELPRO. Killings of minority leaders. Mass arrests of anti-war protesters.

	Revolutionary War	Civil War	World War I	World War II	Vietnam War
Loyalty Oaths	Loyalty oaths instituted by most colonies. Teachers, others required to swear loyalty to revolution.		Loyalty oaths instituted by states and various localities and enforced by officials and private vigilante groups.	FBI investigation of potential subversives. Loyalty oaths required of Japanese-Americans. 20 million screened in Federal loyalty program. State loyalty oaths for teachers, public employees, etc.	
Confiscation of Property	Loyalist property confiscated. Land given to Revolutionary soldiers or sold to raise money for Continental Army. Debts owed to Loyalists cancelled.	Property of Confederates, including slaves, confiscated. Telegraphs confiscated.	$500 million in enemy property confiscated. Eleven industrial plants owned by U.S. citizens seized to aid war effort.	Japanese-Americans interned and property seized. 47 factories seized to prevent labor disputes from affecting war effort; 3 plants seized due to inefficient management. 12 plants seized after war ended.	

Notes on War and Freedom

You are about to enter the underside of the American story of freedom. Abandon all hope that you will ever again blindly accept the contention that the United States has staked its future on faith in freedom and not on power. Add to this tragic tale our consistent mistreatment of the native population, slaves, religious, racial and ethnic minorities, plus the ever-present poor and you must brace against despair that America wants to be free.

This appalling history, which painstakingly documents two centuries of war-justified violations of the principles of the Bill of Rights, cries out for explanation. Throughout our history, government and the mob have crushed freedom of speech, assembly, press, association and non-violent resistance when used in opposition to militarism. Michael Linfield's stunning compilation of these systematic assaults on the exercise of constitutionally protected rights to oppose war is undeniable as historical truth.

The mythology of freedom that the United States has designated as our fictive history agreed upon cannot withstand this revelation. With the heavy rhythm and subtlety of a pile driver, Linfield hammers home fact after devastating fact, forging links that present the truth that these United States have used war and the threat of war to stifle freedom while at the same time proclaiming freedom to be our national purpose. Often, the cry of freedom has been a cover for the use of force. The fiction that U.S. foreign policy has been based on the protection and expansion of freedom depends on our believing what has been said and ignoring what has been done.

As this comprehensive account of repression in defense of war reveals, violations of freedom are often greatest in periods between active wars. Philosophers have observed for millennia that such times are not properly called peace, whenever, as Hobbes wrote, there is the "human disposition" to war. We see the United States has always been disposed to war.

Linfield has done a masterful job of identifying the major forms of governmental restraints on freedom, systematically presenting the violations during each epoch and summarizing them in charts. The suppression practiced has created a web over all social conduct that inhibits the development of any significant restraint on government's continued use of organized violence as a means of dominion.

He has generously employed and credited the efforts of the giants on whose shoulders he stands in the prodigious historical research required to produce this work. More than 1,140 footnotes and ten pages of bibliography attest to the intensity of his desire to document the story he tells and respect the pioneers who have preceded him in presenting this commonly ignored part of American history.

A result in addition to the power of the narration is a reference work that will serve beyond the ordinary reader's inquiry for identifying the best known transgressions of liberty in the pursuit of war in the land of the free. While historians can add instances of substantial suppression and lawyers can find additional ways the government has crushed opposition to its aggression, as a combined presentation of the nature of rights violated and the factual report of the violations, this work will remain an invaluable account of the erosion of freedom when under fire during the first two centuries of the Bill of Rights.

The inclusion in this volume of a brief analysis of a similar struggle between force and freedom during the first decade of the Sandinista government of Nicaragua may seem a *non sequitur*. If so, it is a helpful one. Nicaragua has directly suffered U.S force in the name of freedom for more than a century and a half, from before the tragic reign of William Walker, whose rule restored slavery and made English (which no one spoke) the official language before our Civil War, through the latest threats and economic sanctions of the Bush administration.

Linfield's discussion of Nicaragua is based on a unique and rich personal experience in Nicaragua which both fertilized his appreciation of the history he records and provided a basis for comparative study that he shares with his readers. We see the U.S. government—which has brutalized the people of Nicaragua for generations—condemn Nicaraguan efforts to establish guidelines for constitutional government, civil liberty and social justice while it supports a violent surrogate militarism in El Salvador that murders Archbishops and Jesuit priests because they love and minister to the poor.

The reader ought to wonder about the broader meanings, the general truths and guiding principles suggested by the objective facts laid bare in this book. Some seem inescapable.

War is more destructive of freedom than any other human activity. Any violation of civil liberties is easily justified in times of war and the threat of war, however unnecessary for security, harmful to its victims, irrational, unfair, or even detrimental to the war effort itself.

The unity of purpose war requires is intolerant of any dissent or failure to subordinate individual conscience and desire to military command. Absolute obedience to authority is the first rule of war.

Dehumanization and hatred of enemies are essential to create a human capacity for the horrors of war and the assault on liberty alike. A people willing to support killing will not hesitate to crush freedom.

Sometimes government will derive satisfaction from interfering with liberty as a way of showing its support for war. This may be understandable when the activity suppressed is directed against the conduct of the war. But government intervention also occurs when the hated activity is purely an affirmation of freedom, as when Upton Sinclair was arrested for reading the Bill of Rights. Freedom, after all, is an enemy of war. Sadly, the American people more often than not have applauded the assault on liberty by the war lover.

There is little room for freedom when a people are under fire. Liberty will keep her head down when she is being shot at like everyone else. We can hear a lonely Eugene Debs observe on his way to prison for opposing U.S. involvement in World War I: "It is extremely dangerous to exercise the constitutional right of free speech in a country fighting to make the world safe for democracy."

The antagonism between war and freedom is inherent. War is rule by force. Freedom, as Robert Maynard Hutchins helpfully defined it, is the negation of force. A war-time government will act to crush freedom because a people who wants freedom will resist war.

It follows that in freedom is the preservation of peace. The very quest for freedom involves finding ways of preventing war.

It ought to be clear that the ultimate subversion of the Bill of Rights, and the more comprehensive idea of freedom, is the misbegotten belief that freedom can be either defended, or obtained by force. In war, all participants seek to have their way by violence. Whatever the intentions of the combatants, or the policy of the prevailing party after war, freedom has been diminished.

Far from recoiling at war's inhumanity, the victor and the vanquished seek superior force as the only way to win. Each prepares for the next war while liberty is held in thrall to militarism. Jorge Luis Borges, in his powerful story "Deutsches Requiem," depicts a captured Nazi concentration camp commander awaiting execution who declares ecstatically that although the Fatherland was destroyed, Nazism prevailed because its faith was in the sword and those who destroyed the fatherland adopted its faith.

Throughout history, nation-states have spoken of their commitment to freedom and desire for peace while planning war. In Plato's dialogue *The Laws*, the anonymous Athenian Stranger argues that the good legislator orders "war for the sake of peace." The more candid Cleinas of Crete observes of his own country, "I am greatly mistaken if war is not the entire aim and object of our institutions." The Athenian Stranger, thought by most scholars to represent Plato himself, by others Socrates, by all the wisdom of Attica, saw war as a means with peace as its end. Cleinas, with greater simplicity, saw a world in eternal struggle among nations for domination.

For both views the result has been the same. War has been the dominant experience of nearly every generation for virtually every nation, culture and civilization that history records. And the little bit of uneasy peace and partial freedom that has been known was found despite, and not because of, war.

The ultimate reliance on force has been the nuclear arms race. The Trident II nuclear submarine is a powerful symbol of the mindless will to dominate. Here is a single boat, about the size of the Washington Monument, capable of launching 24 missiles while submerged. Each missile can be equipped with 12 or more independently targeted, maneuverable nuclear warheads. Each warhead may have an explosive force ten times greater than the bomb that destroyed Nagasaki. Each warhead can strike within 300 feet of a predetermined target anywhere within a 7,000-mile radius. Hundreds of cities can be leveled within minutes, a million or more persons incinerated in each. Many more will suffer grievous injury, unbearable pain and shortened lives. Life on the planet may be imperiled.

Where is moral freedom—the freedom most cherished by Thoreau—in the company of a people who would conceive and construct so awful a weapon? Where is economic freedom when more is spent on arms than food while millions starve and hundreds of millions are hungry? Where is civil liberty when a nation bases its security on instruments of terror?

General James Doolittle, who sought to cremate the city of Tokyo in 30 seconds, voiced the military view in the report of a Presidential Commission he chaired: "Hitherto acceptable norms of human conduct do not apply...We must learn to subvert, sabotage and destroy our enemies by more clever, more sophisticated and more effective methods than those used against us..."

Louis D. Brandeis encapsulated the story as far as the rule of law is concerned in a single phrase in a letter to a friend: "During a war...all bets are off."

Most ominous for the fate of freedom is the undeniable fact that U.S. assaults like those on Grenada, Libya and Panama in the 1980s were supremely successful in domestic political terms and met with no significant opposition. President Reagan's popularity reached its peak with the bombing of Libya. President Bush ended his first year in office with a near-record rating for popularity largely because of his tragically wrong invasion of Panama. Overwhelmingly through our history, the American people have supported every use of U.S. military force abroad for so long as we were "winning."

In the longer periods between active military conflict, which have involved foreign tensions, preparation for war and cold war, it has been the politics of preparation and bellicosity that have prevailed. Most often these politics have been portrayed in terms of freedom through force. This statement of political purpose has always recruited legions of civilian soldiers who have patriotically suppressed liberty and every form of opposition to war.

Clearly a people who want freedom must end war. Equally clear, if a nation founded on principles of freedom and democracy engages so consistently in falsehood, deception, suppression, and force, the power of nations to engage in war must be controlled by world law.

International law must prohibit war and remedy its causes by establishing social justice and securing freedom. World government must be capable of effective police action and social programs to fulfill those laws and preserve peace.

Michael Linfield's *Freedom Under Fire* offers a fertile, painful, perhaps too volatile, grist for reflection and beyond—for analysis and action.

Ramsey Clark
New York City
February 1990

Chapter I

Introduction

That is one of the indictments of war; its first casualties are liberty and truth.

Norman Thomas (1927)[1]

History teaches that grave threats to liberty often come in times of urgency, when constitutional rights seem too extravagant to endure.

Justice Thurgood Marshall
Skinner v. Railway Labor Executives (1989)

Press censorship...loyalty oaths...people's tribunals...jailing of opposition leaders...concentration camps...denials of passports...government spying...states of emergency—we associate these violations of basic democratic principles with totalitarian governments. Yet the United States itself has resorted to just such illegal and unconstitutional actions during every one of our wars, from the Revolutionary War through the war in Vietnam.

Most people in the United States view unconstitutional restrictions on civil liberties during war-time as the exception. They are not; such restrictions are the rule. A recent Supreme Court statement is typical of the commonly accepted viewpoint: "Our distaste for censorship—reflecting the natural distaste of a free people—is deep-written in our law." [2] Even Alexander M. Bickel, the noted First Amendment scholar and counsel for the *New York Times* when the government tried to censor the *Times* in the *Pentagon Papers* case, believed that "[t]his country's experience with censorship of political speech is happily almost non-existent. Through wars and other turbulence, we have avoided it." [3]

1

Unfortunately, these statements simply misread American wartime history.

As this book demonstrates, war-time restrictions on civil liberties have not been unusual or isolated incidents. During each war, and for period often lasting as long as ten to fifteen years before and after each war , the civil liberties of U.S. citizens have been trampled under foot as if the Constitution did not exist. Rather than being an exception, war-era violations of civil liberties in the United States are the accepted norm for our government.

*

We are proud of the glorious tradition of civil liberties that we learned in elementary and junior high school history classes:

Our forefathers came to this land to escape political and religious persecution. They created a city upon the hill, to serve as a beacon of tolerance unto the nations. The Bill of Rights encapsulated our people's desire for freedom and individual liberty.

The First Amendment guarantees all Americans the right to speak their mind, to criticize their government, and to believe— or not believe—as conscience dictates. We have, and have always had, a free press. From Thomas Paine's *Common Sense* in 1775 through the printing by the *New York Times* of the Pentagon Papers during the Vietnam War, the First Amendment has guaranteed a free press, and allowed newspaper editors to print the truth as they saw it, protected from the wrath of angry politicians.

We take pride in the guarantees of due process enshrined in the 4th, 5th, 6th, 8th and 14th amendments: guarantees that require probable cause before police can enter our home and arrest us; that ensure the accused the right of counsel at a fair and public trial; that prohibit torture and forced confessions; that prevent repeated arrests for the same crime. We are proud that political opponents are protected, that the United States has no political prisoners, and that people are not arrested and held on trumped-up charges as is the case in totalitarian countries. We feel secure that in our country there is no secret police and no one need fear a knock on their door in the middle of the night.

This is the accepted version of U.S. history that will be celebrated in 1991 with the Bicentennial of the Bill of Rights.

But there is another, darker tradition that has haunted U.S. history. It is rarely mentioned in our history texts, and has been conveniently forgotten—sometimes even by its victims. While constitutional freedoms have been highly praised, most Americans, throughout most of our history, have lived in a society in which they were not in fact protected by the hallowed phrases of the Bill of Rights.

The Constitution was written by wealthy white men in closed session. The majority of Americans living at the time did not get a chance to vote on its adoption. At a time when almost 20 percent of the population was black,[4] the Founding Fathers included ten sections in the Constitution to protect the institution of slavery.[5]

For the greater part of its history, our country has been involved in a massive campaign of genocide against the Native American populations. Our history of broken promises and abrogated treaties with the Indian nations is perhaps unmatched in the world.

Although the First Amendment guarantees freedom of speech, the day-to-day reality for most Americans during 90 percent of our history was as if the First Amendment didn't exist. Throughout our history, people in the United States were harassed, arrested, banished and even killed for speaking out against the current administration or local power structure. Newspapers that offended those in power were banned, their presses seized, their articles censored.

Prior to 1925, states could constitutionally pass any laws they wished denying freedom of speech or of the press. In fact, it was not until the 1960s—175 years after the Bill of Rights was ratified—that the majority of the protections of the Bill of Rights were first applied to the states. Prior to the 1960s, states could legally deny defendants the right to counsel, force defendants to testify against themselves, and place defendants in double jeopardy.

This was the state of our country during its normal peace-time existence. During times of war, conditions were immeasurably worse for anyone who was not considered "100 percent American."

What is Meant by "War-time"?

Through the distorting lenses of hindsight, historians write as if wars begin and end on fixed, ascertainable dates. Human history is often not so neat. When did the Vietnam War—at least as a social reality for the United States—start? In 1959, when the first U.S. "advisor" died in Vietnam? In 1963, when the first anti-Vietnam war demonstrations were held? Or in 1964, when the Tonkin Gulf resolution was passed? And did the Vietnam War "end" when U.S. ground forces returned home in 1973? In 1975, when the U.S. Embassy in Saigon was evacuated? Or was it not until 1982, when the Vietnam War Memorial was dedicated in Washington, D.C., serving as a symbolic end to the domestic conflicts generated by the war?

When using the term "times of war" or "war-time," I intentionally employ imprecise and ill-defined terms. They are meant to include entire eras: the build-up to war, the war itself, and the aftermath of war.

Civil liberties and individual freedoms are one of the first casualties of war. As war approaches, a panoply of restrictions are imposed on the civilian population—restrictions that generally last long after peace is declared. War hysteria, xenophobia and fear of subversion all outlive the shooting war. War-time hatred, fueled by patriotic rhetoric, infects the citizenry. Political opportunists and demagogues have played to these fears, instituting massive restrictions on civil liberties and clamping down on real or supposed dissidents, long after any possible threat to the nation's security has vanished.

In the United States, it has generally taken some ten to fifteen years after the end of each war for the "war era" to finally end. The Alien and Sedition Acts in 1798 are part of the Revolutionary War era; the Palmer Raids of 1920 are associated with World War I; McCarthyism is intimately connected with the World War II and Korean War experience.

Most people think of war as the exception—that the United States has been a nation at peace, only occasionally interrupted by short episodes of war. Yet during the 210 years since the founding of the Republic, the United States has used military force abroad some 200 times.[6] People alive today, who were born around 1900, have lived fully half their lives in times of war.*

Yet all previous studies of U.S. history have analyzed civil liberties as if the norm was peace-time; what has happened during war—half of modern U.S. history—has been ignored as irrelevant, atypical or aberrant. This book is written to correct that misperception.

How Should We Evaluate U.S. War-time Violations of Civil Liberties?

Upon reading the history of war-time repression in the United States, Americans rightly ask, "how are we to judge this history?" Under international law, a country may suspend all but the most fundamental human rights and civil guarantees in times of war or public emergency, as long as the restrictions are proportionate to the danger facing the country.[7] The U.S. Constitution also enshrines this principle: during times of "Rebellion or Invasion," the right to *habeas corpus* can be suspended.[8]

At least in modern times, the United States has not engaged in domestic violations of fundamental human rights when at war. Despite the fact that our government has been complicit in the killing or brutalizing of innocent people, it is generally true that the United States has not had an official policy of domestic murder, torture, disappearances or rape.

In making this assertion, we should not forget that for roughly the first half of our nation's history, slavery was the official policy of our nation; for the first two-thirds of our nation's history, the genocide of Native Americans was condoned; and for virtually our entire history, violence against blacks and other people of color has been tolerated,

---

* The World War I war-time restrictions lasted from approximately 1914-1925; World War II from 1939-1950; Korea from 1950 through the McCarthy era until 1960; the Vietnam War from the mid-1960s until the late 1970s.

and sometimes encouraged. However, as these violations of fundamental human rights were not traceable to war-time activity, nor were they more prevalent or virulent during war-time eras, they are beyond the scope of this book. Similarly, the impact of racism on the denial of human rights to immigrant communities is another thread running throughout U.S. history that I can only deal with here in its most virulent, war-time appearances.

Many human rights proponents believe that we should not compare the record of one country with that of another. They correctly argue that, for instance, the fact that the Guatemalan government has murdered 100,000 Indians during the past decade should not be used to minimize the disappearance of "only" 7,000 in Argentina's "dirty war." For similar reasons, human rights organizations are loath to praise a country because it is doing "better" than previously: that government-sponsored death squads were murdering 35 civilians a week in El Salvador in 1987 should make that country a human rights outcast; the country should not be praised because this was an improvement from some 300-500 civilian deaths per week in the early 1980s.

To compare our own record with that of the Nazis during World War II, or to more recent actions in totalitarian countries, such as the genocide of 100,000 Indians in Guatemala or the annihilation of much of the Cambodian population by the Khmer Rouge, is to trivialize these actual holocausts and do an injustice to the United States.

But having a better record than that of South Africa or El Salvador should be little comfort to those who pride themselves on democratic traditions. If any comparisons are called for, we must compare the United States with other democratic countries. Thus, we might appropriately compare our record with that of England or France. Such a comparison might cast a relatively favorable light on the United States: England suspended elections during World War II, has an Official Secrets Act to muzzle its press and established special tribunals to try suspected Irish Republican Army sympathizers; France censored and closed its dissident press during the Algerian War.

This book, however, looks to yet another comparison in an attempt to judge the civil liberties record of the United States. For most of the 1980s, the United States has been involved in a proxy war to overthrow the Sandinista government of Nicaragua. The stated objective of our support for the contras has been to force the Sandinista administration to become more democratic, more "like us." The U.S. media and the Reagan and Bush administrations have repeatedly pointed to Sandinista censorship of the press and radio, establishment of people's tribunals to try suspected contras and other violations of civil liberties as justification for our arming, training and supporting the contras. The stated justification of both lethal and "humanitarian" aid to the contras has been to force a democratization of the Nicaraguan government.

In an effort to put the civil liberties restrictions currently in effect in Nicaragua in a broader perspective, I made two trips to Nicaragua, funded by the Harvard Law School Human Rights Program, to investigate the record on human rights and civil liberties. During the summer of 1987, I served as the intern for the Chief Justice of the Nicaraguan Supreme Court and, in that capacity, had access to records and personnel in the judicial system. In the winter of 1988, I returned to Nicaragua to analyze the changes in internal civil liberties as a result of the Central American peace process.

The appendix to this book contains a history of the Sandinista record of civil liberties during the past ten years of warfare.

The inescapable conclusion is that the United States record of civil liberties during war-time is no better—in fact, is arguably worse—than that maintained by the Sandinistas during the past ten years. Considering the time, money and national prestige that has been expended on support for the contras, and the national trauma and internal divisiveness that has been engendered by our nation's policy of trying to force, through proxy warfare, a "democratization" of the Nicaraguan government, the comparison is indeed sobering.

In the final analysis, as illuminating as these comparisons may be, they are, after all, not the point. Our measuring stick should reflect what we believe is necessary for a truly functional, liberating democracy. Therefore, when we look at our own history, we need to ask some fundamental questions:

- Under what conditions, if any, might restrictions on civil liberties be justified?
- Are the emergency measures taken by the government proportionate to the threat?

- Were all—or even most—of the war-time restrictions imposed in the United States in fact necessary? Did some—or perhaps all—of these restrictions do more harm than good?
- Is our record the best that can be hoped for in a democracy?

And perhaps most important, if many—perhaps most—of the war-time restrictions were unjustified, how do we prevent such restrictions from being re-imposed in the event of future periods of crisis?

Chapter II

The Revolutionary War Era

A long war for independence is scarcely a propitious time for the birth and nurturing of freedom of expression or any civil liberties. Everywhere there was unlimited liberty to praise the American cause; criticism of it brought the zealots of patriotism with tar and feathers.

Levy, *Legacy of Suppression*[1]

The United States Revolution was a bloody, divisive war, combining elements of struggle against both a foreign imperial power and domestic opposition. Support for the Revolution varied; at the beginning of the Revolution, probably only a minority of the colonists supported it. Many colonists fought on the side of Britain; as many as 100,000 people fled the Colonies during and after the war.

The Revolutionary War lasted seven years, ending with the Treaty of Paris in 1783. Four years passed after the triumph of the Revolution before the newly formed nation developed a constitution. The validity and perhaps legality of the new Constitution was uncertain; the men who wrote it were convened for another purpose—to amend the 1777 Articles of Confederation. The Articles of Confederation required unanimous agreement prior to any amendment taking effect but the new Constitution stated that only "nine States shall be sufficient for the Establishment of this [new] Constitution," [2] far short of the unanimity mandated by law.

A year after the adoption of the Constitution, George Washington, military leader of the Revolution, ran unopposed for the presidency; in 1789 he became the first President. At the time of his inauguration on April 30, 1789, only eleven of the thirteen colonies had delegates seated in the House and Senate; the other two colonies, Rhode Island and North Carolina, had not yet ratified the Constitu-

tion. In 1791, eight years after independence and peace, the ten
Amendments guaranteeing civil liberties, known collectively as the
Bill of Rights, were added to the Constitution. George Washington ran
unopposed for re-election in 1792; not until 1796 was there a contested
election for President of the United States.

Obviously, if civil rights were not guaranteed by legal codifica-
tion, they cannot strictly be said to have been denied. The pre-Bill of
Rights history presented here, however, is important because it
demonstrates a virtually seamless practice of civil liberties' violations
from the earliest days of the European conquest of North America
through today, whether or not these rights were legally "guaranteed."

People's Tribunals and Loyalty Oaths

Political trials occur most frequently during those times when
the legitimacy of a regime is called into question. This is often the case
in times of civil disturbance and national emergency, or when a new
regime has just been established.

Just fifteen years after the Pilgrims landed, and two years after
the heresy trial of Galileo in Italy, the Colonies convened their first
political trial. In 1635, Roger Williams, convicted by the Massachusetts General Court of having "broached and divulged dyvers
newe and dangerous opinions, against the authoritie of magistrates,"
was banished from Massachusetts.[3] He achieved fame in exile by
founding Rhode Island. Two years later, Anne Hutchinson was
similarly convicted by the General Court and banished.[4]

During the colonial era, those who didn't subscribe to the established religious orthodoxies were routinely persecuted. When colonies
enacted conscription laws, Quakers and other pacifists were arrested
for refusing to fight against the Indians.[5]

But until Independence, such trials were generally isolated
incidents. People's tribunals, as we define them today, didn't come into
existence until the start of the Revolution.

At the beginning of the Revolutionary War, the country was
divided, with large sections of the population still loyal to the King. In
1776, the new American government "possessed a dangerously small
base of popular support";[6] in Delaware in 1776, for instance, a petition

opposing independence garnered 5,000 signatures, while a rival petition urging separation from England attracted only 300 signatures.[7]
Perhaps a quarter of the population identified themselves as Loyalists;
in New Jersey, over 35 percent of the population were Loyalists;[8] in
New York, fully half of the population opposed the Revolution.[9] Some
50,000 colonists fought on the side of England against the Revolution.[10]

Given these conditions, it is not surprising that the pro-Revolutionary citizens, their guerilla army and the newly-formed government
would resort to anti-democratic measures to silence the opposition,
strengthen their base of support and ensure their victory.

To deal with what pro-Revolutionary colonists viewed as potentially dangerous disaffection and disloyalty, Committees of Safety
were created in numerous towns and villages throughout New
England. The Committees identified potential anti-Revolutionary sentiment, surveilled and harassed Loyalists, wrote and administered
loyalty oaths, conducted *ad hoc* people's trials to punish those
suspected of committing disloyal acts and issued bills of attainder[*]
against individual Loyalists.[11]

Any colonist who would not pledge allegiance to the Revolution
was deemed a "non-associator" and targeted. The Connecticut General
Assembly, during its first session following the Declaration of Independence, authorized towns to set up commissions with the power to
confine those deemed dangerous to the safety of the state for "such
times as the public security may require."[12] A person could not remain
neutral and be left alone; active support for the Revolution was
necessary. The Committee of Safety in New York ordered that all
weapons of anyone not swearing allegiance to the Revolution be
seized;[13] during interrogation, another Committee of Safety told three
suspected Tories that "you will perhaps say that you are determined
to stay neutral...this will not be a satisfactory answer."[14] "Test laws"
were passed by most state legislatures, compelling a declaration of
allegiance to the Revolution by all colonists.

Given the turmoil of the Revolution, it is not surprising that most

---

[*] A bill of attainder is a legislative enactment that takes away a specific
person's life, liberty or property without the person having been convicted
by a court of law. Today it is considered a legislative usurpation of the
judicial process and is forbidden by Art. I, Sec 9[a] of the Constitution.

state legislatures passed laws making treason punishable by death. What is surprising is the expansive definition given to the term "treason." The Continental Congress defined treason in a fairly modern manner: waging war against the colonies, supporting the "King of Great Britain," or "giving aid and comfort" to England. But in New Hampshire, simply *believing* in the authority of the Crown was deemed treasonable—and hence punishable by death.[15] Although some people charged with treason were tried by civilian courts, many more were either court-martialed or tried by the Committees of Safety. In New York alone, over 1,000 people were tried and sentenced.[16]

Committees of Safety issued bills of attainder against suspected Loyalists. In 1778, some 400 people were attainted in Philadelphia alone.[17] Property of attainted persons was forfeited to the state. The Loyalists were denied access to the courts and loyalist lawyers were disbarred. A Loyalist

> ...had no legal redress until he took an oath that he favored American independence. All legal action was denied him. He might be assaulted, insulted, blackmailed or slandered...yet he had no recourse in law. No relative or friend could leave an orphan child to his guardianship. He could be the executor or administrator of no man's estate. He could neither buy land nor transfer it to another. The legal right to dispose of his own fortune at his death was refused him. Even his deed of gift was invalid.[18]

Under a Massachusetts act of 1776, ministers and schoolmasters were to lose their salaries if they did not swear allegiance to the Revolution; the same applied to the Governors of Harvard College.[19]

In 1777, when Massachusetts was anticipating invasion by British forces, the State Council issued warrants to apprehend all suspicious Loyalists; they were held in prison without bail until released by an order of the Council. South Carolina granted its governor extraordinary powers to arrest disloyal persons and deny them bail or trial until ten days after the next meeting of the legislature. Virginia gave its governor power to relocate or exile Loyalists, while Connecticut and New Jersey gave this extraordinary power to local Committees of Safety.[20] Eleven of the thirteen colonies passed laws quarantining, banishing or exiling Loyalists.[21] Over 400 people were banished from Pennsylvania in 1778 alone. Many of the banishment acts remained on the books for thirty years after the era of the Revolution; they were not rescinded until after the War of 1812.[22]

Expropriation of Property

During the early years of the Revolutionary War, virtually every state enacted laws confiscating the holdings of people loyal to the Crown. Three weeks after the Declaration of Independence, the Continental Congress proposed a law making all property of those siding with the King subject to seizure.[23] On March 6, 1777, New York established a Commission of Sequestration, which was authorized to seize all property of those who joined the British. At the time, as much as two-thirds of all land in New York belonged to Loyalists. The property was to be sold ten days after confiscation at a public auction. The State employed these forced sales to fund the war effort.[24] Making things official, two years later the New York Assembly passed an act "declaring the sovereignty of the people of this state to all property within same." [25]

This "land reform" had the potential for breaking up the large colonial land estates and redistributing the land to family farmers. In some places, this was indeed the result; in general, however, the confiscated land was bought by well-to-do revolutionaries.[26]

Less than a year after the signing of the Declaration of Independence, Thomas Jefferson wrote a bill for the Virginia Assembly confiscating British property.[27] On March 13, 1778, the Vermont Legislature convened for the first time under the new Constitution. Within two weeks, the Governor requested the Assembly to pass a measure to confiscate the property of Tories.[28] Connecticut passed an act declaring that all property, both personal and real, of anyone supporting the enemy was henceforth forfeited to the state.[29] In 1778, Georgia confiscated all real and personal property of British subjects; four years later, 274 people were banished, their property confiscated and they were given sixty days to leave the state on pain of death.[30]

Pennsylvania was home to many religious groups, including substantial numbers of Mennonites and Quakers. These religious people, although not necessarily pro-British, were prevented by their religion from taking loyalty oaths and swearing allegiance to the revolutionary government. Their property, too, was confiscated. In one incident, all personal property of eleven Mennonites was confiscated,

> even their beds, bedding, linen, Bibles, and books were taken from them and sold by the sheriff...From some of them all their provisions were taken and not even a morsel of bread left for their children...As all their iron stoves were taken from them... they were deprived of every means of keeping their children warm in the approaching winter, especially at night, being obliged to lie on the floor without any beds... Some of the men's wives were pregnant and near the time of deliverance, which makes their case the more distressing.[31]

Rhode Island not only confiscated all property of Loyalists, but of anyone who fled during the War.[32] During the course of the Revolution, every one of the thirteen colonies passed confiscatory legislation.[33]

As another means of rewarding revolutionaries and punishing Loyalists, the states of Georgia, Pennsylvania and New Jersey passed laws voiding all debts to Loyalists.[34] A Virginia Act of 1782 stated that "no Debt or Demand whatsoever, contracted with or due to any British Subject...shall be recoverable in any Court of Record within this Commonwealth." [35]

New York and Virginia passed similar laws both to punish Loyalists and to raise money for their bankrupt treasuries. In these states, a person who owed a debt to a Loyalist could instead pay the debt, dollar for dollar, to the state.[36] A similar law, passed by New York in 1782, declared that debts to Loyalists were cancelled, providing that the debtor paid 1/40th of the debt to the State.[37]

To escape persecution, harassment and confiscation of property, Loyalists fled the Colonies during the Revolution. In the winter of 1775, prior to the outbreak of the War, more than 900 men, women and children left Boston by boat for Nova Scotia. Despite tempestuous weather, they arrived in Canada, becoming the first of some tens of thousands of boat-people to make the trip.[38] More than 35,000 Loyalist refugees fled north to Nova Scotia in 1783, overwhelming local resources and pitting established residents against newcomers.[39] It is estimated that as many as 100,000 Loyalists emigrated during this time,[40] with between 35,000 and 60,000 fleeing from New York alone.[41]

As other defeated colonial powers have done in more recent times, the British offered repatriation to loyal supporters wishing to return to England at the end of the War. The majority of Loyalist refugees moved north to Canada, although sizeable numbers did return to England, and more than 1,000 black refugees, many of whom had escaped slavery during the Revolutionary War, settled in Sierra Leone.[42]

When the War ended, thousands of Loyalists filed suit to reclaim their property. One hundred forty-six Loyalists made claims for estates confiscated by the State of Vermont.[43] Total claims for the State of New York were estimated at $3,600,000.[44] Over 5,000 claims, totaling millions of dollars, were presented to a British parliamentary commission established after the War to examine pending claims of American Loyalists.[45]

Censorship of the Press

Attempts at press censorship in the United States pre-date the Revolutionary War. The first newspaper ever printed in America, *Publick Occurrences Both Foreign and Domestick*, was published in Boston by Benjamin Harris in 1690. The premier issue criticized colonial Boston life; four days after its publication, the town council closed the paper.[46] Half a century before independence, on May 13, 1725, Massachusetts passed the first recorded censorship law in the New World, stating that

> The printers of the newspapers in Boston be ordered upon their peril not to insert in their prints anything of the public affairs of this province relative to the war without the order of the government.[47]

As revolutionary fervor increased, so did attempts to silence opponents of the Revolution. In 1776, six months before the Declaration of Independence, the *New Hampshire Gazette* published an editorial opposing independence. The editor was censured for his editorial by the provisional Assembly and, unwilling to chance another jail sentence (he had been imprisoned 22 years earlier for printing another article), he judiciously chose to suspend his paper.[48]

Four months before independence, Samuel Loudon, editor of the *New York Packet,* printed a Loyalist's reply to Tom Paine's *Common*

Sense. Loudon had not accepted the printing job out of ideological support for the King—he himself favored independence—but simply as a way of earning some money. Patriotic vigilantes, however, viewed the job differently and broke into his house, forced him from bed, destroyed the printing plates and burned 1,500 copies of the pamphlet. The next day, all New York printers received the following note:

> Sir, if you print, or suffer to be printed in your press anything against the rights and liberties of America, or in favor of our inveterate foes, the King, Ministry, and Parliament of Great Britain, death and destruction, ruin and perdition, shall be your portion. Signed, by order of the Committee of tarring and feathering.

The threat worked. No more Loyalist publications were printed in New York.[49]

All of the Colonies passed war-time laws prohibiting the publishing of materials supporting the King's authority over the emerging states. To prevent Loyalist attempts at debasing the money supply, laws were passed forbidding any derogatory mention of Continental currency. In 1776, "A Discourse upon Extortion," which denounced the civilian government, was to be published in Connecticut. A literary "bill of attainder" was passed, ordering the seizure of all copies of the book.[50]

The Alien and Sedition Acts

Fifteen years after the end of the War of Independence, the new nation was still weak and insecure. John Adams, running on the Federalist platform, had been elected President in the first contested election in our nation's history. At this time, Presidents did not choose their Vice-President; until adoption of the Twelfth Amendment in 1804, the presidential candidate receiving the second highest number of votes became Vice-President. Adam's Vice-President was his political enemy, Thomas Jefferson.

The Adams administration was worried about the recent revolution in France and persistent rumors of French covert involvement in U.S. domestic politics. They were also searching for a way to quiet the increasingly vocal Jeffersonian opposition. In this atmosphere, the first national censorship law was enacted by the U.S. government.

The Senate version of what was to become the Alien and Sedition Acts passed the Senate on Independence Day, 1797, six years after the Bill of Rights was added to the Constitution. The Act actually consisted of three bills: the "Alien Friends Act," the "Alien Enemies Act," and the "Sedition Act."

The first Alien Act[51] allowed the President "to order all such aliens as he shall judge dangerous to the peace and safety of the United States" deported. The second Alien Act[52] authorized the immediate arrest and deportation of aliens who were citizens of any foreign country with which the United States was at war, or which had "perpetrated, attempted or threatened" any "invasion or predatory action" against the United States. Although the alleged purpose behind the Alien and Sedition Acts was concern over a possible war with France, and the "open secret" that foreign governments were interfering in our domestic affairs,[53] no alien was ever arrested or deported under either of the two Acts.

The third of these Acts, the Sedition Act[54] turned U.S. xenophobia inward and was used to imprison opposition leaders and suppress domestic criticism of the Adams administration. Section 1 of the Act punished by imprisonment of up to five years anyone conspiring "with intent to oppose any measure...of the Government of the United States...or to impede the operation of any law of the United States...[or to] counsel, advise or attempt to procure any insurrection, riot, unlawful assembly or combination..." Section 2 punished the printing, uttering or publishing of:

> any false, scandalous and malicious...writings against the government of the United States, or either house of the Congress...or the President...with intent to defame the[m]...or to bring them ...into contempt or disrepute...or to excite against them...the hatred of the good people of the United States...

with up to two years imprisonment. The Sedition Act had a sunset clause, expiring on March 3, 1800, the last day of the Adams administration. While the Sedition Act criminalized statements against the President or Congress, it conspicuously did not criminalize statements against Vice-President Thomas Jefferson, leader of the Anti-Federalists.

Although only two dozen arrests and seventeen prosecutions

were initiated under the Sedition Act,[55] the effect on domestic dissent was chilling: virtually all of these prosecuted were political leaders or prominent newspaper editors opposed to the Adams administration.

The first victim of the Act was an anti-Federalist member of Congress from Vermont, Matthew Lyons, indicted less than three months after passage of the Act. Found guilty of sedition, he was sentenced to four months in jail and fined $1,000 by Justice William Paterson of the U.S. Supreme Court. While imprisoned, Lyons became the first candidate in U.S. history to run his campaign from a federal jail. He won re-election by a two-to-one margin over his Federalist opponent and assumed his seat in the House of Representatives upon completion of his sentence.[56]

Member of the New York State Assembly Jedidiah Peck was another leading opponent of the Federalists. The "sedition" for which he was arrested consisted of his circulating a petition urging repeal of the Alien and Sedition Acts! Although arrested in 1799, his trial was postponed until April 1800 to coincide with his re-election campaign. Peck's case became a *cause célébrè* and the government dropped the charges against him, fearing a trial would enhance his bid for re-election.[57]

Secretary of State Timothy Pickering launched a campaign to harass and prosecute under the Sedition Act all leading anti-Federalist newspapers in the country. Prosecutions were initiated against four of the five major pro-Jefferson papers as well as four smaller opposition papers. Four of the papers were driven out of business as a result of the prosecutions, including all three New York papers; another suspended publication from April through August 1800 while its editor was imprisoned for sedition.[58]

The campaign against papers that opposed the Adams Administration started even before the Sedition Act cast its shadow over the First Amendment. Three months prior to its passage, Benjamin Franklin Bache, the editor of the Philadelphia *Aurora,* the leading anti-Federalist paper, was tried for libel in an effort to silence his criticism of the Federalists. The *Aurora* had already been the target of economic pressure by the Adams administration, and on several occasions mobs attacked its editor and his home. Bache died of yellow fever during his trial[59]; his successor, William Duane, was indicted for sedition barely three months after his name appeared on the *Aurora's* masthead.[60]

Thomas Adams, the editor of the second most important anti-Federalist paper, the Boston *Independent Chronicle,* was also indicted for sedition and tried before Justice Paterson. Because of the prolonged trial and his own health, Adams was forced to sell the paper. Like Bache, Adams died before his trial was concluded.[61]

One Federalist newspaper in Boston correctly described the reigning Federalist position when it wrote, "It is patriotism to write in favor of the government—it is sedition to write against it." [62]

Most of the Sedition Act prosecutions were clearly intended to silence major critics of the administration. In at least one case, however, the machinery of Federalist justice ensnared not a political leader but a drunken jokester. Luther Baldwin was prosecuted under the Act for stating that he did not care if someone fired a cannon shot at the President's ass. Tried before a Circuit Court presided over by Justice Bushrod Washington of the U.S. Supreme Court, he was convicted of uttering "seditious words tending to defame the President and Government of the United States," fined $150, and sentenced to jail until the fine was paid.[63] Anti-Federalist newspapers had a field day covering the trial of the citizen who was sentenced "for speaking of the president's a--." One paper sagely noted that "joking may be very dangerous even to a free country." [64]

The Sedition Act was uniformly supported by the Federalists,[65] but not surprisingly, it generated tremendous opposition from the pro-Jefferson forces. The major institutional opposition to the Act took the form of resolutions from Virginia and Kentucky, written by Madison and Jefferson respectively, "protest[ing] against th[ese] palpable and alarming infractions of the Constitution," [66] and declaring the Acts "altogether void and of no force." [67] Although the resolutions condemned the Sedition Act's violation of the First Amendment, opposition to the Act centered around perceived federal usurpation of rights guaranteed the states under the Constitution.

The resolution condemning the censorship imposed by the Sedition Act was sent to the other states for their concurrence, but support was not forthcoming. In fact, Federalist-controlled state legislatures castigated the Virginia and Kentucky resolutions and re-affirmed their own "support [for] the government of the United States in all measures" taken against "aggression, foreign or domestic." New

Hampshire opined that the Alien and Sedition Acts "are constitutional, and in the present critical situation of our country, highly expedient"; Massachusetts declared the Act "not only constitutional but expedient and necessary." [68]

Although the Sedition Act was intended to muzzle the anti-Federalist forces, its unintended result was the election to the Presidency of the leading anti-Federalist of the day, Thomas Jefferson. In the election of 1800, the Electoral College was evenly split between Thomas Jefferson and Aaron Burr. According to the Constitution (Article II, Section, Clause 3), a tie in the Electoral College is resolved by a vote of the House of Representatives. When the House voted, Jefferson won by one vote. That deciding vote was cast by Representative Matthew Lyon, the first victim of the Sedition Act. The Sedition Act expired by its own terms on the last day of the Adams administration.*

After his election, President Jefferson pardoned those convicted under the Act. Toward the end of his first term, Jefferson wrote to Abigail Adams, wife of the former President: "I discharged every person under punishment or prosecution under the sedition law, because I considered, and now consider, that law to be a nullity, as absolute and as palpable as if Congress had ordered us to fall down and worship a golden image." [69]

Nonetheless, two years after committing these righteous sentiments to paper, six of Jefferson's political opponents were indicted for common law seditious libel,[70] with Jefferson's apparent approval. Jefferson also helped motivate the impeachment trial of Justice Samuel Chase, based on Chase's statements attacking the Jefferson administration.[71]

Despite his ringing defense of free speech when his party was being muzzled by the Adams' Adminstration, President Thomas Jef-

---

* While serving as Jefferson's Vice-President, Aaron Burr killed Alexander Hamilton in a duel. In 1807, Burr was tried for treason after President Jefferson accused him of plotting to carve out an empire for himself in the Western Territories of the United States. After Burr's arrest, Jefferson attempted to suspend *habeas corpus,* but the House of Representatives refused to go along with this unconstitutional action. Burr was ultimately acquitted of all charges.

ferson urged local officials to retaliate against Federalist papers by initiating common-law prosecutions for seditious libel. Prosecutions were begun in Pennsylvania against the Federalist editor of *The Port Folio,* and in Connecticut targetting not only editors, but also two ministers for preaching seditious sermons. One of the ministers, Reverend Azel Backus, was indicted for the "sedition" of accusing President Jefferson of having seduced his friend's wife some forty years earlier. The case was dropped when it became clear that Rev. Backus had spoken the truth.[72]

After Jefferson became president, his ally, George Clinton, became governor of New York. In 1803, Clinton's administration, with the apparent knowledge and approval of Jefferson, indicted Harry Croswell, editor of the Federalist publication, *The Wasp,* for seditious libel. Croswell's libel consisted of an accusation that President Jefferson had paid someone else to denounce Washington and Adams. Croswell was convicted in the lower court; he was not even allowed to plead truth as a defense. His appeal to the Court of Errors of New York, argued by Alexander Hamilton, was denied.[73]

Forty years later, Congress voted to reimburse people for fines assessed under the Sedition Act. Even though the Supreme Court never ruled on the constitutionality of the Sedition Act, it is generally accepted today that the Sedition Act was unconstitutional. In 1964, the Supreme Court, reviewing the history of Alien and Sedition Acts, stated,

> Although the Sedition Act was never tested in this Court, the attack upon its validity has carried the day in the court of history...[There is] a broad consensus that the Act...was inconsistent with the First Amendment.[74]

Despite this inauspicious beginning, and despite sporadic attempts during the ensuing fifty years to impose press restrictions— President Andrew Jackson, for instance, tried unsuccessfully to persuade Congress to ban abolitionist papers such as William Lloyd Garrison's *Liberator* from the mails[75]—press censorship did not assume major proportions until the Civil War, and Congress did not again impose a Sedition Act until the U.S. entrance into World War I.

Chapter III

The Civil War Era

The Civil War era was, by far, the most traumatic period in U.S. history. For five years the country was at war: state against state, family against family. Some 600,000 people died during the War—an unimaginable catastrophe for a population of only 31,443,000. The equivalent of almost five million deaths in today's United States, the number of people killed during the Civil War was more than ten times as great as that during the second most divisive war in U.S. history, the Vietnam War.

During the Civil War, the Constitution was put into a deep freeze:

- Complete censorship was imposed on all telegraphic communications;
- Anti-administration newspapers were closed, their editors jailed or banished;
- Tens of thousands of civilians were arrested and tried by military tribunals, or were simply arrested and kept in jail without any charges being brought against them;
- Confederate leaders were jailed after the war without ever being brought to trial;
- Property was confiscated from pro-slavery whites; slaves, rather than being freed, originally became the property of the U.S. government;
- *Habeas corpus* was illegally and unconstitutionally suspended.

Censorship of the Press

After the election of President Jefferson and the demise of the censorship of the Alien and Sedition acts in 1800, there was relatively little press censorship until the outbreak of the Civil War. By the 1860s, however, the telegraph had been invented, making virtually instantaneous transmission of information possible. The increased ability to disseminate news about the war frightened the government, and adherence to the First Amendment disintegrated under war-time restrictions.

During the Civil War, not only did President Lincoln seize the telegraph lines and establish censorship over all transmissions, but newspapers that printed articles unfavorable to the Union war effort were censored, prevented from publishing or confiscated.

In August 1861, the War Department issued an order forbidding the printing of any war news about camps, troops or military movements without the express permission of the military officer in charge of the area.[1] Compliance with this order was sporadic. When newspapers printed articles that displeased local authorities, their presses were often seized and closed.

On March 6, 1862, *The Sunday Chronicle,* a Washington paper, published an article that displeased Secretary of War Stanton. The next day, on Stanton's orders, Brigadier General Wadsworth, military governor of the District of Columbia, took possession of *The Sunday Chronicle*'s printing presses, destroyed all of the papers and arrested the editors.[2]

In Missouri, the military accused the *Boone County Standard* of publishing articles that encouraged resistance to the war effort. The editor of the paper was banished from Missouri and its presses were confiscated and sold for the benefit of the army.[3]

A similar incident occurred in Illinois, where the *Chicago Times* incurred the displeasure of General Burnside, the local military commander. Aware that Burnside planned to seize the paper, Judge Drummond issued an injunction forbidding the military from carrying out suppression orders. Ignoring the injunction, military forces nonetheless seized the *Times* office, and on June 3, 1863 prevented the paper from publishing.[4] However, three days later, President Lincoln countermanded General Burnside's orders and the paper reopened.

Two New York papers, the *New York Journal of Commerce* and the *New York World,* fell victim to a similar fate. They were closed for two days for printing a letter, purportedly written by President Lincoln, that called for the drafting of 400,000 men that year.[5]

While the Union government closed pro-Confederate papers, vigilantes attacked and forced the closing of Abolitionist papers both before and during the War. Pro-slavery mobs attacked the Illinois *Observer* several times, on three occasions dumping the paper's presses in a nearby river. Nonetheless, the editor, Reverend Elijah Lovejoy, continued to urge the abolition of slavery. Ultimately, a mob dragged Rev. Lovejoy from his home and murdered him.[6]

The Philadelphia offices of the *Pennsylvania Freeman* were burned three times. Mobs took control of Cassius Clay's *True American* in Kentucky, closed the paper and shipped the presses north to Cincinnati. In a similar manner, the offices of William Lloyd Garrison's *Liberator* were attacked.[7] Local officials were unable, or unwilling, to stop such attacks.

From the very beginning of the war, citizens were arrested for speaking against Lincoln's policies. The Presidential Proclamation of September 24, 1862 that suspended *habeas corpus,* also subjected to military courts-martial not only "rebels and insurgents," but anyone "discouraging volunteer enlistments" in the Union army.

A year later, Congress passed the first national conscription act. Anyone resisting conscription, or even criticizing conscription, was punishable by $500 fine or two years in prison.[8] Mennonites and Quakers, who refused to be drafted for religious reasons, were arrested and jailed until 1864, when Congress passed a law recognizing conscientious objection.

The inability of citizens to protest against the newly-instituted draft, combined with class antagonisms and racism (many blamed the blacks for the war), led to major riots in Northern cities. During July 1863, more than 1,000 people were killed in anti-draft riots in New York City alone.[9] Troops were called in from Gettysburg to restore order. According to one offical army report:

> [With a force of 160 men we] marched to Second Avenue, where we found the mob in great force and concealed in houses. They fired on us from house tops...We soon cleared the streets, and then commenced searching the houses. We searched thirteen houses, killed those within that resisted, and took the remainder prisoners. Some of them fought like incarnate fiends, and would not surrender. All such were shot on the spot.[10]

Violation of Due Process and Suspension of *Habeas Corpus* *

During the Civil War, Lincoln ignored or violated numerous constitutional safeguards in his effort to win the war. "The slow and procedurally difficult process of accusing, trying, and convicting people of treason for aiding the South was replaced by military arrest, trial, and execution, facilitated by the suspension of the writ of *habeas corpus*." [11]

Article I of the Constitution allows for the suspension of *habeas corpus* "when in Cases of Rebellion or Invasion the public Safety may require it." [12] But since Article I deals with powers entrusted to the legislature, it would appear that suspension of *habeas corpus* can only be lawfully accomplished by an act of Congress. Nonetheless, President Lincoln issued at least three executive proclamations during the first two years of the Civil War suspending *habeas corpus*. [13] When Mr. Merryman brought a case challenging its suspension, Chief Justice Taney, sitting as a Maryland circuit judge, repudiated the authority of the President to suspend *habeas corpus*. The Chief Justice stated:

> I can see no grounds whatever for supposing that the president, in any emergency...can authorize the suspension of the privileges of the writ of *habeas corpus*...He certainly does not faithfully execute the laws if he takes upon himself legislative power, by suspending the writ of *habeas corpus,* and the judicial power also, by arresting and imprisoning a person without due process of law...[The Bill of Rights], which Congress itself could not suspend, ha[s] been disregarded and suspended, like the writ of *habeas corpus,* by a military order, supported by force of arms. [14]

---

* *Habeas corpus* is the process by which a person who is illegally arrested can be released from unlawful imprisonment. The Latin term "habeas corpus" means "you have the body." By issuing a writ of *habeas corpus,* a judge commands a sheriff, warden, government, etc. to produce the prisoner so that a determination of the legality of the detention can be made. Known as "The Great Writ" in Anglo-American law, *habeas corpus* is considered essential for liberty and is guaranteed by the Constitution (Art. I, Sec. 9).

President Lincoln's response was simply to ignore the court's decision. He justified his actions by referring to similar conduct of President Andrew Jackson some forty years earlier:

> After the Battle of New Orleans...General Andrew Jackson still maintained martial or military law...Mr. Louaillier published a denunciatory newspaper article, General Jackson arrested him. A lawyer by the name of Morel procured the United States Judge Hall to order a writ of *habeas corpus* to release Mr. Louaillier. General Jackson arrested both the lawyer and the judge. A Mr. Holander ventured to say of some part of the matter that "it was a dirty trick." General Jackson arrested him...[15]

Some of the "disloyal" acts for which federal officials arrested American citizens during one three-week period in 1861 included:

- having secessionist tendencies;
- being an intimate friend of someone arrested for disloyalty;
- expressing gratification over a rebel victory;
- habitually leaving home early and coming home late, and saying that the U.S. government was oppressive;
- displaying Confederate buttons and emblems;
- selling Confederate songs;
- refusing to take an oath of allegiance to the Union.[16]

As was often the case with governmental violations of civil liberties, the public and the press applauded the government's unconstitutional actions and condemned those who sought to require the government to act legally. The *New York Tribune* not only condemned the Chief Justice's decision upholding the Constitution, but virtually accused him of treason:

> The Chief Justice takes sides with traitors, throwing around them the sheltering protection of the ermine. When treason stalks about in arms, let decrepit Judges give place to men capable of detecting and crushing it.[17]

President Lincoln justified his decision to suspend *habeas corpus* on the grounds of national security. In his address to the Special Session of Congress on Independence Day, 1861, he said: "To state the question more directly, are all the laws but one to go unexecuted and the government itself go to pieces lest that one be violated?"[18]

Similar reasoning was used by the President to justify the

banishment and exile of a former U.S. member of Congress. Clement Vallandigham, as the Representative from Ohio, had been a leader of anti-war Democrats in Congress. After his re-election defeat, Vallandigham continued to vociferously condemn Lincoln's conduct of the war. When Vallandigham was arrested for treason and exiled to the Confederacy, Lincoln defended the banishment as follows: "Must I shoot a simple-minded soldier boy who deserts, while I must not touch a hair of a wily agitator who induces him to desert?"

Although it is accepted that a government may use military tribunals to try enemy soldiers, Lincoln found it expedient to extend the use of martial law to the entire Union. As Justice William Brennan recently stated, "[Lincoln] continued to use military arrests and trials throughout the war, relying on the insidious principle that if military detentions are constitutional in places in rebellion, they are constitutional 'as well in places in which they may prevent the rebellion extending.' " [19]

During this time the Confederacy made political capital by accusing the Union of human rights violations. In his inaugural address, Jefferson Davis, President of the Confederacy, stated:

> [The United States] has exhibited [a disregard] for all the time honored bulwarks of civil and religious liberty. Bastilles filled with prisoners, arrested without civil process or indictment duly found; the writ of *habeas corpus* suspended by Executive mandate; a State Legislature controlled by the imprisonment of members whose avowed principles suggested to the Federal Executive that there might be another added to the list of seceded States; elections held under threats of military power; civil officers, peaceful citizens, and gentlewomen incarcerated for opinion's sake."[20]

Oblivious to the horrors of slavery, the Confederacy prided itself in the fact that "through all the necessities of an unequal struggle there has been no act on our part to impair personal liberty or the freedom of speech, of thought, or of the press." [21] The Confederacy never did suspend *habeas corpus.* [*]

During the course of the Civil War, the United States arrested and jailed somewhere between 10,000 and 30,000 people, denying them the benefits of *habeas corpus* hearings.[22] Kept in military custody, without charges, for as long as the government felt necessary, many were never brought to trial. Among those arrested and jailed without charges being filed were the elected mayors of both Washington, D.C. and Baltimore.

During the third year of the Civil War, on March 24, 1863, Congress itself passed a bill suspending *habeas corpus.* Lincoln issued two more proclamations suspending *habeas corpus* on September 15, 1863, and July 5, 1864. The constitutionality of the suspension of *habeas corpus* by Congress was upheld by the Supreme Court a year after the Civil War ended.[23]

Neither the death of Lincoln nor the cessation of hostilities brought an end to the use of military tribunals and the suspension of *habeas corpus.* President Andrew Johnson ordered that the eight people accused of conspiracy to kill Lincoln be tried by military tribunals, even though the civil courts were functioning in Washington D.C.[24]

Many former Confederate leaders were jailed without charges filed against them. At the conclusion of the war, Jefferson Davis was held for two years at Fort Monroe before formal charges were pressed. He petitioned the Supreme Court to quash his indictment; the Supreme Court never heard the appeal as Davis' ultimate release rendered the issue moot.[25]

Even upon release, former Confederate leaders were not allowed to reintegrate into the political life of the Union. The Fourteenth Amendment to the Constitution specifically prohibits any Confederate

---

[*] The relative observance of civil liberties for whites in the Confederacy provides an extreme contrast with the total lack of such rights for the Black population. Slaves had no right to *habeas corpus,* trial by a jury of their peers, freedom of speech or of the press, or any of the other rights guaranteed by the Constitution. Even the slaves' right to life itself was dependent upon the whims of their masters. This was as true in the four slave states that remained part of the union (and to which the Emancipation Proclamation did not apply) as in the Confederate states.

who previously had held office in any state of the United States from ever holding office again.[26]

Two years after the war was over, Congress dissolved several elected state legislatures, replacing them with appointed military governments in an attempt to curb the abuses of all-white southern legislatures and to prevent obstruction of the policies of Reconstruction.[27] The stated reason for the re-imposition of military rule was "efficiency." [28]

Not only was *habeas corpus* suspended—both legally and illegally—during the war, but in at least one instance during the Reconstruction era, Congress passed a law preventing the Supreme Court from having appellate jurisdiction of *habeas corpus* petitions arising under the Reconstruction Act.

After the Civil War, one Mr. McCardle was imprisoned by the military government set up under the Reconstruction Act. He brought a *habeas corpus* action to the Supreme Court challenging the constitutionality of the Act. After oral arguments, but before the Court rendered its decision, Congress passed a law preventing the Court from hearing appeals from Circuit Court decisions under the Reconstruction Act. The Court upheld this limitation of its appellate review of *habeas corpus* actions in 1869.[29]

Expropriation of Property

Between the Revolution and the Civil War, the new country was engaged in several smaller wars, including the War of 1812 and the Mexican-American War of 1848. When the government felt that specific private property was needed during these wars, such property was confiscated. During the Mexican-American war, a large wagon train owned by one Mr. Harmony was seized near El Paso because a U.S. army colonel wanted to add its 300 wagons to a military convoy about to attack Chihuahua, Mexico. The Supreme Court, although upholding an award of compensation to Harmony, affirmed that the military had the power to take private property for public use.[30]

During the Civil War, the Union resorted to confiscation of property as both an economic and political tool. As is well known, the freeing of slaves was undertaken as a means of punishing rebellious whites and hurting the Confederate war effort, not out of abolitionist concerns.

The First Civil War Confiscation Act was passed on August 6, 1861 and declared that all property used by Confederates in their insurrection was forfeited and became the property of the government. If a slave was owned by a "loyal" white, the slave remained a slave. But a slave owned by a Confederate was to be confiscated. These slaves, rather than being freed, became the property of the U.S. government.[31]

To remedy this bizarre situation, General Hunter, Union military commander of Georgia, South Carolina and Florida, issued an order on May 9, 1862 freeing all slaves in areas under his command. Upon hearing of General Hunter's action one week later, President Lincoln immediately revoked the order, thus returning the slaves to their former status as property of the federal government.[32]

On July 17, 1862, the Second Confiscation Act was passed. Recognizing that "confiscated" slaves needed to be treated differently than other confiscated "property," the Second Act freed all slaves of rebellious whites.[33] A few months later, the Emancipation Proclamation was signed, but the institution of slavery remained unaffected. The Emancipation Proclamation freed only slaves within Confederate states—the result, of course, was that no slaves were freed as a result of the Proclamation, since the Union government exercised no control over the Confederate states. The four slave states that stayed in the Union were specifically excluded from the Emancipation Proclamation. Thus, slavery continued unabated in Kentucky, Missouri, Maryland and Delaware, and the Fugitive Slave Law remained in force.[34]

In 1861 and again in 1862, President Lincoln seized control of the telegraph lines and railroads. The railroads were operated under military supervision; telegraph lines were run under both military supervision and censorship. The first seizures in 1861 were apparently undertaken without any statutory authority.[35]

The following year, the government passed a law allowing it to confiscate private property without having to follow cumbersome legal procedures. The Abandoned Property Act did allow Southerners to recover their property two years after hostilities ended, but only if they could prove that they had not supported the Confederacy.[36] Both the Abandoned Property Act and the Confiscation Acts were upheld by the

Abandoned Property Act and the Confiscation Acts were upheld by the Supreme Court after the war.[37]

Chapter IV

The World War I Era

Although World War I was highly profitable for U.S. business and propelled the United States onto the world scene as a major power, the war was not hugely popular with the American people. Prior to our entrance into the war, anti-war sentiment was widespread. Fifty-six members of Congress voted against the declaration of war; in comparison, only one voted against declaring war against Germany in World War II.[1]

In an effort to "make the world safe for democracy," and to counter indigenous anti-war sentiment and a growing labor and radical movement, the U.S. government trampled on virtually every democratic principle guaranteed by the Constitution. Not since the Civil War had the government engaged in such wholesale violations of civil liberties of citizens and residents.

Despite the promise of a return to "normalcy" after the Armistice, the United States experienced severe race riots in 1919, rampant inflation (prices were double pre-war levels), a crime wave (the homicide rate was double the pre-war rate), an economic recession and a deadly flu epidemic. In addition, the union movement was increasingly successful in organizing previously unorganized men and women. Workers, whose demands had been held in check by the war, launched a series of strikes to recoup lost wages. There were 3,600 strikes involving 4 million workers in 1919. One in every five workers went on strike that year, a record still unsurpassed.[2]

Fears of an increasingly radical labor movement and the specter of communism that was supposedly sweeping all Europe, fanned by war-induced hysteria and xenophobia, led to massive civil liberties violations during the World War I era:

- Citizens' committees and people's tribunals were established to try individuals suspected of disloyalty;
- Vigilante organizations, with the support and approval of the Department of Justice and local police, kidnapped, "arrested" and incarcerated thousands without trial;
- "Neutrality" was equated with treason;
- Religious people opposed to war were thrown in jail, kept in chains and given a diet of bread and water until they renounced their religious convictions;
- The Attorney General, with the help of his assistant, J. Edgar Hoover, illegally arrested 4,000 resident aliens, deporting over 1,000—many of whom had lived virtually all of their lives in the United States—without due process or trial;
- The first official federal censorship board was established and given complete control over all printed material;
- Over one hundred publications were suspended and prevented from printing;
- The government directed 75,000 people around the country to deliver official propaganda speeches written in Washington;
- Unions were targeted for harassment and destruction; to be a member of the Industrial Workers of the World (IWW or "Wobblies") was itself a deportable offense;
- Elected officials were denied seats in Congress and state legislatures because of their political beliefs.

The Historical Context: The Use of Martial Law in the Pre-War Decades

As World War I began, U.S. business and political leaders, eager for profits and fearful of militant labor organizations, incited a particularly jingoistic patriotism and encouraged vigilante justice and the formation of right-wing citizens' committees.

These violations of basic due process built on a pre-war foundation of harassment and suppression of dissent. On numerous occasions throughout the decades prior to the war, the U.S. government found that censorship of the media, declaration of martial law and the substitution of military trials for constitutional due process was a convenient way to silence and punish those who challenged the *status quo*.

President Hayes sent federal troops to Maryland, West Virginia,

Pennsylvania, Illinois and Missouri to break the railroad strike of 1877. President Cleveland used troops to crush the 1895 Pullman strike in Illinois led by Eugene Debs.[3] Federal troops were ordered to break the strike even though there had been virtually no violence prior to their appearance and Governor Altgeld of Illinois not only didn't request their use, but protested to President Cleveland against their unnecessary deployment.[4] The troops were accompanied by the issuance of an "omnibus injunction" against Debs' union, virtually prohibiting any strike or boycott against the railroads.[5] Debs was sentenced to six months imprisonment for violating the injunction.[6]

Probably the clearest example of the misuse of the judiciary to repress labor was an injunction issued by Federal District Judge James Jenkins. In December 1893, when the Northern Pacific Railroad company cut wages between 15 and 30 percent, workers struck demanding restoration of their salaries. Judge Jenkins issued an injunction on December 22, 1893 ordering workers to stay on the job.[7] The injunction was enforced, although this judicial coercion of involuntary servitude was later condemned as a "gross abuse of judicial authority" by the House Judiciary Committee.[8]

During the 1907 recession, Governor Sparks of Nevada tried unconstitutionally to obtain federal troops to help put down a labor strike in the mines. The Constitution states that federal troops can only be sent to quell domestic violence "on Application of the [State] Legislature, or of the Executive (when the Legislature cannot be convened)."[9] The Nevada legislature hadn't requested troops, and there was no reason that the legislature couldn't convene. Nonetheless, the day after receiving Governor Sparks' appeal, President Theodore Roosevelt cabled his readiness to send "two companies" to suppress the miners. A week later, Elihu Root, former Harvard Law professor and advisor to the President, notified Governor Sparks that his request called for an unconstitutional act:

> If such action should be desired under the Constitution...to suppress an insurrection a call must be made by the legislature of the State unless circumstances are such that the legislature cannot be convened...A mere statement of domestic disturbance would not seem sufficient."[10]

The President did not send the requested troops.

In 1914, the same week that marines landed in Veracruz, Mexico,

President Wilson sent federal troops to aid the state militia and John D. Rockefeller's mine guards in a battle against the miners in Colorado. Sixty-six people died in the Ludlow massacre, including two women and eleven children who were burnt alive when state troopers set fire to their tents. Six months later, Wilson sent federal troops to enforce an injunction against striking miners in Arkansas.[11]

The judiciary countenanced these derogations of civil liberties and due process, supporting the Executive's substitution of martial law for constitutional guarantees.[12] In *Moyer v. Peabody,*[13] an official of the Western Federation of Miners brought an action under the Civil Rights Statute of 1871 against the Governor of Colorado for holding him in preventive detention. Even though martial law had not been declared, the Supreme Court assumed that a state of insurrection existed. Justice Holmes, writing for the Court, stated:

> When it comes to a decision by the head of the State upon a matter involving its life, the ordinary rights of individuals must yield to what he deems the necessities of the moment. Public danger warrants the substitution of executive process for judicial process.[14]

Three years later, martial law was declared in response to strikes in the West Virginia coal fields. Labor organizers, arrested during the strike, were tried and convicted by military courts, even though the civil courts were still functioning. The West Virginia Supreme Court upheld the convictions.[15]*

---

* The use of federal troops to enforce the status quo during the decades between World Wars I and II is beyond the scope of this book. It is interesting to note, however, that labor was not the target of the largest single use of federal troops in the post-World War I era—veterans were. In 1932, 15,000-20,000 unemployed veterans formed the Bonus Expeditionary Force which camped in Washington, D.C. to demand payment of a bonus promised by President Coolidge. On June 28, 1932, President Hoover ordered federal troops to remove them from federal property, claiming that he was doing so to preserve the Constitution. The demonstrators were routed by troops using tanks, tear gas, cavalry and fixed bayonets. Four people died in the attack ordered by Chief of Staff Douglas MacArthur and led by Majors Dwight D. Eisenhower and George S. Patton.

Citizens' Committees and Tribunals

Given this history of due process violations, it is not surprising that vigilante justice and massive violations of civil liberties became commonplace as war hysteria swept the nation.

While Congress passed the Espionage and Sedition Acts, and George Creel's Committee on Public Instruction was propagandizing the country,[16] numerous semi-official national and local citizens' groups were established to enforce patriotism. These groups frequently took the law into their own hands with the acquiescence, and often the encouragement, of local, state and national officials.

In Nevada, for example, local citizens held a "people's trial," finding an unpopular resident guilty of "lukewarmness toward the cause of the United States and their allies." Led by the sheriff, the citizens' group tarred and feathered the "defendant." The governor of Nevada, admitting that the citizens might have been a little rough, condoned the action because "it all helped the cause." [17]

Many "patriotic" vigilante groups had official status. In some states, the legislatures gave statutory authority to vigilantes to conduct warrantless searches and issue subpoenas and contempt citations. In other states, people were appointed to Councils of Defense by the governor, although they had no formal authority to act. However, the absence of legal authority didn't seem to deter the Councils.[18]

The South Dakota Council made sure that all South Dakotans purchased their quota of Liberty Bonds to finance the war effort. Those who didn't, the State Council said, "come under our classification as 'slackers', and where they can afford to take certain amounts of bonds, can justly be suspicioned as being in opposition to the policy of our government." County councils were urged to subpoena and interrogate "slackers" regarding their ability to purchase bonds. In Iowa, "slacker" courts were established to hear charges against people who had not bought the requisite number of bonds.[19] In Cleveland, Oklahoma the council built a "slacker pen," announcing that anyone who failed to buy their quota of war stamps would be thrown in the pen until they changed their minds.[20] In Minnesota, the Commission of Public Safety virtually ran the state.

In August 1916, Congress created the Council of National Defense, to coordinate local and state committees. By the end of the war, it claimed a nationwide network of 184,000 organizations.

The American Protective League (APL), a privately-organized patriotic association whose goal was to aid the Bureau of Investigation (the forerunner of the FBI), was originally formed by wealthy Chicago businessmen for the purpose of lending their automobiles to motorless federal agents. By the end of the War, the APL had expanded into a citizens' secret service, with 250,000 members in 600 cities and towns. The Attorney General authorized the APL to state on its letterhead: "Organized with the Approval, and Operating under the Direction, of the U.S. Department of Justice, Bureau of Investigation." Anyone who could pay the required $1 dues could become a member and receive a badge stating "Secret Service Division." [21] The tentacles of the APL were so widespread that Attorney General Thomas Gregory stated:

> After the first six months of the War, it would have been difficult for 50 persons to have met for any purpose, in any place, from a Church to a dance hall in any part of the United States, without at least one representative of the Government being present. [22]

Although they had no legal authority to make arrests, League members surveilled, harassed, intimidated and detained those whose loyalty they questioned. People were sometimes held for weeks while the APL tried to determine if they were draft evaders. In addition to "arrests," kidnappings and harassment, APL members infiltrated, burglarized and opened the mail of radical organizations. [23] Fully aware of the APL's methods and tactics, Attorney General Gregory said of dissenters, "May God have mercy on them, for they need expect none from an outraged people and an avenging government." [24]

Although the APL's mission was presumably to combat foreign subversion, its main efforts were targeted against labor and progressives. A published report of APL activity in the Northwest from May 1 through November 1, 1918 indicated that, of twenty-five categories of arrests and investigations, the largest—over 10 percent of all APL activity—was directed against members of the radical labor union, the Industrial Workers of the World. [25]

With the Attorney General's approval, the American Protective League staged a series of "slacker raids," designed to apprehend young men who had not signed up for the military draft. In dozens of cities, government officials and APL volunteers raided movie houses, factories, union halls, offices and private homes, herding young men into detention centers until their draft status could be verified.[26] Some 10,000 men were "arrested" during the slacker raids in New York City; in one instance, the exits to a movie theatre were blocked and anyone who could not produce a draft card was arrested.[27] During one such raid in 1918, the United States Marshal for New York, Thomas McCarthy, impounded the badge of an APL member and released his eighty-five prisoners on the grounds that a private citizen had no authority to take slackers into custody. In response, the head of the Bureau of Investigation denounced McCarthy and expressed complete support for APL activities.[28] The New York raids in September 1918 prompted even the pro-Wilson *New York World* to condemn the raids as "Amateur Prussianism in New York." [29]

The APL "arrested" over 40,000 young men for the War Department. Interestingly, there were no legal cases testing the constitutionality of these detentions and arrests during the war. It was not until 1922 that the Circuit Court of Appeals for Northern California held that detentions by private citizens violated due process. The court relied on *Ex parte Milligan*[30] in ruling that the war did not suspend due process, and that warrantless arrests were unconstitutional.[31]

Lawyers and judges were also attacked. Lawyers were disbarred for speaking at meetings of the Industrial Workers of the World (IWW).[32] A Montana federal district court judge avoided impeachment by one vote after he had acquitted a defendant accused of violating the Espionage Act.[33] The Illinois Bar Association passed a resolution condemning a lawyer's defense of a draft evader as unpatriotic and unprofessional.[34] The American Bar Association supported such activity. At its first annual meeting following the U.S. entry into the war, Elihu Root proposed a resolution stating:

> We condemn all attempts in Congress and out of it to hinder and embarrass the government of the United States in carrying on the war with vigor and effectiveness.
> Under whatever cover of pacifism or technicality such attempts are made, we deem them to be in spirit pro-German and in effect giving aid and comfort to the enemy.[35]

The resolution passed unanimously.

Attorney General Gregory stated that the greatest danger to the

United States was not the German spy, but the "respectable pacifist." Calling the male pacifist a "physical and moral degenerate," he proclaimed that "[t]here is no room for neutrality in this country." [36]

The National Civil Liberties Bureau reported 280 incidents of mob violence against people accused of disloyalty in the thirteen months from April 1917 to May 1918.[37] This vastly underreports the actual number. "During World War I, physical violence and murder seemed to become legal, as long as the victim was allegedly disloyal or pro-German." [38] One U.S. Senator, after hearing a report of the lynching of a German miner, stated, "Of course, I would rather not have mob law, but if we can't take care of them any other way, popular justice will do it." [39]

The extent of war-time violations of due process and civil liberties can be inferred from the following incidents:[40]

- Aliens were prevented from holding licenses and permits to do business within the city of Cleveland, Ohio.
- Five hundred citizens of Collinsville, Illinois, having decided that a neighbor was a German spy, dragged him into the street, wrapped him in an American flag and murdered him.
- Two thousand striking IWW members in Bisbee, Arizona were routed from their beds, herded into cattle cars by armed mine officials and abandoned in the Arizona desert without food or water.[41]
- A man in Thetford Township, Michigan was tarred and feathered because he had only purchased $1,500 worth of Liberty Bonds instead of the $3,000 that the mob thought he should have bought.
- Wesley Everest, a decorated war hero, was lynched by a mob of "patriots" in Centralia, Washington. "They first 'smashed his teeth with a rifle butt', then drove him to a railroad bridge, [where] he was mutilated, hanged three times and his body sprayed with bullets..." The coroner's report listed his death as suicide.[42]
- A small-town Minnesota newspaper editor was attacked and his presses destroyed because he refused to publish editorials critical of the Non-Partisan League.
- The Los Angeles Board of Education forbade all discussion of peace in classrooms.
- The Austrian-born violinist Fritz Kreisler was denied access to U.S. music halls.

• Beethoven's music was banned in Pittsburgh for the duration of the war.

While most arrests and due process violations during World War I involved pacifists and socialists protesting the war, feminists were also targeted by the government. During the war, women continued to struggle for equality and suffragists picketed the White House throughout 1917 demanding the right to vote. Although originally tolerated, these demonstrations proved embarrasing to the Wilson administration, especially when the women began carrying banners emblazoned "Kaiser Wilson" and "20,000,000 American women are not self-governed." Although their picketing was peaceful and legal, the government began to arrest suffragists shortly after the U.S. entrance into the war.

Various Independence Day celebrations took place in Washington, D.C. in 1917. At one, former Speaker of the House Champ Clark told a cheering, patriotic crowd that "Governments derive their just powers from the consent of the governed." At a smaller demonstration held in front of the White House, thirteen suffragists unfurled a banner proclaiming the very same words from the Declaration of Independence. The suffragists were arrested; Rep. Clark and his crowd were left unmolested.[43]

After a group of women was arrested and sentenced to sixty days for picketing, they carried their struggle inside the jailhouse itself. Although separated, the suffragists managed to write and sign the earliest known appeal issued in the United States demanding special treatment for political prisoners. Their letter read, in part:

> As political prisoners, we, the undersigned, refuse to work while in prison...
> This action is a necessary protest against an unjust sentence...
> We ask the Commissioners...to grant us the rights due political prisoners. We ask that we no longer be segregated and confined under locks and bars in small groups, but permitted to see each other...
> We ask exemption from prison work, that our legal right to consult counsel be recognized...to supply ourselves with writing materials...to receive books, letters, newspapers, our relatives and friends.

Our united demand for political treatment has been
delayed, because on entering the workhouse we found
conditions so very bad that before we could ask that the
suffragists be treated as political prisoners, it was necessary to make a stand for the ordinary rights of human
beings for all the inmates.

The appeal was ignored, their leader put in solitary confinement and
the women denied privileges granted ordinary criminals.[44]

During World War I, the federal government instituted the first
national draft since the Civil War. Conscientious objection was
equated with treason; former President Theodore Roosevelt
proclaimed in 1917 that pacifists "showed themselves traitors to
America."[45] The Secretary of War ordered that any conscientious
objector who was "sullen and defiant" or "active in propaganda" be
court-martialed. Some 450 conscientious objectors were found guilty
in these courts-martial: seventeen were sentenced to death (although
the death sentences were eventually commuted); 142 were sentenced
to life imprisonment; seventy-three were given twenty-year terms.[46]
By mid-1918, several hundred conscientious objectors were in solitary
confinement in military prisons in Fort Jay and Fort Leavenworth.
Conditions were barbaric:

Most solitary confinement cells are in the cellars of
prisons. They are small and all but completely dark. Light
and air comes in from a very small opening on the top, and
through a small iron grating [in the door...Prisoners were
found with their] wrists shackled to the iron bars of the
small opening in the door.

They are given two slices of bread three times a day and
a pitcher of water three times a day. They are given no
water with which to wash. If they wish to wash, they must
use some of their drinking water.

After 14 days of such confinement, the prisoners are
released into the prison yard for 14 days. They are given
raw food, an ax for chopping wood, cooking utensils, and
shelter at night. Otherwise they are regarded as men on a
desert island, bound to shift for themselves. If after these
14 days of desert island life, they are still unwilling to yield
their conscientious convictions, they are placed in solitary
confinement again for another 14 days. This can go on

indefinitely for the term of 20 or 30 years, to which these men have been sentenced, or until they are broken, either physically or mentally.[47]

Beatings by prison guards were common. "Coffin cages," measuring the length of a man's body, but only twenty-three inches wide and twelve inches high, were used to punish conscientious objectors. Some Russian immigrant prisoners stated that conditions in jail under the Czar were better than those they were subjected to as conscientious objectors in the States.[48] Amish prisoners, who refused to wear military garb—their religion prohibited the wearing of clothing with buttons—were similarly mistreated. On December 6, 1918, the military announced that it would stop the practice of manacling prisoners, although the rest of the ill-treatment cited above continued.[49]

Violations of the First Amendment

The Espionage and Sedition Acts

By 1917, Congress began considering numerous bills to prevent the expression of "disloyal" thoughts. On February 5, 1917, the chair of the House Judiciary Committee introduced a bill that would penalize with life imprisonment anyone who, in war-time, communicated reports that were "likely...to cause dissatisfaction, or to interfere with the success of, the military or naval forces of the United States." [50] The bill passed the House but died when the Senate adjourned for the season.[51] Another bill was introduced into the Senate that would have made the entire United States a war zone, and declared that any person publishing anything that hurt the morale of our armed forces could be tried as a spy before a military tribunal.[52]

Although these draconian measures failed to become law, four months later, on June 15, 1917, Congress enacted the Espionage Act,[53] which is still in force today. The Act gave the government power not only to punish the transmission of information injurious to national security, but also allowed the imposition of penalties for anti-war commentary and opinions.

However, as hysteria heightened, it was felt that the Espionage

Act was not strong enough, and it was amended the following year to include nine more offenses. The amended version, commonly known as the Sedition Act, made virtually any criticism of the government a crime. The Sedition Act made illegal in war-time:

- "Disloyal advice" regarding the purchase of U.S. bonds;
- Saying or printing anything "disloyal…scurrilous, or abusive" about the government;
- Saying or doing anything to bring the armed forces into "contempt, scorn…or disrepute";
- Advocating "any curtailment of production" of any goods necessary to the "prosecution of the war"; or
- "Favor[ing] the cause of any country with which the United States is at war." [54]

Anyone violating these acts could be sentenced to twenty years in jail and/or a fine of $10,000. The Sedition Act was not repealed until three years after the end of hostilities; the original Espionage Act was left intact and was used again during World War II.[55]

The Espionage and Sedition Acts were defended on two grounds: to protect the nation and to protect the dissenters themselves. It was argued that the Acts were a means of protecting dissenters—after all, proponants said, if disloyal acts were allowed, it would be impossible to protect dissenters from mob violence.[56] (From the dissenters' perspective, imprisonment for twenty years may have seemed a less-than-desirable form of protection.)

The Espionage and Sedition acts of 1917-18 are classic forms of suppression of speech. Mere advocacy was illegal. The breadth of the acts appears from a few examples of prosecutions under them:

- D.H. Wallace was sentenced to twenty years in jail for saying, "That when a soldier went away he was a hero, and that when he came back flirting with a hand organ he was a bum…" [57]
- D.T. Blodgett was sentenced to twenty years in jail for urging the people of Iowa not to re-elect members of Congress who voted for conscription.[58]
- Rose Pastor Stokes was sentenced to ten years in prison for saying "I am for the people, and the government is for the profiteers." [59]
- John White was sentenced to twenty-one months in prison for stating that U.S. soldiers were "dying off like flies" and that the "murder of innocent women and children by German soldiers

was not worse than what United States' soldiers did in the Philippines."[60]

- Kate Richards O'Hare was sentenced to five years in the Missouri State Penitentiary for stating that "the women of the United States are nothing more or less than brood-sows, to raise children to get into the army and be turned into fertilizer."[61]
- Twenty-seven South Dakota farmers were convicted for sending a petition to the government calling the war a "capitalist war" and objecting to the draft quota for their county.[62]

There were some 2,000 prosecutions under the Espionage Act; approximately 45 percent of the prosecutions led to conviction.[63] Although the purported rationale for the Espionage and Sedition Acts was to protect the nation from enemies and foreign agents, not a single person was ever convicted of spying.[64]

Many extremely harsh sentences were imposed, with at least thirty people condemned to twenty years in prison and seventy people to ten-year sentences.[65] By comparison, the longest sentence imposed under George III's sedition prosecutions was four years; under the Alien and Sedition Acts, the longest terms were eighteen months.

Zechariah Chafee summed up the use of the Espionage and Sedition Acts:

> It became criminal to advocate heavier taxation instead of bond issues, to state that conscription was unconstitutional though the Supreme Court had not yet held it valid, to say that the sinking of merchant vessels was legal, to urge that a referendum should have preceded declaration of war, to say that war was contrary to the teachings of Christ. Men have been punished for criticism of the Red Cross and the YMCA, while under the Minnesota Espionage Act it has been held a crime to discourage women from knitting by the remark, "No soldier ever sees these socks."[66]

For his own criticism of the Espionage Acts in a *Harvard Law Review* article,[67] Chafee, then a 34-year-old Harvard Law Professor, was brought up before an "academic inquisition" by Harvard's Board of Overseers to determine if he was fit to continue teaching. He was acquitted on a six-to-five vote. Although unknown at the time, it was recently discovered that the charges against Chafee had been prepared by the Justice Department, whose conduct Chafee had criticized in his article.[68] The man in charge of the "anti-radical" unit of the Department of Justice, which had developed dossiers on Chafee and other Harvard faculty, was J. Edgar Hoover.[69]

Censorship of the Press

During the smaller wars preceding World War I, press censorship had been routinely invoked, with or without legal authorization, when the military deemed it necessary.[70] With the coming of World War I, however, formal statutory press censorship appeared.

Two years before the U.S. entrance into the war, the U.S. War Department (later renamed the Department of Defense) began to consider what legislation might be "necessary to control the press in times of war." [71] A year later, on June 9, 1916, in preparation for hostilities, the War Department established a censorship office, known as the Bureau of Information, headed by Major Douglas MacArthur.[72]

Under the Espionage Act, the Postmaster General could bar from the mails any material deemed "subversive." As interpreted by the courts, the banning decree was conclusive "unless proved clearly wrong."

The most famous censorship case was probably that of *The Masses*. After the Postmaster barred the August 1917 issue from the mails, the magazine appealed. Judge Learned Hand issued an injunction barring enforcement of the Post Office's order, noting that nothing in the issue advocated violence or opposition to the war. When the Post Office appealed, the Court of Appeals voided the injunction;[73] from then on, the Postmaster had virtually complete discretion in the role of censor.

The *Milwaukee Leader* was also banned by order of the Postmaster. On appeal to the U.S. Supreme Court,[74] the Court ruled that the Post Office could ban a publication even if there had been no conviction under the Espionage Act. In effect, one lawyer in the Post Office, the solicitor, had complete authority over the entire press of the nation.

Not once since Judge Learned Hand was reversed in *The Masses* case was a decision to censor a paper during World War I overturned by a court. In all, over one hundred publications were censored.[75] The Post Office quickly moved from concern over anti-war and potentially treasonable issues to any criticism of the government: the *Freeman's*

Journal and Catholic Register was censored for reprinting a statement by Thomas Jefferson to the effect that Ireland ought to be a republic; the *Nation* for attacking Samuel Gompers, labor's representative on the Council of National Defense; *The Public* for stating that the government should "raise more money by higher taxes and less by loans"; the *Irish World* for saying that Palestine would not be a Jewish kingdom. Lenin's *Soviets at Work* was censored (even though we weren't at war with Russia), as was *Imperial Germany and the Industrial Revolution* by Thorstein Veblen, a book which even the Committee on Public Information—the government's official censorship board[76]—had approved as being patriotic.[77] Virtually all IWW literature was banned from the mails.[78] Due to a combination of official persecution and general anti-German feeling, the German-American press at the end of the War was half its pre-war size.[79]

Even after the Armistice, criticism of the government continued to be suppressed. In 1919, the Attorney General raided the *Seattle Record,* suppressing the paper for its anti-government views. The *New York Call* was still being banned from the mails thirteen months after peace had been declared.[80]

Censorship of Other Media

On April 6, 1917, President Wilson issued an order authorizing seizure of all wireless establishments and instituting censorship of cable communication.[81]

Press censorship was authorized, not only under the Espionage Act but also under the Trading with the Enemy Act, passed on October 6, 1917.[82] All cable messages between the United States and any foreign country had to be authorized. No magazine or periodical could print a foreign language article "respecting the government of the United States...its policies, international relations, the state or conduct of the war or any matter relating thereto," without first submitting a sworn translation to the Postmaster.[83]

Prior restraint was also imposed on the fledgling film industry; an interesting example is that of the case ironically known as *United States v. The Spirit of '76.*[84] Robert Goldstein, who worked with D.W. Griffith on "Birth of a Nation" decided to film a similar treatment of the American Revolution. "The Spirit of '76" contained scenes of

Patrick Henry's speech, Valley Forge and other patriotic settings. After one and a half years of work and $100,000, the film was previewed just prior to the outbreak of World War I. Because the movie contained scenes of British troops attacking North American colonists, the government indicted the director for producing a film "intended to arouse antagonisms, hatred and enmity between the American people and the people of Great Britain." The film was confiscated, driving the company into bankruptcy and Goldstein was sentenced to ten years in prison. His sentence was later commuted to three years.

Another example of the absurd lengths of censorship during the war involved a patriotic film produced by William Randolph Hearst known as "Patria." The film featured racist anti-Japanese and anti-Mexican propaganda combined with a plea for "preparedness." However, by the time the film was to be released, we were allies with Japan against Germany. President Wilson personally called Hearst to demand that all anti-Japanese references be deleted. Without changing any of the footage, Hearst simply reshot all of the title cards. The actors, still wearing Japanese uniforms but now given Mexican names, were allowed to be seen.[85] Racism against Mexicans was acceptable; racism against Japanese was temporarily off-limits, not to be officially sanctioned until the next World War.

The Committee on Public Information

On April 14, 1917 the Committee on Public Information (CPI)—the official U.S. censorship board—was created by President Wilson. The Committee, chaired by George Creel, included the Secretaries of Army, Navy and State. It was the first censorship board in the history of the United States. Its reach was pervasive:

> [E]very item of war news [Americans] saw—in the county weekly, in magazines, or in the city daily picked up occasionally in the general store—was not merely officially approved information but precisely the same kind that millions of their fellow citizens were getting at the same moment. Every war story had been censored somewhere along the line...in accordance with "voluntary" rules issued by the CPI.[86]

Creel's CPI also established a highly centralized, highly effective network of some 75,000 people throughout the country to present the government's official message.[87] These men and women were known as the Four Minute Men, a reference to both the Revolutionary Minutemen, and the maximum length of time that any speech was to last. The Four Minute Men were active from May through December 1917, proclaiming the government's "official line" before the showing of movies, plays and anywhere else large groups assembled. The topic of each day's speech was coordinated from Washington, D.C. Topics included a twenty-five-day campaign touting the "Liberty Loan," twenty-eight days on "What Our Enemy Really Is," thirteen days on "Why We Are Fighting" and thirty days on "The Meaning of America."[88] All told, there were thirty-six distinct drives during the seven months of the Four Minute Men program.[89] In New York City alone, over 500,000 people heard the Four Minute Men speeches each week given by some 1,600 people in three different languages. It is estimated that over 1,000,000 speeches were given, reaching a cumulative audience of over 400,000,000 people.[90] Total cost to the government of this propaganda blitz was barely $200,000.[91]

The CPI helped convince the population that war-time restrictions on civil liberties were acceptable. An entry titled "Freedom of the Press" in the CPI-published *War Cyclopedia* stated:

Congress may establish a censorship of the press in war time if circumstances render such a measure "necessary and proper." For Congress has the power to pass all laws that are "necessary and proper" to prosecute successfully a war which has been declared; and the subjection of the press to the powers given Congress by the Constitution can hardly be said to *abridge* the freedom there recognized. Also, of course, Congress may penalize publications which are calculated to stir up sedition, to obstruct the carrying out of the laws, or to "give aid and comfort to the enemy" (which is treason). Freedom of the press in war time rests, therefore, largely with the discretion of Congress.[92]

These sentiments were echoed by the leading jurists of the time. Professor Wigmore claimed:

Where a nation has definitely committed itself to a foreign war, all principles of normal internal order may be suspended. As property may be taken and corporal service may be conscripted, so liberty of speech may be limited or suppressed, so far as deemed needful for the successful conduct of the war...all rights of the individual, and all internal civic interests, become subordinated to the national right in the struggle for national life.[93]

The efforts of the CPI and other censorship boards had the effect of setting the stage for the "spy hunts" and Palmer Raids that followed the war. Whether they had any actual effect on the U.S. ability to wage war is highly doubtful.

George Creel, chair of the censorship board, called the experiment "disastrous." [94] The ludicrous nature of the effort to censor the entire country may be gleaned from Creel's own analysis:

> There were many instances where papers were denied permission to give the location of aviation plants although the information was to be found in every telephone and city directory. A powder factory was being built in plain view of a large city, an enterprise lauded by the Chamber of Commerce, but reporters were ordered to ignore its existence. Printing of ship news was forbidden, although notices of arrivals and departures were posted in hotel lobbies.[95]

Unfortunately, Creel's "fervent prayer that just as I had been American's first official censor so would I live in history as the last" [96] was not to be answered.

The Supreme Court Response

The Supreme Court never ruled on the validity of the Espionage Acts during World War I, but in the years immediately following the War, the Court upheld the constitutionality of censorship on six separate occasions.

The first three cases were all decided unanimously in 1919. In *Schenck v. United States,*[97] the Supreme Court upheld the conviction of Charles Schenck for printing a leaflet opposing the draft, even though, in the Court's words, the defendant had "confined [himself] to peaceful measures such as a petition for the repeal of the act." It was in this case that Justice Oliver Wendell Holmes first delineated his "clear and present danger" test to determine when speech could be restricted, but then used this test to uphold Schenck's conviction.

Rather than an affirmation of freedom of speech, the "clear and present danger" test, as developed in *Schenck* and the subsequent Sedition Act cases, served as an "apology for repression." [98]

Exactly one week later, the Court upheld the convictions of Jacob Frowerk[99] and Eugene V. Debs.[100] Frowerk was a small publisher who printed pamphlets "to the general effect that [the U.S. government is] in the wrong and [is] giving false and hypocritical reasons for [World War I]." [101] Frowerk was sentenced to ten years even though he had made no effort to distribute his pamphlets to enlisted men.

The same day as *Frowerk,* the Supreme Court unanimously upheld the ten-year conviction of Eugene V. Debs for a speech he gave at a Socialist Party convention in Canton, Ohio deploring the war, prophesizing a socialist society and criticizing the Sedition Act conviction of Rose Pastor Stokes.[102] The most incendiary statement made by Debs during his speech was to the effect that "you need to know that you are good for something more than slavery and cannon fodder." [103]

Like Representative Matthew Lyons 120 years previously,[104] Eugene Debs ran for office while serving his prison term. He received more than 919,000 votes for President of the United States on the ticket of the Socialist Party in 1920.*

The Supreme Court upheld the Sedition Act on three other occasions, but in these decisions the Court split seven-to-two, with Justices Holmes and Brandeis dissenting. In *Abrams v. United States,*[106] Jacob Abrams received a twenty-year jail sentence for printing a leaflet urging a strike at a munitions plant and protesting the landing of 7,000 U.S. soldiers in Vladivostok to fight against the newly-created Soviet republic. In 1919, the Court upheld Abrams' conviction even though we were not at war with the Soviet Union and the Espionage and Sedition Acts only applied to actions supporting

---

* In a phrase echoed some seventy years later by President Bush, Clarence Darrow once described Eugene Debs as follows: "There may have lived somewhere a kindlier, gentler, more generous man than Eugene Debs, but I have not known him." [105]

nations with which we were at war. Justices Holmes and Brandeis dissented, stating that a "silly leaflet by an unknown man" [107] could not possibly pose any threat to the government's war effort.

The next year, in *Schaefer v. United States,* [108] the Court upheld the conviction of a German-language newspaper editor for taking news dispatches from other papers and publishing them with omissions, additions and changes. Examples of Schaefer's seditious writings cited by the Court included the statement that "[t]he army of ten million and the hundred thousand airships which were to annihilate Germany have proved to be American boasts"; and "Germany...has never done this country any harm...the sooner the American people come to their senses and demand peace, the better and more honorable it will be for this country." [109] The Court ruled in *Schaefer* that the Espionage Act's "restraints are not excessive nor ambiguous." [110]

The last of the six Espionage and Sedition Act cases to reach the Supreme Court was *Pierce v. United States,* [111] which upheld a conviction for publishing "The Price of War," a pamphlet produced by the national office of the Socialist Party. Among the seditious statements cited by the Court was the pamphlet's contention that "[t]he Attorney General of the United States is so busy sending to prison men who do not stand up when the 'Star Spangled Banner' is played, that he has no time to protect the food supply from gamblers." [112]

By the time Brandeis wrote his dissenting opinions in *Abrams, Schaefer* and *Pierce,* he had moved beyond the "clear and present danger" formulations with which he had concurred in *Schenck, Frowerk,* and *Debs.* Although he had come to believe that "in peace the protection against restrictions of freedom of speech [should] be unabated," Brandeis still recognized that "during a war...all bets are off." [113]

On June 21, 1920, Charles Evans Hughes gave a speech at the Harvard Law School. (Four years previously, Hughes had resigned as Associate Justice of the Supreme Court to run on the Republican ticket for President against Woodrow Wilson; he was later re-appointed to the Court as Chief Justice.) In his address, Hughes stated:

> We have seen the war powers, which are essential to the preservation of the nation in a time of war, exercised broadly after the military exigency has passed and in conditions for which they were never intended, and we may well wonder, in view of the precedents now established,

whether constitutional government as heretofore maintained in this republic could survive another great war
even victoriously waged.[114]

Although the Espionage and Sedition Acts were written to deal
with war-time emergencies, they were also used to prosecute people
for acts committed after the war was over. In 1920, for example,
activists were convicted for passing out handbills announcing a meeting to protest the previous convictions of conscientious objectors.[115]

In *Gilbert v. Minnesota*,[116] the Supreme Court upheld a person's
conviction for saying "We are going over to Europe to make the world
safe for democracy, but I tell you we had better make America safe for
democracy first." The Court held that since "every word he uttered in
denunciation of the war was false,...[i]t would be a travesty on the
constitutional privilege [of free speech] to assign him its protection." [117]

Judge Van Valkenburgh summed up the situation quite well
when he stated that freedom of speech meant protection for "criticism
which is made friendly to the government, friendly to the war, friendly
to the policies of the government." [118]

Throughout the 1920s, freedom of the press usually meant
freedom to express support for those in power. But by the 1930s, as
the war hysteria receded, the courts began to fashion a more inclusive
concept of freedom of expression.

On nine occasions in the fall of 1927, the anti-Semitic *Saturday
Press* published articles accusing the local power structure of graft and
corruption. The paper was enjoined from printing "malicious, scan-
dalous and defamatory" statements, although the editors were permitted to publish a newspaper "with good motives and for justifiable
ends." [119] The Minnesota Supreme Court upheld their conviction,
stating that freedom of the press only meant "the right to publish the
truth...with good motives, and for justifiable ends..." [120] The U.S.
Supreme Court overturned this ruling by a five-to-four vote, in the now
classic case of *Near v. Minnesota*.[121] Although the Court held that the
First Amendment prevented prior restraint except in the case of war,
Near more accurately represented a condemnation of the concept of
seditious libel.[122] *Near* is as famous for its pronouncements against
prior restraint as it is for its dictum that such restraint would obviously
be tolerated in times of war:

"When a nation is at war many things that might be said
in time of peace are such a hindrance to its effort that their
utterance will not be endured so long as men fight and that
no Court could regard them as protected by any constitutional right" *Schenck v. United States* 249 U.S. 47, 52. No
one would question but that a government might prevent
actual obstruction to its recruiting service or the publication of the sailing dates of transports or the number and
location of troops.[123]

This dictum would serve to legitimate the only example of peace-time
prior restraint in modern history some four decades later.[124]

Invalidating Elections

Toward the end of the war, workers became increasingly successful in electing their representatives at the ballot box. By 1917, the
Socialist Party of America had scored remarkable gains: in New York
City, the Socialist candidate received 21 percent of the vote; in Chicago
34 percent; in Buffalo 25 percent; in Dayton, Ohio 44 percent.[125] The
government's response was the initiation of the first major Red Scare
in U.S. history. As one historian noted,

At the very moment American socialism appeared on the
verge of significant organizational and political success, it
was attacked by the combined resources of the Federal and
various state governments.[126]

As a result of the war hysteria, free speech came under attack in the
legislatures as well as in the streets.

Victor Berger, an editor of the *Milwaukee Leader,*[127] had served
as the first Socialist member of Congress from 1911-13.[128] In 1918,
Berger was indicted under the Espionage Act.[129] Before the trial began,
however, he was elected to Congress from the Fifth district in Wisconsin on the Socialist ticket, winning 17,920 votes against 12,450 for the
Democrats and 10,678 for the Republicans. On the same day that the
Supreme Court unanimously upheld the convictions of pamphleteers
in *Abrams v. United States,* Berger went to claim his seat in the House
of Representatives. The House, by a vote of 319 to 1, refused to seat
him.

The next month the Governor of Wisconsin ordered a new

election. The Democrats and Republicans, haunted by the specter of another Socialist victory, together nominated a consensus candidate. Nonetheless, Berger ran again, increased his vote and outpolled his opponent 25,802 to 19,800. On January 10, 1920, the House again refused to seat him.[130]

Within the hour, the Socialist Party in Milwaukee announced his renomination for a third contest. However, afraid that Berger would win again, the Governor of Wisconsin refused to hold another election. Several cities forbade Berger from speaking publicly about this travesty of the electoral process.

New York had a large Socialist Party that grew out of the abysmal conditions of the large working class and immigrant sections of the city. In 1917, Morris Hillquist, Socialist candidate for mayor of New York, polled 141,000 votes. The next year, a Socialist candidate for governor received 121,000 votes. However, it was only when the Socialist Party was successful in winning office, that the Democrats and Republicans united to illegally deny them power.

On January 7, 1920, five days after the Palmer raids, and three days before Berger's second exclusion from Congress, five elected Assemblymembers—including four incumbents—were denied their seats in the New York Assembly.[131] Their only "crime" was that they had been elected on the Socialist Party ticket.[132] Despite criticism of their expulsion from former Justice Charles Evans Hughes, Governor Alfred E. Smith and the Bar Association of the City of New York,[133] the five were not allowed to serve in the Assembly and their seats remained vacant throughout the legislative session. Although the war had ended 14 months before, the *New York Times* supported their expulsion as a measure of national defense, calling the vote to expel the Socialists "patriotic" and "courageous." [134]

Expropriation of Property

The Trading with the Enemy Act was passed by Congress at the outbreak of World War I and amended four times during the following three years. It allowed the United States not only to confiscate property owned by "enemies," but also property of *allies* of enemies.[135] Under the Act, the government confiscated property of citizens of Turkey and

Bulgaria, both allies of Germany but against whom we were not at war. Neither of these countries confiscated U.S. property. The Alien Property Custodian seized $555,939,263.85 during the course of World War I,[136] the confiscations ranging in size from $1 (taken from two separate individuals)[137] to million dollar corporations owned by German citizens.[138] Three years after the end of the War, the Supreme Court upheld the Trading with the Enemy Act.[139]

Enemy property was not alone in being confiscated; the property of loyal citizens was seized if it was felt that such action would help the war effort. President Wilson seized at least eleven industrial plants to facilitate the war effort. Among these facilities were: the railroads, because of labor difficulties and ineffective operations; the telegraph lines and Smith & Wesson Co., in order to raise wages and end anti-union discrimination; and the Jewel Tea Co. and Hoboken Land Co., so they could be used by Remington Arms Co.[140]

On November 1, 1919, a year after the War's end, a miners' strike was called in North Dakota, disrupting fuel supplies to the western half of the state. A few days after the start of the strike, the weather plummeted to eight degrees below zero. The governor called out the militia and seized the mines to restart coal production. Affirming the need to prevent people from "freezing to death and dying of disease because of the failure of fuel supplies," the court refused to issue an injunction holding the act of the government illegal or unconstitutional.[141]

The Palmer Raids

Many countries have used banishment and exile as both a criminal sanction and a convenient way of eliminating political opposition. Exile has rarely been ordered in the United States,[142] but noncitizens have routinely been deported for violations of the law and excluded or deported in times of war for having opinions contrary to the reigning political orthodoxy. While not viewed under U.S. law as exile,[143] the effect is much the same.

Although the United States had long excluded Chinese and other immigrant groups on grounds of race and ethnicity, it was not until 1903 that aliens could be excluded because of their opinions. By 1920, aliens could be excluded or deported if they were anarchists or belonged to "subversive organizations." [144] Not only could such people be excluded, they could be deported, no matter how long they had lived in the United States, nor how long ago they had held (and perhaps discarded) the proscribed opinions.

During the winter and spring of 1919-20, Attorney General A. Mitchell Palmer, assisted by a twenty-four-year old lawyer named J. Edgar Hoover, conducted one of the most massive campaigns of civil liberties violations against non-Third World minorities in U.S. history. On the night of December 21, 1919, Palmer's agents arrested 249 Russian-born aliens and deported them to the Soviet Union. [145] On January 2, 1920, 2,700 people in thirty-three cities were seized. [146] Aliens were summarily deported. What became known as the Palmer Raids continued until May of that year.

Although the stated purpose of the raids was to protect U.S. citizens from dangerous radicals who were allegedly about to engage in violent revolutionary activity, the total weaponry seized during the entire course of the nationwide raids consisted of just three pistols. [147]

In 1920, Judge George Anderson heard a *habeas corpus* petition of some twenty aliens arrested in the Palmer Raids. He stated:

> I refrain from any extended comment on the lawlessness of these proceedings by our supposedly law-enforcing officials. The documents and acts speak for themselves. It may, however, fitly be observed that a mob is a mob, whether made up of government officials acting under instructions from the Department of Justice, or of criminals, loafers, and the vicious classes. [148]

A few excerpts from Judge Anderson's opinion, granting the *habeas corpus* petitions, should suffice to give an idea of the violations of civil liberties that occurred:

- [The] total number of persons arrested on this raid was [between 600 and 1,200]. The circumstances under which the raid was carried on make it impossible...to know with any approximate accuracy the number of persons arrested.
- Thirty-nine people at a meeting to discuss a cooperative bakery were arrested by Lynn, Massachusetts police.
- Mrs. Vasilierwska was confined for 6 hours in a dirty toilet room; then taken to Deer Island where she was kept 33 days.

- Private rooms were searched in omnibus fashion; trunks, bureaus, suit cases, and boxes broken open, books and papers seized. I doubt whether a single search warrant was obtained or applied for.
- The arrested aliens, in most instances perfectly quiet and harmless working people, many of them not long ago Russian peasants, were handcuffed in pairs, and...chained together.
- Deer Island [prison] conditions were unfit and chaotic...The place was cold, the weather severe...For several days the arrested aliens were held practically incommunicado.[149]

In Detroit, more than one hundred aliens were kept for over a week in a police bull-pen that measured twenty-four by thirty feet.[150] With substantially less than one square yard per person, it is no wonder that the mayor described the conditions as "intolerable in a civilized city." [151] Another 800 people were held for up to six days in the windowless corridor of the federal building where they were forced to share a single toilet.[152]

Virtually every prominent leader of both the Socialist and Communist parties was arrested.[153] A not unintended effect of the Palmer Raids can be seen from the decline in monthly dues to the Communist Party. In December 1919, the month before the raids, 23,624 members had paid dues; in January 1920, dues-paying membership had dropped over 90 percent to just 1,714.[154]

By the time the raids were over, warrants were issued for 6,000 aliens; 4,000 were arrested and approximately 1,000 were deported. One of those arrested was an Italian immigrant named Andrea Salsedo. After being held incommunicado for eight weeks in the office of the New York Bureau of Investigation, his crushed body was found on the pavement below the building. Bureau agents stated that he committed suicide by jumping out of the fourteenth-story window. Two of the more vocal critics of the treatment of Salsedo were Nicola Sacco and Bartolomeo Vanzetti. Their criticisms were silenced when they were framed, arrested and ultimately executed in 1927 on trumped-up murder charges.[155]

The Beginnings of a Secret Police

Napoleon's grand-nephew created the first permanent political surveillance organization in the United States. On July 1, 1908, Attorney General Charles Joseph Bonaparte established the Bureau of Investigation (later to become the FBI) within the Justice Department.[156] Since its inception, the FBI has engaged in massive and illegal spying on U.S. citizens. Starting at the end of World War I, the Bureau engaged in investigations, break-ins, wiretapping and various other illegal activities against political opponents of the administration. By the 1920s, J. Edgar Hoover's General Intelligence Division had an index of 450,000 names.[157] Included among those monitored were Helen Keller, Bertolt Brecht, Henry Steele Commager and future Supreme Court Justices Felix Frankfurter and Arthur Goldberg.[158]

The Army and Navy each developed their own politicized spy organizations. Two years after the Russian Revolution, the Office of Naval Intelligence (ONI) issued a report claiming that there was a Bolshevik conspiracy to take over the entire United States within the year. According to ONI, the leaders of the plot included anarchists Emma Goldman and Alexander Berkmann, "German and Russian Jews," Mexican bandits, IWW subversives and a "Japanese master spy." [159]

The Army created its own Military Intelligence Division (MID) in 1917 to prepare reports on "labor agitators and anarchists." During World War I, MID began amassing dossiers on hundreds of thousands of peaceful U.S. dissidents. These files continued to be updated and used by Army intelligence to spy on people as late as 1970.[160]

In 1922 Senator Burton K. Wheeler of Montana, who had been elected with the help of the progressive "Non-Partisan League," began making speeches attacking corruption in the Department of Justice. Bureau agents staked out his home to spy on him, ransacked his Senate office and tried to lure him into a compromising position with a woman in an Ohio hotel. With Bureau prodding, a federal grand jury eventually brought a criminal indictment against him. Sen. Wheeler was acquitted of all charges, while Attorney General Dougherty was ultimately dismissed from office when the Teapot Dome Scandal broke in 1924.[161]

That same year, the Director of the Bureau of Investigation in the Department of Justice testified that:

> Twenty-seven thousand four hundred and thirty-six reports have been received as to ultra-radical activities; 2,724 cases, approximately, under investigation...Many reports have been received upon violations of laws against syndicalism which have been referred to the State authorities, resulting as follows: 115 convictions and 114 cases pending; 611 radical publications are in circulation, including anarchist, communist, and ultra-radical dailies, weeklies and monthlies. This is an increase of 358 publications over last year...We find this radical propaganda being spread in churches, schools, and colleges throughout the country...Their propaganda principally consists in urging working men to strike...[162]

When visitors came to see their friends who were being held in the Hartford jail for attending a meeting of the Communist Party, the visitors were arrested. According to the Attorney General, their coming to inquire was *prima facie* evidence that they too were Communists.[163] Even though the Communist Party was not an illegal organization, any alien who was a member of the Party was liable to deportation.[164]

In a practice repeated many times in the ensuing fifty years, the government even spied upon and infiltrated churches. The government placed Secret Service agents in the congregation of the Community Church of New York to monitor the speech of the Church's minister.[165]

Sometimes the spies themselves fell victim to the government's violations of civil liberties. Herbert O. Yardley was a pioneer of the science of cryptography and during World War I became one of the founders of modern intelligence gathering. His manuscript, *Japanese Diplomatic Secrets,* was seized by U.S. government marshals at the offices of the Macmillan Company prior to publication. The book was never allowed to be published.[166]

The Industrial Workers of the World

Aliens, Jews and labor organizers were targeted by the various secret police agencies for harassment and illegal treatment. A concerted effort was made to destroy the most important union of the era, the Industrial Workers of the World. The IWW held the belief that all working people should be united in one single union. At a time when most unions were professional or craft unions, this was a radical idea. The Wobblies—as members of the IWW were called—believed that by creating one large union, socialism could be achieved peacefully. After all workers were organized, a general strike would be called, the country would come to a standstill and a new society would be born.

At its peak in 1912, the IWW had 100,000 members. When the IWW began winning rights for working men and women—and particularly after the successful 1912 strike of 30,000 previously unorganized textile workers in Lawrence, Massachusetts—the establishment set out to destroy the IWW.[167] Because they were successful, because they were radical and because the Wobblies opposed U.S. entrance into World War I, the IWW was targeted for elimination by the federal government. Being a member of the IWW became a deportable offense.[168] IWW members were forcibly expelled from scores of towns in the Midwest and West during 1917.[169]

The case of James Rowan provides one example of the length to which the government would go to deport an IWW organizer. Born in Ireland and naturalized as a U.S. citizen in Massachusetts in 1907, Rowan joined the IWW and became an organizer. He was arrested and convicted in the mass Chicago trials of the Wobblies. While in prison, the government attempted to revoke his citizenship. These attempts at nullifying Rowan's citizenship continued even after President Coolidge unconditionally commuted Rowan's sentence in 1923. The government's theory was that even though Rowan hadn't been a member of the IWW in 1907 when he became a citizen, the fact that he joined the union five years later provided proof of his unexpressed reservations about supporting the Constitution when naturalized.[170]

IWW leaders were constant targets of government repression. William D. "Big Bill" Haywood, secretary-treasurer of the Western Federation of Miners and an organizer for the IWW, was arrested countless times on a variety of trumped-up charges. In 1905, Governor Fran Steunenberg of Idaho was killed by a bomb attack. When Haywood was charged with the murder he hired Clarence Darrow as his defense lawyer. Haywood spent eighteen months in jail awaiting trial, during which time he ran for governor of Idaho on the Socialist Party ticket. He was found innocent after an eleven day trial. During

World War I, Haywood was arrested for sedition. He jumped bail and fled from the United States to the Soviet Union.

IWW organizer Joe Hill was not so lucky. Framed on a trumped-up murder charge, he was found guilty and executed before a firing squad in Utah.[171] Before dying, Joe Hill requested that his ashes be scattered throughout the entire United States except for the state of Utah; he did not want to be found dead there.

One judge described the "reign of terror," similar to that directed against aliens in the Palmer Raids, that was unleashed against members of the IWW:

> ...the Industrial Workers of the World was dissatisfied with working places, conditions, and wages in the mining industry, and to remedy them was discussing ways and means, including strike if necessary. In consequence, its hall and orderly meetings were several times raided and mobbed by employers' agents, and federal agents and sol-diers duly officered, acting by federal authority and without warrant or process. The union members, men and women, many of them citizens, limited themselves to oral protests, though in the circumstances the inalienable right and law of self-defense justified resistance to the last dread extremity. There was no disorder save that of the raiders. These, mainly uniformed and armed, overawed, in-timidated, and forcibly entered, broke, and destroyed property, searched persons, effects and papers, arrested persons, seized papers and documents, cursed, insulted, beat, dispersed and bayoneted union members by order of the commanding officer." [172]

Within a month, 2,000 IWW members were in jail awaiting trial. Mass trials were held: 165 IWW defendants were tried together in Chicago, 146 in Sacramento. Most were found guilty; many were sentenced to between ten and twenty years in prison.[173] The Chicago trial of 165 Wobblies lasted four months. After one hour of deliberation, the jury returned guilty verdicts against all the defendants. Fines in this one trial alone cost the IWW over $2 million.[174]

California may have been the most anti-IWW state in the Union. In Eureka, California, a person could be jailed for six months for distributing "membership cards, pamphlets, handbills or songs" of the IWW.[175]

At one trial in April 1922 in Sacramento, California, Anita Whitney, the niece of former U.S. Supreme Court Justice Stephen J. Field and an active member of the Oakland branch of the Socialist Party, was called as a witness for the defense to describe the aims of the IWW. She was rejected as a witness, however, as she was not a member of the organization. Thereupon, ten Wobblies were brought in as witnesses. Upon conclusion of their testimony, they were arrested, since they had admitted on the stand that they were IWW members. All ten were convicted and sentenced to between one and ten years in San Quentin.[176]

Anita Whitney would gain legal fame in 1927 as the defendant in *Whitney v. California,*[177] the case in which Justices Brandeis and Holmes wrote their famous concurrence justifying freedom of speech:

> Those who won our independence...knew that...it is hazardous to discourage thought, hope and imagination; that fear breeds repression; that repression breeds hate; that hate menaces stable government;...and that the fitting remedy for evil counsels is good ones...[T]hey eschewed silence coerced by law—the argument of force in its worst form. Recognizing the occasional tyrannies of governing majorities, they amended the Constitution so that free speech and assembly should be guaranteed.
>
> Fear of serious injury cannot alone justify suppression of free speech and assembly. Men feared witches and burnt women. It is the function of speech to free men from the bondage of irrational fears...To justify suppression of free speech there must be reasonable ground to fear that serious evil will result if free speech is practiced...The wide difference between advocacy and incitement, between preparation and attempt, between assembling and conspiracy, must be borne in mind.[178]

Anita Whitney had been convicted for violating California's Criminal Syndicalism law through her attendance at a peaceful convention of the Communist Labor Party in 1919. It is often forgotten that despite the ringing encomium on free speech written by Justices Brandeis and Holmes in *Whitney v. California,* both Justices voted to uphold her conviction.

In 1923, the state of California succeeded in obtaining an injunction against the IWW, virtually prohibiting its very existence within the state.[179]

The U.S. Post Office refused to deliver any mail that contained either symbols or ideas considered to be subversive. However, the Post Office's list of proscribed ideas was secret—one could never know in advance whether their mail would run afoul of Post Office censorship. The IWW emblem was one such forbidden symbol—the Post Office refused to deliver virtually anything mailed by the IWW.[180]

In their zeal to destroy the IWW, the federal government created fictitious Wobbly locals, lured people into joining the "union" and then arrested the newly-enrolled members. Roger Baldwin, founder of the American Civil Liberties Union (ACLU), wrote that once when he was in an FBI office, an FBI agent "showed me...a whole setup for forming an IWW local—forms, membership cards, literature. Thus the FBI could catch the 'criminals' they made." [181]

As a result of the attacks by local, state and federal officials, the IWW was effectively destroyed.

Only rarely did the judiciary attempt to require the government to act within the bounds of the law. One of the few judicial condemnations of the kangaroo trials of IWW members was from a federal district judge in Montana, who stated:

> [n]o emergency in war or peace warrants...violation [of civil liberties] for in emergency, real or assumed, tyrants in all ages have found excuse for their destruction.
> Assuming [the defendant, a Wobbly] is of the so-called "Reds"...he and his kind are less a danger to America than are those who [under cover of law have attacked him]. These latter are the mob and the spirit of violence and intolerance incarnate...Far worse than the immediate wrongs to individuals that they do, they undermine the morale of the people, excite the latter's fears...incline the people towards arbitrary power, which for protection cowards too often seek, and knaves too readily grant...They advocate and teach, not only unlawful destruction of property, but in addition unlawful destruction of persons, and they engage in the practice of both...
> ...They are no new thing, these present excesses. They are the reactions of all great wars, and in due time run their course...[182]

In 1924 there were 121 political prisoners in state prisons, serving terms of between one and twenty-eight years. None were "charged or convicted of any crime against person or property." [183] All but four were members of the IWW; 105 of the 121 were convicted in California. [184]

State and Local Laws

States throughout the country followed the lead of the federal government by passing anti-sedition, criminal syndicalism and criminal anarchy statutes. These laws made it a criminal offense to advocate, teach, publish, advise or in any way further any doctrine that promoted the use of force to bring about social or political change. The laws were designed to make it criminal to be a member of the IWW and to cripple unionization efforts by making advocacy of strikes, boycotts or picketing illegal. None of these laws punished actual damage to life or property; such overt acts were already illegal. These laws simply punished advocacy and speech in support of such actions.

By 1921, thirty-three states had passed "red-flag" statutes, making it a crime to display a red flag or any other "anti-government" symbol. Penalties ranged from a $10 fine to twenty-one years in jail. [185] Not until 1933 was California's red flag statute declared unconstitutional; it was re-enacted four years later by the California legislature in a successful effort to get around the Supreme Court ruling. [186]

Criminal syndicalism acts were used to jail socialists, anarchists and pacifists. Penalties for sedition ranged up to twenty years in Colorado, Delaware, Iowa, New Jersey and Pennsylvania; the penalty for criminal syndicalism was twenty-five years in South Dakota, twenty-one years in Kentucky, fourteen years in California, and ten years in another eleven states. [187] Within five years of passage of California's criminal syndicalism statute, 504 people had been arrested and 264 tried under the act. [188] The Constitution itself was deemed subversive: Upton Sinclair was arrested for reading the Bill of Rights at a rally in San Pedro, California; [189] across the country, Roger Baldwin, founder of the ACLU, was arrested in Patterson, New Jersey for reciting the Constitution.

In 1902, following the assassination of President McKinley by

Polish-born anarchist Leon Czolgosz, New York passed a criminal anarchy statute that read, in part:

> Every editor...of a book [or] newspaper...is chargeable with the publication of any matter contained in such book [or] newspaper.
> Whenever two or more persons assemble for the purpose of advocating or teaching the doctrines of criminal anarchy...such an assembly is unlawful...and every person voluntarily participating therein by his presence...is guilty of a felony.[190]

The law lay dormant until the 1920s when it was used to arrest Abraham Gitlow for publishing *The Left Wing Manifesto*. The case, *Gitlow v. New York*,[191] reached the Supreme Court in 1925. Prior to this case, the Court had held that the First Amendment did not apply to the states; individual states could infringe upon freedom of speech with constitutional impunity.[192] In *Gitlow*, the Court recognized for the first time that the First Amendment applied to the states;[193] nonetheless, the Court upheld Gitlow's conviction for publishing the *Manifesto*, stating that it was not even open to question:

> [t]hat a State in the exercise of its police power may punish those who abuse [their] freedom by utterances inimical to the public welfare, tending to corrupt public morals, incite to crime, or disturb the public peace...[194]

It is estimated that at least 14,000 people were arrested under state sedition, syndicalism and red flag laws during 1919-20.[195]

A 1921 survey of eighty-eight chiefs of police[196] showed that in only eleven of the cities was there an unrestricted right for citizens to meet on public streets.[197] In twenty-one of the cities, even meetings on private property required a permit. Permits generally were not given to dissident speakers. As the Chief of Police of Lowell, Massachusetts explained, "No radical meetings on public or private property" are permitted. In twenty-five of the cities, no police protection was given to radical meetings, thus allowing right-wing thugs to attack at will. The Mayor of Toledo, Ohio prohibited any meeting anywhere in the city "where it is suspected a man of radical tendencies will speak." [198] Mayor Baker of Portland, Oregon felt he had everything under control when he replied:

Owners of halls in this city are notified that they are held
responsible under the criminal syndicalism law for violations in their halls. This has stopped the majority of meetings of radicals. Street permits are refused the IWW and
no radical street meetings have been held for 18 months.[199]

Similar conditions lasted throughout the 1920s in Boston. Any
building that allowed a meeting which was opposed by the mayor
would have its license revoked. Meetings of the Ku Klux Klan, of
Margaret Sanger discussing birth control and of people protesting the
frame-up of Sacco and Vanzetti were all prohibited.[200] "The Old South
Meeting House, historic focus of free speech in colonial Boston, refused
to permit a Sacco and Vanzetti memorial meeting within its walls,
although agreeing to its use by the same committee to protest against
other halls closing their doors to them!"[201] Even outdoor speeches were
censored or banned in Boston. The Boston Common was off-limits to
all speakers and meetings about Sacco and Vanzetti. In 1929, two
years after Sacco and Vanzetti's execution, the National Secretary of
the Socialist Party acquired a permit to speak on the Boston Common.
His permit was revoked in the middle of his speech when he mentioned
the names of Sacco and Vanzetti and he was immediately arrested.[202]

Nonetheless, by the end of the 1920s, state repression began to
decrease. On the one hand, this was due to the gradual end of
war-induced hysteria; on the other, it was a curious, but logical, result
of the success of the repression itself:

The reason for the decrease in repression is that there is
little to repress. Militancy in the labor movement has
declined; the radical movements do not arouse fear. Insur-
gency of any sort is at a minimum...No new repressive laws
have been passed, probably for the simple reason that it
would be difficult to suggest any.[203]

It took a full ten years after World War I for the courts to stem
the tide of unconstitutionality swept in by "patriotic fervor." By the
1930s, the Supreme Court finally overturned California's red flag
statute,[204] recognized limits on a state's ability to declare martial law,[205]
and overturned Oregon's criminal syndicalism statute.[206] At least one
district court, in a case which has never been overruled, recognized a
constitutional right to grant reprieve from deportation.[207]

Chapter V

The World War II and
Korean War Era

Although prior to the attack on Pearl Harbor there was opposition to the U.S. entrance into World War II, afterwards there was overwhelming support for the allied cause. During no other war before or since has the population been so united in their support for the government's war effort.

World War II is often considered the last of the "good" wars. Nonetheless, it was not a war that was good for civil liberties. Violations of civil liberties—at least in terms of the number of people affected—were vastly greater in World War II than in World War I.

> In the First World War the number of victims of mob attacks, the people suppressed under the Sedition Act, all of those arrested and ordered deported, all of those sent to prison for conscience, total...about eight to ten thousand. The interned Japanese and Nisei alone numbered one hundred twenty thousand in 1942. The likelihood of a CO [conscientious objector] being jailed, which was four times greater in [World War II than World War I] resulted in six thousand men being imprisoned for conscientious objection. The victims of mob violence ran into the thousands...Thus, for every person falling foul of official or spontaneous persecution in the First World War, there were more than ten times as many victims in the Second.[1]

In addition, given the relative lack of opposition to World War II, the ratio of repression to dissent during the war may have been higher than during any other war-time era in U.S. history.[2]

Unlike previous wars, the United States did not demobilize its forces nor fully return to a peace-time economy at the war's end. Within two years of V-J Day, the Cold War was underway; two years later, we were involved in a "police action" in Korea.

In 1946, there were more labor strikes than in any previous year in U.S. history. Just as the government had repressed rising union militancy and radicalism through Red Scares at the close of World War I, so too the Truman and Eisenhower administrations unleashed a second and even more virulent Red Scare against the new labor militancy.

Proof of one's "loyalty" became essential to avoid harassment, loss of employment and even imprisonment. All three branches of government—separately but equally—violated with impunity the basic constitutional liberties guaranteed to American citizens. During the World War II and Korean War era, the United States:

- Interned 110,000 Japanese-Americans, most of whom were U.S. citizens, in concentration camps;
- Established strict censorship over all media, extending not only to war-related news but to any reports that might lower home-front morale;
- Closed down the pro-Nazi press;
- Enacted three peace-time sedition acts, making criticism of the government a crime;
- Denied passports to hundreds of progressives, including one member of Congress and a U.S. Supreme Court Justice;
- Prevented foreign writers and artists who held opinions disliked by our government from entering the country;
- Initiated a federal loyalty oath program, screening over 20,000,000 citizens for "subversion";
- Established federal loyalty boards that were empowered to determine if someone was "disloyal" using anonymous accusations and interrogations containing questions such as "Do you ever have Negroes in your home?";
- Established a dozen concentration camps and allowed for the internment of innocent people without trial during any future national emergency;
- Expropriated private factories due to "inefficient management";
- Allowed states to prohibit "subversives" from acquiring a birth certificate or a high school diploma, or becoming a pharmacist or living in public housing.

Censorship of the Press and Radio

Engaged in a world-wide struggle to defeat fascism, the U.S. government again saw the utility of imposing press censorship to aid the war effort. The day after Pearl Harbor, President Roosevelt gave FBI Director J. Edgar Hoover emergency authority to censor all news and control all communications going into or out of the country.[3] Later, the Office of Censorship was created and placed an "absolute restriction upon news of day-to-day fighting," [4] clearing an average of twenty-six stories daily.[5]

An elaborate code of war-time restrictions for both press and radio was issued by the Office of Censorship. These restrictions were voluntarily accepted by the press; no statute was ever enacted to enforce their provisions.[6] According to the Press Codes, issued by the Office of Censorship on February 20 and June 25, 1942, censorship extended not only to any information related to troop movements and ship sinkings, but also to:

- Reports of air raids;[7]
- "The civil, military, industrial, financial or economic plans of the United States" or its allies;
- "Criticism of equipment, appearance, physical condition or morale" of the armed forces of the United States or any of its allies;
- "Any other matter...which might directly or indirectly bring aid or comfort to the enemy, or which might interfere with the national effort, or disparage the foreign relations of, the United States or any anti-Axis nations." [8]

In addition, the publication of rumors and unconfirmed reports was prohibited. Publishers were cautioned that "[t]he spread of rumors in such a way that they will be accepted as fact will render aid and comfort to the enemy...[E]qual caution should be used in handling so called 'atrocity' stories."

The Revised Radio Code, issued on June 24, 1942 by the Office of Censorship, had equally strict rules regarding broadcasts. In addition to the rules covering the press, radio broadcasters were cautioned that "the most important censorship function [is] keeping the microphone under the complete control of the station management." All "open-mike" programs were considered "dangerous and should be

carefully supervised." [9] For the same reasons, popular "quiz
programs...should be discontinued." All foreign language programs
were required to submit, prior to broadcast, the text of the show along
with an English translation. This was not only due to fear that the
enemy might glean useful information, but also because of prejudice
against and distrust of non-English speaking people.

The National Association of Broadcasters issued their own
voluntary code of censorship on Dec. 18, 1941, less than two weeks
after Pearl Harbor. This Wartime Guide warned:

> DO NOT take chances with *ad lib* broadcasts...an open
> microphone accessible to the general public constitutes a
> very real hazard in times of war.
>
> DO NOT broadcast personal observations on weather
> conditions. Watch sports broadcasts for this. A late
> night...comment that 'it's a fine, clear night...' might be
> invaluable information to the enemy.
>
> DO NOT broadcast any long list of casualties. This has
> been specifically forbidden.

As censorship became a way of life during the war, articles
seemingly far removed from the war effort were censored. The *Los
Angeles Times* was censored at the post office before being sent to
subscribers overseas. Censors laid the paper on a table, and cut out
offending articles with razor blades. Unfortunately, the razor would
normally go through several pages, thus not only excising "dangerous"
articles, like the one on the funeral of Carole Lombard, but also
destroying the articles on the pages underneath. [10]

Articles on a race riot at Fort Dix, New Jersey on April 3, 1942
were banned, as were articles about a similar riot several months later
at a Louisiana base. [11]

Although they could print local weather reports, newspapers
were prohibited from reporting weather conditions in more than one
area of the country, presumably to prevent the enemy from gaining
information useful for planning an attack. In one particularly absurd
application of this policy, an account of a major snowfall in New York
City was censored from the *New York Times*. The front page of the
paper had a picture and article about the previous day's snowstorm in
Washington, DC. Accompanying the article was the following para-
graph:

Because of censorship restrictions which allow mention of
storms in only one area of the country in any one issue of
a newspaper, the *New York Times* does not print this
morning a report of weather conditions which obtained in
New York yesterday afternoon and last night.[12]

Of course, censorship restrictions fell hardest on the pro-Nazi
press. During the first year of the war, seventy newspapers were
banned from the mails under the Espionage Act passed during World
War I. Entire papers were closed. In the spring of 1942, for instance,
Social Justice, the anti-Semitic paper of Rev. Charles Coughlin was
censored, as was the *Philadelphia Herald* for reprinting *Social Justice*
articles critical of entry into the war. Also censored or prevented from
publishing were *The X-Ray,* because of articles that disparaged the
motives of our ally, Great Britain; and the *Townsend National Weekly*
and *Publicity,* accused of obstructing the war effort through their
publications.[13] The newspaper of the Socialist Workers Party, *The
Militant,* was also banned.[14]

The war-time restrictions resulted in what was probably the first
example of a censored shareholders' report. United States Steel's
annual report for 1941 showed production figures as "00,000 thousand
tons." A footnote to the report notified shareholders that the actual
figures were "omitted at the suggestion of the United States Office of
Censorship." [15]

Multiple censorship of a reporter's copy before release was the
norm from the battlefield. Censorship was often done for reasons of
morale. The news of the U.S. naval defeat at Savo Island, for example,
was not allowed to be announced until nine weeks after the battle, so
as not to affect morale on the home front. The enemy, of course, knew
of the defeat at the time it occurred.[16]

Battlefield news was also censored for purely political reasons.
The most notable example involved Charles DeGaulle and news from
North Africa. In late 1942, the U.S. State Department, opposed to
DeGaulle's government-in-exile, preferred to work with General Henri
Giraud. While behind the scenes talks between DeGaulle, Giraud and
the United States were taking place, General Eisenhower imposed a
six-week blackout on all news from the area in order to prevent public
speculation regarding the negotiations. Because of the success of the
censorship in North Africa, military officers specially trained in cen-

sorship subsequently were assigned to units in Europe.[17]

Personal mail was censored under both the Trading with the Enemy Act, passed during World War I,[18] and the War Powers Act of 1941. On December 19, 1941, ten days after war had been declared with Germany, a man sent a letter to his wife, a U.S. citizen living in Budelsorf, Germany. The letter had been routed through an intermediary in Barcelona, Spain. The husband mailed the letter without having obtained the necessary authorization from the President or Treasury Department, as required by law. He was tried, convicted and sentenced to ten years in jail for violating the Trading with the Enemy Act.[19]

At the beginning of the Korean War a voluntary system of press censorship was again established. But as politically troublesome stories began to appear, mandatory restrictions were imposed.[20] All news copy and film had to pass inspection by Eighth Army censors. Reporters were not allowed to print articles about food shortages, panics, inferior U.S. equipment or the rampant corruption in the South Korean government. As one example of such political censorship, reporters were not allowed to:

> ...mention the actions of South Korean police who black-mailed innocent farmers, threatening to arrest them as Reds unless they paid off. Hundreds fled into the mountains and joined guerrilla units because of police blackmailing tactics, but stories concerning this were killed...[21]

Throughout the Korean War, material that was deemed foreign "political propaganda" was prohibited from the U.S. mails. The Customs Bureau and the U.S. Post Office based their authority to exclude such publications on the Foreign Agents Registration Act[22] and the 1917 Espionage Act.[23] Publications as varied as *Lenin's Selected Works* and *Happy Life of Children in the Rumanian People's Republic* were banned. Little of the proscribed material was "anti-American;" none posed the slightest danger to the security of the country.[24]

After John F. Kennedy became President, he rescinded the State Department regulations authorizing this censorship. Representative Walters (co-sponsor of the repressive McCarran-Walters Act) then led a successful effort in Congress to pass a law banning "foreign propaganda." In 1965, the Supreme Court, in *Lamont v. Post Master General*,[25] ruled the statute unconstitutional. This was the first time since the adoption of the Bill of Rights 174 years previously that any federal statute had been found to violate the First Amendment.

Although state and local censorship flourished throughout the 1950s and early 1960s,[26] most forms of federal censorship ended with the truce at Panmunjom. However, during the anti-communist hysteria of the Korean War era, it became dangerous to be seen owning or reading any book that someone—anyone—might label subversive. At one point, the State Department began removing "dangerous" books from its own libraries. As President Truman recounted,

> [Senator Joseph] McCarthy began to say in his speeches that overseas libraries funded by the United States were full of Communist and pro-Communist books. So a number of cowardly fellows in the State Department immediately started destroying a lot of books, just as Hitler had done a few years earlier.[27]

At the end of the Korean War, the Army, Navy and Air Force jointly developed the *Field Press Censorship* manual, outlining the procedures for military censorship should it be reimposed. Less than an hour after President Kennedy's television announcement regarding the Cuban missile crisis on October 22, 1962, the Army's press censorship detachments were mobilized. These units were not abolished until 1977.[28]

Free Speech Restrictions

In 1800, the first federal sedition act, the Alien and Sedition Act, expired. For the next 140 years, there was no peace-time sedition act on the books. During the fourteen years between 1940 and 1954, however, Congress would enact three new sedition acts.

The Smith Act

In 1935, four years prior to World War II, the U.S. Congress began debate on the first federal peace-time sedition law since 1798. One month before Germany's invasion of Poland, the bill passed the House by a vote of 272 to 48 and became law on June 28, 1940. This act, formally known as the Alien Registration Act of 1940, was "the

most drastic restriction on freedom of speech ever enacted in the
United States during peace." [29] Title I of the Act did not deal with aliens
at all; it was modeled after New York's Criminal Anarchy Act of 1902[30]
and named after Representative Howard W. Smith of Virginia. Its
purpose was to:

> 1) Prohibit the advocacy of insubordination, disloyalty,
> mutiny or refusal of duty in the military, [and]
> 2) To prohibit the advocacy of the overthrow or destruc-
> tion of any government in the United States by force or
> violence.

The Smith Act's reach was far and undiscerning, yet was milder
than many of the other forty alien and sedition bills debated by
Congress in 1939 and 1940. One bill would have made communists
per se deportable.[31] Another bill passed by the House of Representatives would have mandated the deportation of aliens who advocated "any change" in the U.S. form of government.[32] A third bill would
have had all "sympathizers" with the Communist Party deported.[33] On
May 15, 1940, a bill to deport labor leader Harry Bridges overwhelmingly passed the House of Representatives, even though the Secretary
of Labor—on the advice of Harvard Law School Dean James M.
Landis, acting as special examiner in the case—had found him not
deportable. Had the bill been enacted, "it would [have been] the first
time that an Act of Congress ha[d] singled out a named individual for
deportation. It would [have been] the first deportation in which the
alien was not even accused either of unlawful entry or of unlawful
conduct while here." [34]

In the words of Zechariah Chafee, the original form of the Smith
Act provided for:

> ...the deportation of any alien who "advocates a change in
> the form of government of the United States" (with no
> violence whatever), or "engages in any way in domestic
> political agitation" (like attending a Democratic rally or a
> trade-union meeting to urge the passage of a wages and
> hours law). [parenthetical comments in original][35]

The Smith Act was challenged repeatedly in the courts; the
courts consistently upheld the Act. One of the first such cases involved
the arrest of eighteen Socialist Workers Party members prior to the

U.S. entrance into World War II.[36] Although the Circuit Court recognized that the Smith act "appears on its face to limit exercise of a right specifically protected by the Constitution," [37] the Act was upheld. The court found that the Smith Act didn't "limit the constitutionally protected individual liberties of the citizen to any greater extent than is reasonably necessary and proper to accomplish the important allowable ends of preserving the life of the Government and the States and their orderly conduct." [38]

The Supreme Court continued this line of reasoning in its ruling in the most famous of the Smith Act prosecutions, *Dennis v. United States*.[39] Twelve members of the Central Committee of the Communist Party of the United States were indicted under the Smith Act in 1948. All of the defendants (except for one whose case was severed due to bad health) were convicted. The Supreme Court upheld restrictions on free speech using a greatly weakened "clear and present danger" test. Adopting an approach usually used for civil wrongs,[40] not constitutional guarantees, the Court held that "In each case [courts] must ask whether the gravity of the 'evil,' discounted by its improbability, justifies such invasion of free speech as is necessary to avoid the danger." [41] The Court thus turned a "clear and present danger" test into a not too improbable danger test. Or as Chafee put it, the Court reinterpreted the First Amendment to mean: "Congress shall make no law abridging the freedom of speech and of the press unless Congress does make a law abridging the freedom of speech and of the press." [42] As late as the mid-1970s,the Supreme Court reaffirmed its adherence to this First Amendment balancing test.[43]

After the Court's ruling in *Dennis,* the Department of Justice initiated twenty-one other Smith Act prosecutions, involving 131 defendants. One died during trial; three were severed for reasons of ill health; a few became fugitives. Only ten were acquitted. Of those tried, 89 percent were convicted.[44] Courts of appeals affirmed every conviction that came before them.[45]

At least two lower court judges offered banishment to the Soviet Union as an alternative to imprisonment. The defendants declined the offer, stating "We feel we belong here and have a political responsibility here. We feel we would be traitors to the American people if we turned our backs on them just to escape jail." [46]

During the ensuing decade, the Supreme Court continued to

uphold the constitutionality of this peace-time sedition act. As war-
time hysteria began to recede, the Court started to require stricter
evidentiary proof for convictions,[47] and by 1961, in the last Smith Act
case to reach it, the Supreme Court held that mere membership in
"subversive organizations," without personal intent to overthrow the
government, was not enough for conviction under the Act.[48] These more
demanding requirements, combined with a lessening of the Cold War,
brought an end to Smith Act prosecutions. The *Dennis* decision has
never been overruled, however, and the Smith Act remains the law of
the land.

Lawyers who represented Smith Act defendants were targeted
for governmental and judicial harassment. These attacks were pre-
saged by Attorney General Tom Clark, who warned that lawyers
should be careful whom they chose as clients, and urged that lawyers
who represented Communists should be taken "to the legal woodshed
for a definite and well-deserved admonition." [49] After being appointed
to the Supreme Court, Clark again repeated his call that lawyers who
defended Communists should be closely "scrutinized by grievance
committees of the bar and the courts." [50] Two years later, in 1951, the
American Bar Association recommended that all lawyers be required
to swear to an anti-communist loyalty oath[51] and that local bar groups
expel lawyers who were members of the Communist Party. This was
the first time since 1867, when the U.S. Supreme Court struck down
an attempt to purge the bar of Confederate sympathizers, that a
loyalty oath for lawyers was seriously considered.[52]

The campaign to purge the bar found its target in the counsel for
the *Dennis* defendants.[53] After the conviction of the eleven defendants,
all five defense attorneys were charged with contempt of court and
served sentences ranging from thirty days to six months. The contempt
citations were upheld by a divided Supreme Court.[54] The lawyers
served their sentences under harsh conditions; one lawyer, ordered to
serve his sentence in Texarkana, Texas, was driven across the country
for nearly seven weeks, handcuffed and in leg irons.[55] Due to their
representation of unpopular defendants, two of the five lawyers were
later disbarred, their careers ruined. The Supreme Court eventually
overturned their disbarment,[56] although one lawyer continued to be
disbarred from state court practice for another decade.

The bars in at least twenty-one states asked questions pertaining to a future lawyer's loyalty, political affiliation or membership in subversive organizations. The Indiana Bar, for example, asked applicants' references, "Have you ever heard any question raised as to the applicant's adherence to and support of the principles of the Constitution of the United States?" They also required the applicants' law schools to complete an affidavit stating, "During [his attendance] the reputation of the applicant for honesty, morality, fair dealing, truthfulness and loyalty to the United States was [excellent, fair, bad]."

The Hawaii Bar, after requiring applicants to attest to whether or not they had contact with any of the organizations on the Attorney General's list, asked the following question:

> (8) If you were to be listed as a "Communist" in the records of any federal investigative agency, what past actions or organizational affiliations of yours not already listed by you might be used by such investigative agency to support its conclusion? In answering this question, assume that all of your past actions and organizational affiliations are known to such investigative agency.[57]

The McCarran Act

Congress enacted the third federal peace-time sedition law on September 23, 1950. This sedition act, officially known as the Subversive Activities Control Act of 1950, is more commonly called the McCarran Act. President Truman stated in his veto message that the McCarran Act:

> ...would put the United States into the thought-control business. It could give government officials vast powers to harass all of our citizens in the exercise of their rights of free speech.[58]

Despite opposition by the Department of Justice, the Department of Defense, the Department of State and the CIA, Congress overrode President Truman's veto and enacted the McCarran Act as the law of the land.

The fifty-six pages of the McCarran Act contain several major provisions:

1) *Denial of habeas corpus.* The Act violated constitutional restrictions on denial of *habeas corpus*[59] by allowing the imprisonment

of innocent citizens during any presidentially-declared "Internal Security Emergency." Such an "emergency" could be declared in times of invasion, insurrection or war—including, for instance, a localized conflict thousands of miles from the United States—and would last until terminated by the President or Congress. This section of the Act, known as the Emergency Detention Act of 1950, authorized "the detention of each person as to whom there is reasonable ground to believe that such person probably will engage in, or probably will conspire with others to engage in, acts of espionage or sabotage..." [60] The government established concentration camps to be used for the mass internment envisioned by the Act.[61] These unused concentration camps were maintained by the government through the 1960s; the Emergency Detention Act of 1950 was not repealed until 1971.

2) *Immigration Restrictions.* The McCarran Act required the exclusion or deportation of aliens based on their political ideology. Under the Act, no visa could be issued to anyone who "ever has been" affiliated with any organization that advocated any form of totalitarianism.[62]

The Supreme Court avoided any problems of due process surrounding arbitrary denial of entrance of aliens into the United States by tautologically defining that due process for aliens is whatever Congress says it is.[63] In one particularly glaring example, an alien who had lived legally in the United States for twenty-five years had left the United States to visit his dying mother in Rumania. He was refused readmittance to the United States without a hearing, even though no other country would take him; his summary exclusion was upheld by the Supreme Court.[64]

A majority of the people deported during this period had lived in the United States virtually all their lives. One study showed that 60 percent of the people deported for political reasons in 1956 had lived in the United States for more than forty years; 81 percent had resided here more than thirty years.[65] Unfortunately, the reigning philosophy of the time was that expressed by Attorney General (and later Supreme Court Justice) Tom Clark in 1948: "[t]hose who do not believe in the ideology of the United States shall not be allowed to stay in the United States." [66]

3) *Subversive Activities Control Board.* The McCarran Act created the Subversive Activities Control Board, consisting of five

members, who could declare any organization "Communist" or "Communist-front," thus requiring it to register with the Attorney General and subjecting it and its members to various adverse legal consequences, including:

a) *Registration.* The Act required that every "Communist-front organization" must file a report listing all officers and full financial statements including all contributions received. The penalty for failure to register was draconian: a $10,000 fine and five years in prison for *every* day the report was delayed, *every* name willfully left off the list, or *every* item found by a jury to be deliberately omitted.

A 1954 amendment to the McCarran Act added another requirement to the registration forms:

"A listing...of all printing presses and machines included but not limited to rotary presses, flat bed cylinder presses, platen presses, lithographs, offsets, photo-offsets, mimeograph machines, multigraph machines, multilith machines, duplicating machines, ditto machines, linotype machines, intertype machines, monotype machines, and all other types of printing presses, typesetting machines or any mechanical devices used or intended to be used, or capable of being used to produce or publish printed matter or material..."[67]

b) *Restrictions on right to travel.* The Act denied passports to "subversives." Any knowing member of a "Communist-front organization" who applied for a passport could be punished by five years in prison and $10,000 fine.

c) *Restrictions on use of the mail.* It became a crime for any "communist-front organization" to send anything by mail that was intended to be read by two or more people, unless the envelope contained the warning, "Disseminated by _____, a Communist organization." Similar warnings were required to be announced on any radio or television broadcast made by such organizations. Again, the penalty was a $10,000 fine and/or five years in prison.

d) *Restrictions on employment.* No member of a "Communist-front organization" could "hold any nonelective office or employment under the United States," or work in any "defense facility."

Other Federal Measures

The Smith Act and the McCarran Act were neither the first nor the last of the World War II and Korean War era federal measures to target non-violent expression of beliefs.

One month before Germany's invasion of Poland, Congress passed "An Act to Prevent Pernicious Political Activities," [68] commonly known by the name of its sponsor, Senator Carl Hatch. Section 9A of the Hatch Act prohibited federal employees from being members of "any political party or organization which advocates the overthrow of our constitutional form of government." The Civil Service Commission interpreted this to include the Communist Party and the German Bund. By 1942, the Civil Service Commission had concluded that being a "follower" of Communism raised a "strong presumption" against one's loyalty to the United States.[69]

In 1946, after a four-year war-time hiatus on labor strikes, more than 4.5 million workers engaged in 4,700 walkouts.[70] The next year, over President Truman's veto, Congress passed the Taft-Hartley Act[71] to curb the power of organized labor. Among other provisions, the Taft-Hartley Act was designed to purge unions of communist influence by withdrawing National Labor Relations Board recognition from any union whose leadership refused to swear they were not communists. The Act stated that the NLRB shall not investigate or accept union recognition petitions or investigate complaints by any union:

> unless...each officer of such labor organization and the officers of any national or international labor organization of which it is an affiliate...[has filed an affidavit with the NLRB] that he is not a member of the Communist Party or affiliated with such party, and that he does not believe in, and is not a member of or supports any organization that believes in or teaches, the overthrow of the United States Government by force or by illegal or unconstitutional methods." [72]

Four years after passage of the McCarran Act, when not one organization had registered under its provisions, Congress enacted the fourth national sedition act in our history, known as the Communist Control Act of 1954.[73] The Act declared the Communist Party an outlaw organization.

In 1954, Congress also passed the Expatriation Act,[74] which would have turned any member of the Communist Party or "Communist-front" organizations into a "Man Without a Country." The Act provided for the automatic loss of U.S. citizenship for any person convicted of certain crimes, including violations of the Smith Act. Since lower courts at the time ruled that mere membership in the Communist Party was sufficient to constitute a violation of the Smith Act, this Act potentially meant the expatriation of perhaps 70,000 U.S. citizens for mere expression of political beliefs.[75] Loss of citizenship would have meant a denial of basic constitutional rights. Aliens were granted only limited procedural due process rights regarding deportation hearings: aliens could be compelled to testify against themselves, could not complain of illegal searches and seizures, could be held without bail at the discretion of the Attorney General prior to a deportation hearing, and, if found deportable, could be detained for up to six months after such a hearing.[76] It took the Supreme Court another thirteen years before ruling that U.S. citizenship could not be revoked by the government.[77]

Three years later, still in the throes of a national anti-communist hysteria, Congress enacted the Landrum-Griffin Act,[78] which lumped together robbery, bribery, extortion, grand larceny, murder, rape and being a member of the Communist Party as equally heinous crimes of turpitude.[79]

As a curtain call to this closing era of the Red Scare, Congress, when passing Title VII of the landmark 1964 Civil Rights Act,[80] specifically exempted any member of the Communist Party or Communist-front organizations from being able to file discrimination charges under Title VII.[81]

Federal Loyalty Oaths

A year and a half after World War II ended, President Truman issued Executive Order 9835, which initiated a comprehensive Federal Employees Loyalty Program.[82] The Attorney General compiled a list of 275 "subversive" organizations; over 20,000,000 citizens were screened before the security program ran its course.[83] Not one of the millions screened under this program was indicted for a crime.[84] People accused of disloyalty were not given the right to hear the specific charges made against them by anonymous informers. Loyalty boards were established which asked questions regarding political and social beliefs, including such questions as, "Do you ever have Negroes in your home?"; "Do you read Howard Fast? Tom Paine? Upton Sinclair?"; and "There is a suspicion in the record that you are in sympathy with the underprivileged. Is this true?" [85]

Loyalty boards accused people of the following breaches of loyalty:

> ...the employee advocated the Communist Party line, such as favoring peace and civil liberties...
> ...the employee's convictions concerning equal rights for all races and classes extend slightly beyond the normal feeling of the average individual...
> You have during most of your life been under the influence of your father, who...was an active member of the Communist Party. [86]

Absurd hearings took place, in which people tried to disprove accusations of disloyalty. One young man suggested that his landlady find a boarder through the community chest; to her, "community chest" sounded like "communism," and the young man ended up trying to save his job in a hearing before the loyalty board. Another man, an employee in the Government Printing Office, was denied work when a security officer overheard "left-wing talk" from him. The security officer testified that he heard the employee—a black man—describe himself as a "second-class citizen." In a hearing before the board, it became clear that the employee had said he would "rather be a second-class citizen in Mississippi than a first-class citizen in Russia." [87]

An incident demonstrating how the loyalty program worked—unusual only in the fact that the case ultimately reached the Supreme Court—involved one Miss Bailey, a low-level civil servant whose loyalty was put in doubt by an anonymous accusation that she had been a member of the Communist Party. In her hearing before the Loyalty Review Board, she produced "affidavits of some 70 persons who knew her including bankers, corporate officials, federal and state officials, union members and others" testifying to her loyalty. No one testified against her, and she was never told the supposedly incriminating evidence that the board had received. "Against all this, there were only the unsworn reports in the secret files to the effect that unsworn statements of a general sort, purporting to connect [Miss Bailey] with Communism, had been made by unnamed persons." [88] Nonetheless, Miss Bailey was fired. Her firing was upheld by an equally divided Supreme Court. [89] Justice William O. Douglas later remarked, "How could anyone prove that he was not disloyal?"

As one commentator wrote:

> To enumerate the features of the loyalty program is to suggest the description of an authoritarian society. Any American hearing of a foreign country in which the police were authorized to search out the private lives of law-abiding citizens, in which a government official was authorized to proscribe lawful associations, in which administrative tribunals were authorized to condemn individuals by star-chamber proceedings on the basis of anonymous testimony, for beliefs and associations entailing no criminal conduct, would conclude without hesitation that the country was one in which tyranny prevailed. [90]

Three years later Congress passed a law giving the executive branch "absolute discretion" to fire any employee "when deemed necessary in the interest of national security." [91] President Eisenhower enlarged the loyalty investigations in 1953; [92] in the last six months of that year, over 2,200 government employees were fired and another 4,315 resigned their jobs rather than submit to security investigations. [93]*

---

* This is not to condemn all loyalty oaths as insidious. Oaths given to office holders to uphold the Constitution have generally been considered appropriate. [94] Other oaths, such as a new South Dakota pledge, effective July 1, 1987—"I pledge loyalty and support to the flag and state of South Dakota, land of sunshine, land of infinite variety" [95]—are relatively innocuous.

Congressional Inquests

> The House Un-American Activities Committee is the most un-American thing in America.
>
> —President Harry Truman[96]

While the executive branch was trampling on individual liberty through its loyalty purges, the legislative branch established its own inquisition under the guise of conducting legislative investigations.

As fascism was advancing in Europe, and the Continent was veering towards another war, the U.S. Congress created a temporary subcommittee to deal with "subversion." Known as the House Committee on Un-American Activities, (HUAC) it was authorized to investigate:

> 1) the extent, character and objects of un-American propaganda activities within the United States, 2) the diffusion within the United States of subversive and un-American propaganda that is instigated from foreign countries or of a domestic origin and attacks the principle of the form of government as guaranteed by our Constitution...

Six years later, while chaired by Representative Martin Dies, HUAC became a permanent committee of the House of Representatives.

From the beginning, HUAC was an anomaly—a House Committee whose only purpose was harassment, intimidation and exposure of "incorrect" ideas. Committees of Congress are supposed to exist for the purpose of preparing legislation. But exposure, not legislation, was the unconstitutional purpose of HUAC. From 1951 to 1960, 41,776 bills were introduced in the House of Representatives and referred to committees. Of these, only thirty-one were referred to HUAC—even though HUAC's budget during this period was greater than that of any other House committee. HUAC held no legislative hearings on the twelve bills referred to it between 1951 and 1958.[97]

Despite the fact that the House Committee on Un-American Activities served no legitimate legislative function, HUAC "spent the most money, called the most witnesses, published the most pages, visited more places, [and] ruined more lives...[than] any Committee in Congress."[98] Between 1945 and 1960, HUAC produced more pages of reports and hearings, issued more subpoenas—over 5,000—and cited for contempt five times as many witnesses as all other House committees combined.[99] During this time, HUAC interrogated over 3,000 witnesses at 230 public hearings.[100] Of the 187 contempt citations issued by the House of Representatives between 1945 and 1971, 174 came out of HUAC hearings. Of these 174, 142 failed in court.[101]

HUAC had an ultra right-wing view of what constituted un-American ideas. The 1939 report of HUAC stated that "Americanism recognizes the existence of a God." According to HUAC, un-American beliefs included beliefs in:

- Absolute social and racial equality;
- The destruction of private property and the abolition of inheritance;
- The belief that it is the "duty of government to support the people." [102]

Not surprisingly, the chairs of HUAC came from the far right of the political spectrum. Representative John Wood, chair from 1945-46 and again from 1949-53, considered the Ku Klux Klan "an old American custom." Representative Harold Velde, chair of HUAC in 1953, had previously opposed mobile library services in rural areas, explaining:

Educating Americans through the means of the library service could bring about a change of their political attitude quicker than any other method. The basis of Communism and socialistic influence is education of the people. If we are opposed to socialism in America as we all say we are, we must all conscientiously oppose this bill.[103]

While investigating supposed communist subversion, HUAC refrained from any inquiries into violence motivated from the Right. Racist violence, beatings and lynchings in the South were never investigated; only during the very early years of HUAC was fascist "subversion" investigated or exposed.

As World War II ended and the Cold War began, even the mildest political statements could generate accusations of "subversion." The counsel to HUAC wrote to columnist Drew Pearson in 1946:

Several people have called my attention to the closing line of your Sunday night broadcast, "Make democracy work."

I should like very much to have your definition of
"democracy" as you are using it over the radio. If you will
be good enough to supply this information, I will give the
matter further consideration to determine whether it
should be called to the attention of the members of the
committee for such action as they deem proper.[104]

HUAC worked in collusion with the mainstream press, private
employers and local thugs and vigilante groups. The Committee's
witnesses were divided into two groups: "friendly" witnesses, including
former Communists and communist infiltrators, who were willing to
name names and inform on others; and "unfriendly" witnesses, who
refused, on First or Fifth Amendment grounds, "to cut [their] conscience to fit this year's fashions..." [105] The names of unfriendly witnesses subpoenaed to testify before the Committee, or the names of
those mentioned by friendly witnesses, would be prominently
publicized in the local media, accompanied by local addresses and
places of employment. Unfriendly witnesses were often fired from their
jobs even before testifying.

Witnesses returning home after appearing before HUAC were
frequently attacked by local vigilantes, who were encouraged, or at
least condoned in their illegal actions, by the Committee. One witness
wrote the following letter after appearing before a HUAC hearing
organized by Representative Kit Clardy of Flint, Michigan:

> I am earnestly seeking your help to stop the violence
> against me that was instigated by Representative Clardy's
> hearings.
> I have been a responsible citizen for forty-three years...I
> have an unchallenged record as an employee at Chevrolet
> Manufacturing Company for twenty years. I served con-
> scientiously as a soldier in World War II, and was decorated
> with the Bronze Star Medal...
> Since the hearings I have worked only two weeks. I was
> severely beaten on returning to work and was placed under
> a doctor's care for thirty days with broken ribs and con-
> tusions. Again last Wednesday I was viciously beaten by a
> small but well organized gang of hoodlums at the factory
> gates...

Upon hearing that workers had been beaten, Rep. Clardy stated "This

is the best kind of reaction there could have been to our hearings." [106]
HUAC relied on "friendly witnesses"—often self-proclaimed ex-communists—to name names and accuse others. The case of Matthew Cvetic, a friendly witness in 1950, was not atypical. Cvetic was an FBI undercover agent who had infiltrated the Communist Party. In his testimony before HUAC, Cvetic named over 300 people as Communists or communist sympathizers. Their names, addresses and places of employment were prominently publicized by the media. As a result of his testimony, over one hundred people named by Cvetic lost their jobs.[107] On March 9, 1950, Judge Michael A. Musmanno dismissed a grand juror whom Cvetic had named as a Communist. The grand juror was also fired from her job. Although the Pennsylvania Supreme Court condemned the judge for his action, the juror never got her job back.[108] Five years later, it was revealed that Cvetic was an unreliable witness with a long history of mental illness.[109]

For the first time in U.S. history, the informer became a hero. One FBI informer proudly reported that he had recruited friends and relatives to join the Communist Party and then turned their names over to the FBI.[110]

Witnesses appearing before HUAC were not given even the most elementary due process protections designed to ensure a fair hearing. Witnesses were often not given notice of the charges against them, nor were they allowed to confront or cross-examine witnesses against them.[111] As Committee Chair J. Parnell Thomas lectured a witness, "The rights you have are the rights given you by this Committee. We will determine what rights you have and what rights you have not got before the Committee." [112]

In 1947, HUAC began highly-publicized hearings into "communism" in Hollywood. Forty-one witnesses were subpoenaed in September; nineteen were expected to be unfriendly witnesses. Ten of the nineteen were eventually summoned to testify. The "Hollywood Ten" were: Alvah Bessie, Herbert Biberman, Lester Cole, Edward Dmytryk, Ring Lardner, Jr., John Howard Lawson, Albert Maltz, Samuel Ornitz, Adrian Scott and Dalton Trumbo. They refused to answer questions before HUAC, citing their First Amendment rights of freedom of association. Within a month of the hearings, five had been fired from their jobs. The Hollywood blacklist had begun.[113] Within a year, the Hollywood Ten had been found guilty of contempt of Congress; after the Supreme Court refused to hear their case, all ten went to prison.[114]

Of the 204 artists who signed the *amici curiae* brief to the Supreme Court on behalf of the Hollywood Ten, eighty-four were blacklisted. As a result of the HUAC hearings, over 250 of Hollywood's most talented writers, directors and actors were blacklisted.[115] The blacklist was not confined to the big screen; by 1954, some 1,500 radio and television artists were affected.[116]

Advertising agencies, production companies, directors and producers all capitulated to the blacklist. Most producers would routinely submit the name of any actor they planned to employ for "clearance" to one of the blacklisting agencies. From April 1955 through March 1956, producer David Susskind submitted some 500 names, one-third of whom were rejected. After blacklisted actor John Randolph appeared in the television program "Danger," one of the advertisers apologized profusely, emphasizing that CBS had given assurances that in the future "they will be meticulous in their screening." [117]

Folksinger Pete Seeger was blacklisted from network television from 1950 until 1967. When he finally appeared, CBS refused to let him sing a song critical of U.S. involvement in the Vietnam War.[118]

One of the more subtle results of the blacklisting was a change in the content of movies and television programs. One study showed that in 1947 (before the HUAC Hollywood Hearings), 28 percent of the movies had a "serious social bent"; in 1953, only 9 percent did.[119]

The print media also capitulated to the blacklist. Little, Brown stopped publishing the works of Howard Fast. The *New York Times* refused to carry paid advertising protesting the sentencing of the Rosenbergs. *American Sports Annual* rewrote history in an attempt to obliterate the fact that Paul Robeson was an All-American football player at Rutgers University in 1917 and 1918.[120]

The annual reports of HUAC listed the names of all witnesses called by the Committee during the previous year—another method of ensuring that witnesses would continue to be harassed. In 1952 and 1953, HUAC reports listed more than 1,000 witnesses each year. By 1960, HUAC was calling fewer than 100 witnesses per year.[121]

HUAC compiled cumulative indices of names. These indices list over 45,000 names of individuals and thousands of organizations mentioned in testimony. HUAC also printed "Appendix IX," which listed the names of some 250,000 individuals who allegedly were members of "communist-front" organizations. In addition, HUAC maintained files on "subversive" individuals and organizations. In 1948, HUAC had 300,000 files on individuals; by 1949, there were 1,000,000 entries.[122]

As late as the Kennedy administration, HUAC had access to an individual's income tax returns. An Executive Order issued by President Kennedy provided that "any income, excess-profits, estate, or gift tax return for the years 1945-1961, inclusive, shall...be open to inspection by the Committee on Un-American Activities..." [123]

Because of the "success" of HUAC, the Senate created its own Un-American Activities committee in 1951, known as the Senate Internal Security Subcommittee (SISS). Its first chair was Democratic Senator Pat McCarran of Nevada, co-author of the McCarran-Walters Act.[124]

Perhaps the most infamous of all the congressional hearings were those of the Senate Committee on Governmental Operations, chaired by Senator Joseph McCarthy. Starting in 1952, McCarthy's hearings attacked "subversion" in the State Department, the Voice of America, the International Information Agency, the Governmental Printing Office and the United Nations. Two years and thousands of ruined lives later, the Senate finally voted sixty-seven to twenty-two to condemn[125] McCarthy after he began to accuse the United States Army of subversion.[126]

The Japanese-American Internment and Violations of Due Process

As World War II began, the U.S. government again resorted to various restrictions on the rights of aliens, due process violations and the imposition of military law for national security reasons.

On December 7, 1941 the Japanese attacked Pearl Harbor; the same day, the Governor of Hawaii declared martial law and suspended *habeas corpus*. Under the authority of the Hawaiian Organic Act, military tribunals took over the functioning of the civil courts. During the ensuing years of the war, the civilian courts began to resume authority over criminal trials; nonetheless, "only military tribunals were to try 'Criminal Prosecutions for violations of military orders.' "[127] Sentences handed down by such military tribunals were not subject to appellate review.[128] The imposition of martial law was upheld after the war by the Supreme Court in *Duncan v. Kahanamoku*, although the Court ruled that the use of military tribunals in place of civilian courts was unconstitutional.[129]

The day of the Japanese attack on Hawaii, President Roosevelt issued Proclamation Number 2525[130] restricting travel by Japanese aliens and authorizing "summary apprehension" of any alien enemy "deemed dangerous." The next day, the United States declared war on Japan. Subsequent proclamations restricted movement of German and Italian aliens when war began with those countries.

During the first year of World War II, 12,071 aliens were arrested, of whom 3,646 were interned for the duration of the war.[131]

Two months later, on February 19, 1942, President Roosevelt issued Executive Order 9066, establishing defense zones within the United States and giving military commanders complete authority to exclude persons from such zones.[132] Executive Order 9066 gave no authority to confine people after their exclusion. Nonetheless, under the presumed authority of this order, 119,803 Japanese-American men, women and children—70,000 of whom were native-born citizens—were rounded-up, herded to temporary collection points and interned in concentration camps for the duration of the war. "Attainder of blood," prohibited by the Constitution,[133] had been reinstituted.[134]

Even at the time, it was fairly clear that the internment was not needed as a security measure. Referring to the internment, Senator Matsunaga stated in 1980:

> It is significant to note that the Military Commander of the then Territory of Hawaii, which had actually suffered an enemy attack, did not feel that it was necessary to evacuate all individuals of Japanese ancestry from Hawaii...
> Moreover, no Military Commander felt that it was necessary to evacuate from any area of the country all Americans of German or Italian ancestry, although the United States was also at war with Germany and Italy.

FBI Director J. Edgar Hoover, who could hardly be

accused of being soft on suspected seditionists, opposed the
evacuation of Japanese Americans from the West Coast,
pointing out that the FBI and other law enforcement agencies were capable of apprehending any suspected saboteurs
or enemy agents. Indeed, martial law was never declared
in any of these Western States...[135]

Admiral Ernest Stark, chief of Naval Operations, stated that a
full-scale Japanese attack on the West Coast was "impossible." The
week prior to the issuance of Executive Order 9066, the army's general
staff had recommended against mass evacuation.[136] Nonetheless, the
internment was ordered.

The evacuation was hasty, and internees were permitted to bring
with them only the most basic personal possessions. Each person was
allowed to bring "bedding and linens (no mattresses)...toilet articles...extra clothing...sufficient knives, forks spoons, plates, bowls
and cups...[and] essential personal effects." [137] Everything else had to
be left behind.

The average Japanese-American internee spent 900 days behind
barbed-wire. Reading material was censored, Japanese phonograph
records were confiscated and arbitrary searches and harassment were
everyday occurrences.[138] Conditions were harsh, with numerous incidents of government brutality against internees. Cold-blooded killings
were rare, but did occur; four Japanese-American internees were slain
by prison guards, including one sixty-three-year-old man shot down
while walking towards the barbed-wire enclosure in broad daylight.[139]
In November 1943, guards at Tule Lake Concentration Camp went on
a ten-day rampage. A security guard described one incident:

> None of the three Japs were unconscious but all three were
> groggy from the blows they received, especially the one
> [questioner Q] had hit with the baseball bat. We picked the
> three of them up and got them on their feet and took them
> into the Administration Building... [where] we ordered the
> Japanese to lie down on the floor. They refused to do so
> whereupon I knocked my Jap down with my fist. He stayed
> down but was not unconscious. [Q] hit his Jap over the head
> again with the baseball bat...[During the interrogation of
> another inmate] I had been itching to take a sock at the
> Jap so I shoved [Q2] aside and hit [Y] a hard right blow to
> the jaw with my fist. [Y] went down and out. I reached down

and shook him hard in an effort to revive him. I even grabbed him by the hair and shook his head. After about three minutes he came to...[At one point] I did hear screams which seemed to emanate from one of the back rooms.[140]

Inmates accused of violating camp regulations were sentenced to the stockade without benefit of counsel or trial by jury. Some inmates were sentenced for as long as 370 days in the stockade.[141]

Under regulations issued by the War Relocation Authority, the internees were to be tested for loyalty. Among the questions asked under oath were:

Will you assist in the general resettlement program by staying away from large groups of Japanese?

Will you try to develop such American habits which will cause you to be accepted readily into American social groups?

Are you willing to give information to the proper authorities regarding any subversive activity...both in the relocation centers and in the communities in which you are resettling?

Have you been associated with any radical groups, clubs, or gangs which have been accused of anti-social conduct within the center?

Can you furnish any proof that you have always been loyal to the United States?[142]

Those who were deemed disloyal were to be confined indefinitely. However, even Japanese-Americans citizens who were found loyal and released "were required to have official approval of their homes, jobs and friends before they were allowed to move. They had to report subsequent changes of address, and remain under scrutiny almost amounting to parole."[143] Loyal citizens, if they were of Japanese descent, were treated as criminals. Yet white citizens could have pro-Axis sympathies; no statute had made "disloyalty" a crime.[144]

When the internment was ordered, approximately 150 Japanese-Americans loudly and noisily protested the evacuation orders. These 150 people were confined in a mental hospital for the duration of the war.[145]

As with the imposition of military rule during the Civil War, the legality of Executive Order 9066 was suspect—after all, there had been no domestic violence, rebellion, invasion or declaration of martial law preceding its issuance. To prevent possible legal challenges, Congress passed a law on March 21, 1942 making disobedience to Executive Order 9066 a criminal offense.[146]

A year later, the first challenge to what is often referred to as the most massive violations of civil liberties in U.S. history reached the Supreme Court.* In *Hirabayashi v. United States*[147] the Court, lending legitimacy to what George Hirabayashi recently called the "rampant, vicious and overt racism against Asians on the West Coast," [148] upheld the imposition of a 8:00 p.m. to 6:00 a.m. curfew on all Japanese and Japanese-Americans. Paying lip-service to the idea that racism is "odious," the Court found nonetheless that:

> the adoption by Government in the crisis of war and of threatened invasion, of measures for the public safety...is not wholly beyond the limits of the Constitution and is not to be condemned merely because in other and in most circumstances racial distinctions are irrelevant.[149]

In 1944, the Supreme Court decided *Korematsu v. United States*.[150] Fred Korematsu, a native-born U.S. citizen, challenged his arrest for refusing to comply with the military order to evacuate his home. There was never any evidence that Korematsu was disloyal. Nonetheless, the Court upheld the evacuation orders, noting that "[p]ressing public necessity may sometimes justify the existence of such restrictions." [151]

The Court ignored the fact that whatever emergency may have existed at the beginning of the war had certainly ended by the time of *Korematsu,* yet the concentration camps were still in existence and scores of thousands of loyal American citizens were still imprisoned. This situation was addressed later that year in *Ex Parte Endo*.[152] While freeing Mitsuye Endo, whose "loyalty" was not doubted, the Court

---

* Yet the horrors of the Japanese-American internment pale in comparison to the genocide of Native Americans and the enslavement of African Americans.

refused to find the original Executive Order 9066 constitutionally infirm.[153] Executive Order 9066 was not rescinded until April 19, 1976, by President Gerald Ford—thirty years after World War II.

It has since come to light that the government engaged in a massive effort to fabricate and suppress evidence in the *Hirabayashi* and *Korematsu* cases. Evidence recently uncovered shows that the government knew that the Japanese-Americans on the West Coast posed no danger to national security.[154] As Justice Murphy noted in his dissent in *Korematsu,* "not one person of Japanese ancestry was accused or convicted of sabotage after Pearl Harbor while they were still free." [155]

Racism, not national security, was the motive force behind the internments. General DeWitt, the moving force behind the internments, wrote at the time, "[t]he very fact that no sabotage has taken place to date is a disturbing and confirming indication that such action will be taken[!]" [156] In testimony before the House Naval Affairs Subcommittee, DeWitt stated, "A Jap's a Jap...There is no way to determine their loyalty...It makes no difference whether he is an American; theoretically he is still a Japanese and you can't change him." [157]

California Attorney General (and later Chief Justice) Earl Warren stated before the House Select Committee Investigating National Defense Migration in February 1942, "We believe that when we are dealing with the Caucasian race, we have methods that will test the loyalty of them...But when we deal with the Japanese, we are in an entirely different field and we cannot form any opinion that we believe to be sound." [158]

John McCloy, Assistant Secretary of War during the internment, testified before Congress in 1981 that the internment had been undertaken "in the way of retribution for the attack that was made on Pearl Harbor." [159] After extensive hearings, the Congressional Commission on Wartime Relocation unanimously concluded in 1983 that "Executive Order 9066 was not justified by military necessity" but rather had been prompted by "race prejudice, war hysteria and a failure of political leadership." [160]

Some thirty-five years after the evacuation, on May 27, 1979, the State of California made the site of the Tule Lake camp an historical landmark. Its memorial plaque, California Registration Landmark No. 850-2, reads:

Tule Lake was one of ten American concentration camps established during World War II to incarcerate 110,000 persons of Japanese ancestry, of whom the majority were American citizens, behind barbed wire and guard towers without charge, trial or establishment of guilt. These camps are reminders of how racism, economic and political exploitation, and expediency can undermine the constitutional guarantees of United States citizens and aliens alike. May the injustices and humiliation suffered here never recur.

The incarceration of Japanese-Americans was the most notorious example of mass deprivation of liberty without due process during World War II; nonetheless, the Japanese-Americans were not the only minority group so treated. After Japan's invasion of the Western Aleutian Islands, the U.S. military ordered some 900 Aleuts to leave their homes. The relocated Aleuts were forced to live in abandoned mines and fish canneries.[161] During the relocation, U.S. soldiers looted and destroyed the Aleutian village and the village church.[162] Congress recently voted to provide tax-free payments of $12,000 to each Aleut who was forcibly relocated, $5 million as reimbursement for destruction of village and community property, and $1.4 million in compensation for destruction of church property.[163]

In addition to mass violations of due process directed against Japanese-Americans, Hawaiians and Aleuts, individual violations occurred against white Americans. One such case of questionable due process involved one of the twentieth century's greatest poets, Ezra Pound. Although born in Idaho, for the two decades prior to World War II Pound lived in Italy, where he broadcast Fascist propaganda to the United States. At the end of the war, he was indicted for treason and returned to the United States to stand trial. But it was difficult to convict someone of treason. Just the year before, the Supreme Court, although we were still at war, carefully reviewed and then overturned a treason conviction,[164] in marked distinction to its treatment of prosecutions under military tribunals. Rather than face a potentially difficult trial, the government found after five minutes of deliberation that Ezra Pound was incompetent to stand trial.[165] Confined to St. Elizabeth's mental hospital, he remained under guard for twelve years. During that time he wrote the *Pisan Cantos,* for which he was awarded the prestigious Bollingen Prize in 1949.[166]

Sedition Prosecutions

The Espionage Act of 1917,[167] amended and recodified as Section 2388 of Title 18, continued in force throughout World War II. The Act was first used during the war to prosecute the author of several mimeographed tracts. His pamphlets attacked the President, Jews and the war effort for diverting the attention of whites from what he felt were the real threats: racial mixing and communism. His conviction was overturned by the Supreme Court in 1944.[168]

During the course of the war, some two hundred people were charged with sedition or counselling opposition to the draft.[169] At least seven other sedition trials were held.[170] Pro-Nazi defendants were convicted of publishing articles attacking the war effort, accusing President Roosevelt of selling-out to Jewish or communist conspiracies, and stating that Germany and Japan were powerful while the United States and the allies were weak and morally corrupt.

Despite the Cold War, sedition trials went out of style for almost a decade. In 1956, however, as an aftermath of the communist revolution in China and the Korean War, the government indicted three U.S. citizens for sedition and treason. John William Powell, his wife Sylvia, and Julian Schumann published the *China Monthly Review,* an English-language magazine printed in Beijing. The three were charged with falsely accusing the United States of: 1) aggression in Asia, 2) committing atrocities and using germ warfare against Korea and China, and 3) deliberately under-estimating U.S. casualties during the War. The indictment also cited articles the three had published which attacked the United States for having morally reprehensible and aggressive policies. These articles accused Chiang Kai-Shek of being a U.S. pawn while stating that the Chinese people were "peace-loving, honest, and just." In order to effectuate the provisions of the Sedition Act, which only applied to actions occurring in times of war, the government resorted to the 1953 statute which declared the Korean "police-action" to be a "war."

From 1949 until their indictment in 1956, the three were the subject of FBI investigations, U.S. Senate Internal Security Subcommittee hearings and State Department harassment.[171] Three years later, on January 9, 1959, the sedition trial of the Powells and Schumann began. Within three weeks, a mistrial was declared. Although the government quickly filed new charges—this time for treason—no indictments were issued. In 1961, Attorney General Robert F. Kennedy finally dismissed the sedition and treason charges against all three.[172]

The Rise of a Secret Police

On August 23, 1936, five years before the U.S. entrance into World War II, President Roosevelt authorized the FBI to spy on "subversive" organizations. This presidential directive was used by the FBI to justify its domestic spying during the next forty years.[173]

Although the Supreme Court held that it was unconstitutional for the government to bug homes or conversations without a warrant, the FBI circumvented the ruling when President Roosevelt advised J. Edgar Hoover that the Court's decision did not apply to "grave matters involving the defense of the nation." Roosevelt issued another executive order in 1940 authorizing the FBI to wiretap anyone *"suspected* of subversive activities" [emphasis added] without a warrant.[174]

In the decade before World War II, the FBI had been investigating some thirty-five espionage cases per year. In January 1940, the Bureau predicted in testimony before the House Appropriations Committee that it would be involved in as many as 70,000 espionage cases a year.[175]

Under the guise of investigating espionage, the FBI continued to conduct political investigations. For several years, the FBI had been investigating the Veterans of the Abraham Lincoln Brigade—U.S. volunteers who fought in Spain from 1936 to 1939 against the fascist forces of Franco. In February 1940, the Bureau's investigations culminated in a grand jury indictment of eleven men and one woman on charges of raising a foreign army in the United States. As in many such cases brought for purposes of political harassment, all charges against the defendants were eventually dropped.[176]

The American Civil Liberties Union had been targeted by the FBI since the mid-1920s, as was the American Friends Service Committee, a Quaker organization which received the Nobel Peace Prize in 1947. The National Association for the Advancement of Colored People came under FBI surveillance in 1941.[177]

In 1939, a year before the U.S. entry into World War II, J. Edgar
Hoover began a program to identify people with Communist or Nazi
tendencies and arrange for their possible "custodial detention." In
1941, Congress authorized $100,000 for the FBI to investigate all
public employees who were members of subversive organizations.
Together with the Hatch Act (passed two years previously), this
became the impetus for the first Attorney General's list of subversive
organizations.

After the war ended, Attorney General Tom Clark instructed
the FBI to prepare an Emergency Detention Program which envisioned the detention of suspected "subversives," the suspension of
habeas corpus and wholesale summary arrests pursuant to one master
warrant signed by the Attorney General. In 1948, over 26,000 people
were identified for summary arrest in the event of a national emergency. Subsequent lists were compiled into the early 1970s; in 1972,
the Administrative Index contained over 15,000 names.[178]

Throughout World War II and the Korean War, the FBI kept
dossiers on at least one Congressman, Vito Marcantonio, and one legal
political party, the American Labor Party.[179] In 1942, they broke into
the New York City offices of the American Youth Congress to
photocopy Eleanor Roosevelt's correspondence with the organization.[180]

By June 1940...Bureau informers had penetrated every
"principal radical organization," "all groups of pronounced
nationalistic tendencies," and "other groups of un-
American principles." As of July 18, 1942, an additional
20,718 "confidential sources" were deployed in some 4,000
industries producing war materials.[181]

But it was only with the start of the Cold War that J. Edgar
Hoover could give full reign to his obsession with rooting out socialism
and communism within the United States. In 1947, Hoover announced
that there was "one Communist for every 1,814 persons in the United
States."[182] Hoover made the destruction of the Communist Party a goal
of the FBI.

During this time, the FBI maintained a widespread network of
informants, including one Ronald Reagan, known to the FBI as agent
"T-10." While serving as President of the Screen Actors Guild, Reagan
was secretly reporting to the FBI on the very union members he was

elected to represent.[183]

The goal of eliminating "subversion" justified all means. In 1954, a commission headed by World War II hero James Doolittle concluded that, in the fight against communism:

> Hitherto acceptable norms of human conduct do not apply...We must learn to subvert, sabotage and destroy our enemies by more clever, more sophisticated and more effective methods than those used against us...another important requirement is an aggressive covert psychological, political and paramilitary organization more effective, more unique, and if necessary, more ruthless than that employed by the enemy. No one should be permitted to stand in the way of prompt, efficient and secure accomplishment of this mission."[184]

The FBI's files on domestic dissidents were filled with details about the individuals' personal and sexual habits. An even more secret "Hoover file" concentrated on the personal peccadillos of members of Congress, the White House, and other high government officials.[185]

The FBI had a special program to target writers for surveillance. Eventually, 134 American writers, including Carl Sandburg, Thomas Wolfe, Theodore Dreiser, Edna St. Vincent Millay, Dorothy Parker and James Baldwin, along with Nobel Laureates Sinclair Lewis, Pearl S. Buck, William Faulkner, Ernest Hemingway, John Steinbeck and Thomas Mann, were subjects of secret FBI investigations.[186]

Between March 1947 and December 1952, the FBI conducted 6.6 million "security investigations" of peaceful citizens—more than 3,000 security investiations a day.[187]

The FBI secretly supplied HUAC with information from its extensive dossiers.[188] Starting in 1951 and continuing throughout the Korean War, the FBI maintained an active informant within the Harvard Law School chapter of the National Lawyers Guild, who provided the FBI with Guild membership lists and correspondence.

On June 9, 1954, during the televised Senate Army-McCarthy Hearings, Sen. Joseph McCarthy interrupted chief counsel Joseph Welch to ask a "point of order": whether Frederick Fisher, a member of Welch's law firm, "has been for a number of years a member of an organization which was named...as the legal bulwark of the Communist Party?" Welch's scathing reply, "Have you left no sense of decency?" marked the beginning of the end of Sen. McCarthy's crusade.

The organization to which McCarthy was referring was the National Lawyers Guild; Fisher had been a member of the Guild while a student at Harvard Law School, and McCarthy apparently received his information on Fisher via the FBI's informant.[189]

The FBI's infiltration of the Harvard Law School may well have occurred with the knowledge and approval of the University. During the Korean War era, the FBI had a mutual arrangement with Harvard in which they shared information regarding suspected subversives on the faculty.[190] In 1953, the Bureau ran a check on every faculty and staff member at Harvard and MIT.[191] Both the FBI and CIA made use of campus informants, paid and volunteer. In July 1953, for example, Harvard Professor Henry A. Kissinger opened a letter sent to one of his students, and notified the Boston FBI of its contents.[192]

Expropriation of Property

During World War II, the United States government again resorted to various forms of confiscation and expropriation of property when it was felt necessary to help the war effort.

Most such seizures took place to prevent labor disputes that the government feared would interrupt the production of war materiel. President Roosevelt seized three factories prior to the attack on Pearl Harbor and the outbreak of the war. The first seizure, of the North American Aviation Co., occurred on June 9, 1941, six months before the United States entered the War, as workers at the California airplane plant went on strike. Because the strike was viewed as an "insurrection, a Communist-led political strike against the Government's lend-lease policy," seizure of the plant was not objected to by the Supreme Court.[193] No statutory authority was cited for any of the three seizures.[194]

During the war itself, at least forty-seven industrial facilities were seized by President Roosevelt to prevent labor disputes from affecting the war effort. These included: the coal mines (to force an eight-hour day, six-day workweek);[195] the railroads (to force acceptance of a compromise wage package); textile plants (to force agreement to seniority provisions); the Los Angeles Department of Water and

Power; Montgomery Ward (first in Chicago, and later nationwide);[196] Midwest Trucking Operators; Humble Oil & Refining Co.; the Scranton Transit Co.; and Goodyear Tire & Rubber Co.[197] In contrast to most of U.S. history, in which the government intervened in labor disputes on the side of big business, Roosevelt's interventions were often beneficial to labor.

Seizures of private property not only began prior to the war, but continued after the ending of hostilities. At least a dozen plants were seized in the two years following V-J Day. These included seizures by President Truman of the meatpacking industry, the Illinois Central Railroad, and the bituminous coal mines (during which time the United States, as owner of the mines, recognized the United Mine Workers Union).[198]

Other governmental seizures of private industry took place unrelated to labor disputes. These included the seizure of Remington Rand because deliveries were behind schedule; and the seizures of the York Safe & Lock Co., the Howarth Pivoted Bearings Co. and the Brewster Aeronautical Corp. due to "inefficient management"![199]

The Supreme Court, although requiring that compensation be paid for appropriations of private industry, never held such actions unconstitutional. The only time such an action was overturned was during the Korean War, when President Truman seized the steel mills to prevent a strike and reduction of war materiel.[200] In this case the seizure was declared illegal when the Supreme Court held that the Executive did not have the power to take such action without a declaration from Congress. Nonetheless, the Court noted that "[t]he power of Congress to adopt such public policies as those proclaimed by the order is beyond question," [201] and Justice Frankfurter in his concurrence, noted that "Congress has frequently—at least 16 times since 1916—specifically provided for executive seizure of production, transportation, communications, or storage facilities." [202]

Probably the largest cumulative confiscation was that of property taken from the 110,000 Japanese-Americans interned in concentration camps during the war. The Federal Reserve Bank estimated that Japanese-American internees lost $400 million in property.[203]

In 1948, Congress enacted the Japanese-American Evacuation Claims Act to compensate internees for those losses. Claims filed under the Act totaled $148 million. But since the Act only allowed compensation for property losses that could be proved by records, only $37 million was repaid to some 26,500 internees—less than ten cents on the dollar.[204] By comparison, the Foreign Claims Settlement Commission awarded $213 million to U.S. companies for property damage abroad during World War II—approximately seventy-five cents on the dollar for claimed losses.[205]

In 1988, Congress passed legislation authorizing compensation of $20,000 to each of about 60,000 Japanese-Americans interned during World War II. Those internees who are still living will begin receiving the reparations payments in July 1990, 45 years after the end of World War II.

Travel Restrictions

Denial of Passports to U.S. Citizens

Passports were first required for travel into war zones during the War of 1812, and their use was re-instituted during the Civil War. But it was not until 1941, at the start of the World War II, that U.S. citizens were required to have a passport in order to *leave* the country. Since the nineteenth century, the government has occasionally denied passports for political reasons—in 1917, for instance, the passport application of several American socialists who wanted to attend a conference in Stockholm, Sweden was denied[206]—but until the 1950s, this had always occurred during times of actual hostilities.

During the Korean War, the Secretary of State again began to deny passports to U.S. citizens. Although Congress has never sanctioned the denial of passports for political reasons,[207] there have been more than one hundred cases in which passports of U.S. citizens have been denied or revoked by our government for "national security" reasons.[208]

In 1955, half a dozen passports were denied for political reasons; by 1956, the number had increased to fifty-seven.[209] Under regulations passed by the Secretary of State which allowed denial of passports to anyone whose travel would be "prejudicial to the interests of the United States," scores of prominent U.S. artists and scientists were denied passports. Among those whose travel was deemed "prejudicial to the interests of the United States," were Howard Fast, Edward G. Robin-son, Ring Lardner, Jr., Arthur Miller and Carl Foreman.[210] Dr. Otto Nathan, the executor of Albert Einstein's estate, was denied a passport for two years.[211] Dr. Linus Pauling was denied a passport for two and one half years. The State Department finally granted him a passport after Dr. Pauling won the Nobel Prize—continued denial had become too great an embarrassment to the government.

Paul Robeson, the famous black singer, was prevented from leaving the United States and entering Canada in February 1952 to attend a convention of the Mine, Mill and Smelter Workers, even though no passport was needed to enter Canada.[212]

At least one member of the House of Representatives, Leo Isaacson, was denied a passport to leave the country. While still serving in Congress, he wanted to attend a conference being held in Paris in support of the Greek partisans. The United States at the time was opposing the partisans and denied Isaacson a passport to leave the country.[213]

A Federal Appeals Court judge was deprived of his passport and had to sue the government to get it back.[214] Security fears stretched so far that the loyalty of a sitting U.S. Supreme Court Justice was suspect—Justice William O. Douglas was denied a passport to attend a conference in China.[215]

Not surprisingly, such restrictions on the right to travel were defended on national security grounds. Harvard Law School Professor Louis Jaffe's defense was typical:

> In the Civil War and again in World War I, the United States set up a rigid system of passport control…It is asserted that the precedents of "war" have no relevance to "peace." But the critical consideration is defense against an external enemy…[since] the Communist International is a foreign and domestic enemy…the United States is…justified in denying passports to persons whose journey abroad is presumptively in furtherance of the Communist "conspiracy." [216]

Artist Rockwell Kent had been denied a passport for seven years by the time he initiated his suit against the Secretary of State.[217] When he applied for a passport in 1955 to attend an artists conference in Finland, the Department of State denied his request, stating that "it has been alleged that you were a Communist." [218] Among the charges leveled against Kent by the U.S. government were that he had been "a speaker at a dinner in 1954 in honor of ...Paul Robeson," that he had sponsored a "four page petition addressed to [the] Attorney General...criticizing the use of paid informers," that he had "signed a petition...urging [a] ban on use of [the] atomic bomb," that he had "urged clemency for [the] Rosenbergs" and that he had supported "the candidacy of Vito Marcantonio, Congressman...[and] the re-election of Congressman Benjamin Davis, Jr." [219] The Supreme Court, over-turning the lower court's ruling, finally granted Kent his passport, but its reasoning was not based on the fact that denying Kent his passport on political grounds was unconstitutional. Rather, the Court simply held that Congress had not given the State Department the authority to withhold passports; hence, the State Department acted illegally. [220]

Denial of Visas to Foreign Citizens

The Voorhis Act of 1940 gave the Executive virtually complete discretion to deny entry into the United States to anyone whose ideas were found dangerous. [221] From the start of the Cold War, this meant the exclusion of progressives, socialists and communists; nazis and fascists, however, normally could enter the country without problem. As Mr. L'Heureux, head of the State Department's Visa Department stated in 1948, "under normal immigration laws, there is nothing that would exclude a Nazi or a Fascist." [222]

Among the "dangerous" people prevented from entering the United States during this decade were such artists as Graham Greene, Alberto Moravia, Czeslaw Milosz and Pablo Picasso. [223] In 1952, Charlie Chaplin's re-entry permit was indefinitely delayed while Immigration Department investigators went to Europe to interrogate him regarding his loyalty. Finally granted a re-entry permit, Chaplin refused to return to the United States in order to avoid an appearance before the Immigration Board of Inquiry. [224] During this time the Dean of Canterbury was denied admission to the United States [225] and the brilliant if somewhat eccentric emigré mathematician Paul Erdös, who had been living in the United States since before the war, was prevented from returning after attending a mathematics conference in Amsterdam in 1954. [226]

State and Local Laws

At the start of World War II, there were some thirty federal statutes and several hundred state statutes still on the books that limited free speech; fifteen states had statutes against opposition to war, thirty-three states had statutes making it illegal to display a red flag, thirty-five states had laws against criminal syndicalism, criminal anarchy or sedition, and five states excluded radicals from the ballot.[227]

Although it is not the states' function to protect national security, local legislators, bowing to the winds of fear and sensing that there were political careers to be made, jumped on the anti-subversion bandwagon. By 1952, forty-seven of the forty-eight states passed anti-subversion statutes: thirty-four states had anti-anarchy or criminal syndicalism laws; thirty-one states had laws against sedition (twenty-four enacted after 1945); thirty-two states required special teachers' loyalty oaths; twenty-eight states passed laws prohibiting subversives from public employment; twenty-six states barred communist or subversive organizations from the ballot; and two states outlawed the Communist Party altogether. In 1950, Michigan imposed life imprisonment for writing or speaking subversive words; the next year, Tennessee decreed the death penalty for unlawful advocacy. In addition, six states had functioning state un-American activities committees. In fact, the only state that did not have a major anti-subversive statute on its books by 1952 was the state that thirty-five years before had become infamous for the frame-up and execution of Joe Hill: the state of Utah.[228]

Municipalities too passed anti-subversion ordinances. On September 13, 1950, Los Angeles passed three ordinances preventing any member of a Communist organization, anyone supporting a "Muscovite model of police-state dictatorship," and anyone believing in the forcible establishment of a "totalitarian dictatorship" over the people of Los Angeles from possessing any weapon, including a knife, gun, pistol or billy club.[229]

On July 18, 1950, Birmingham, Alabama passed an ordinance which made it illegal for any member of the Communist Party to be within the city limits. Under Birmingham's law, people were presumed to be a member of the Communist Party if they spoke in private with anyone who was or had been a member of the Communist

Party. The penalty for violating the law was 180 days in jail. Jackson-ville, Florida passed an ordinance prohibiting any member of the Communist Party from being within the city limits "[d]uring the Period of Hostilities in Korea Against the Armed Forces of the United States." [230] Each day's violation of the ordinance was a separate offense, punishable by ninety days in jail. Miami, Florida required com-munists, both alien and citizen, to register their intent to enter the city. Violation of Miami's ordinance could be punished by "hard labor on the streets or other works of the City of Miami for a term not exceeding sixty (60) days." [231] Seattle prevented any member of a subversive organization from using its Civic Auditorium.[232]

Fear of subversion spread to all levels of government and all levels within government. "Loyalty" was not only demanded of employees in security-sensitive positions, but from municipal employees of all types—including janitors, secretaries and trash col-lectors. In 1951, the Supreme Court, viewing public employment to be a privilege, upheld the use of loyalty oaths in Los Angeles and the termination of public employees who refused to swear that they had no present or past affiliation with the Communist Party.[233]

At the beginning of World War II, the Board of Regents of the University of California passed a resolution excluding members of the Communist Party from teaching at the University. The resolution lay dormant until June 24, 1949, when the Regents required that all University employees swear to an anti-Communist oath. The faculty senate overwhelmingly approved institution of this oath.[234] Within a year, the University of California lost 110 professors because of the controversy surrounding this oath: twenty-six were dismissed, thirty-seven resigned in protest against the institution of a loyalty oath and forty-seven refused offers of appointment to the faculty of the Univer-sity of California.[235]

In 1952, a New York law requiring all teachers to swear that they were not members of any organization deemed "subversive" by the Board of Regents was challenged as a violation of free speech and assembly. The Supreme Court, in *Adler v. Board of Education,* upheld the law, maintaining that "school authorities have the right and duty to screen…teachers" since a "teacher works in a sensitive area." [236]

Even after the Court ruled in 1956 that an employee could not be fired for invoking the Fifth Amendment,[237] public employees asserted their constitutional rights at their own peril. In 1953, the Philadelphia Board of Education fired a teacher who refused to answer questions about his affiliation with an allegedly communist organization. The teacher was fired, not for asserting the Fifth Amendment, but rather for "incompetency"—refusing to answer his supervisor's questions. The Supreme Court upheld the teacher's dismissal in 1958.[238]

As late as 1960, the Court continued to uphold the firing of Los Angeles public employees for refusing to answer questions regarding their loyalty. In that case, the appellants had asserted their Fifth Amendment rights not to answer questions put to them by the House Un-American Activities Committee. Their employer, the Los Angeles Board of Supervisors, ordered them to answer all questions asked of them and fired them when they did not fully comply. The Court ruled that they had not been fired for asserting their constitutional rights, but rather for insubordination in refusing to carry out an order of their employer![239]

In 1963, Governor Barnett of Mississippi banned a book called *English in Action, Course No. 2* from the State's high schools, since one passage in it mentioned "world government" in a favorable light. The same year, Levittown, New York banned *The Subcontinent of India*, because its author had once belonged to an organization on the Attorney General's list. The *Los Angeles Herald and Express* (later the *Los Angeles Herald-Examiner*) printed a series of editorials urging that thirteen schoolbooks be banned as un-American. The newspaper even found one music book subversive, as it contained a song entitled "Swing the Shining Sickle." As it turned out, the song was not a hymn of praise to the Soviet Union; it had been written twenty years before the Russian revolution as a Thanksgiving harvest song.[240]

As late as 1965 hundreds of state laws relating to subversion and state security were still on the books. Thirty-one states had laws making it a crime to be a member of a subversive organization; ten states outlawed the Communist Party by name and nine made it a crime to be a member of the Communist Party; seventeen states prevented the Communist Party or their candidates from appearing on the ballot; three states excluded members of subversive organizations from being admitted to the practice of law;[241] seventeen states mandated loyalty oaths for teachers; two states had oaths requiring teachers to "refrain from...teaching any theory of government or economics or of social relations which is inconsistent with the fundamental principles of patriotism and high ideals of Americanism";[242] and four states required teachers to refrain from teaching communism.[243]

Other state laws required that every textbook state whether each author of any work cited therein was a communist[244] and banned textbooks containing disloyal statements;[245] denied public housing to anyone who refused to swear to a loyalty oath;[246] prohibited bequests to any subversive association;[247] denied tax exemptions to anyone advocating the forceful overthrow of the government;[248] denied subversive persons a birth certificate,[249] workers compensation,[250] unemployment benefits[251] or public assistance;[252] prohibited members of the Communist Party from serving on jury duty,[253] being a pharmacist[254] or speaking on college campuses;[255] and denied a high school or college diploma to any student not "satisfying the examining power of his loyalty." [256]

Although never "question[ing] the power of a State to take proper measures safeguarding the public service from disloyal conduct," [257] by the mid-60s, the Court began to recognize that First Amendment concerns are inherent in loyalty oaths. A year after Dr. Martin Luther King, Jr.'s "I Have a Dream" speech and the assassination of President Kennedy, the Court for the first time struck down a loyalty oath on grounds of vagueness and overbreadth.[258] Two years later, the Court invalidated a loyalty oath because it didn't require the individual to have personally subscribed to the unlawful goals of the organization.[259] Finally, twenty-two years after the end of World War II, fourteen years after the armistice at Panmunjom ended the Korean War, and three years after the Free Speech Movement at the University of California, Berkeley, the Supreme Court overturned, on grounds of vagueness, the New York teachers' loyalty oath that had been upheld fifteen years earlier in *Adler*.[260]

While we think of the McCarthy era as ending in the late-1950s, perhaps it is better to identify 1967 as the year it was finally buried. The same year that the Supreme Court threw out the New York teachers' loyalty oath, a federal appeals court held that the requirement that the Communist Party register as a subversive organization was a violation of the Fifth Amendment.[261] Later that year, stating that "[t]he concept of 'national defense' cannot be deemed an end in itself," the Supreme Court overturned a law preventing any and all Communist Party members from working in the defense industry. The Court stated that "[i]t would indeed be ironic if in the name of national defense we would sanction the subversion of one of those liberties—the freedom of association—which makes the defense of the nation worthwhile." [262]

These rulings marked the functional end of the Subversive Activities Control Board which had been created in 1950 as part of the McCarran Act. Six years later, beset by Watergate, President Richard Nixon—who had built his political career on anti-communism—quietly decided not to request renewed funding for the Board.

Chapter VI

The Vietnam War Era

The era from 1960 through the late 1970s is generally viewed as one during which U.S. activists fought for, and achieved, an expansion of our civil rights and civil liberties: millions marched for the realization of constitutional rights, the courts overturned restrictive precedents, legislatures passed civil rights statutes, and the federal government seemed to put its weight behind the cause of freedom.

Great advances certainly were made during the 1960s in abolishing the framework of Jim Crow laws that formed the legal buttress of U.S. apartheid. Those who remember President Lyndon Johnson's repression of anti-war demonstrations might be surprised to learn that he greeted civil rights protestors at the White House as "fellow revolutionaries" and urged them to "go out into the hinterland and rouse the masses and blow the bugles and tell them that...we are on the march against the ancient enemies and we are going to be successful."[1]

During this era—175 years after the passage of the Bill of Rights—many of its most important provisions were finally applied to activities of the states. Prior to the 1960s, defendants in state felony trials were not protected by the fourth amendment prohibition against warrantless seraches and seizures;[2] were not protected by the fifth amendment prohibition against compulsory self-incrimination[3] and double jeopardy;[4] were not protected by the sixth amendment right to a speedy trial,[5] a trial by jury,[6] the assistance of counsel,[7] the right to confront adverse witnesses,[8] or the right to compulsory process;[9] and were not protected by the eighth amendment prohibition against cruel and unusual punishment.[10]

Repressive or unconstitutional actions of the federal government—the murder of four students by the National Guard at Kent

State, the attempted censorship of the *New York Times* over the *Pentagon Papers,* Nixon's "enemies list" of Watergate fame—are considered infamous and glaring, but nonetheless isolated, examples. The brutal behavior of many Southern whites in beating, terrorizing and murdering civil rights workers is considered a shameful episode—but one confined to rural towns and local racist police.

Unfortunately, this standard view of the Vietnam War era is not accurate. While the civil rights movement did make great strides and the Supreme Court did extend the legal framework of civil liberties, this era was one of a massive, continual and conscious program of war-time repression by the federal, state and local governments.

When the target of federal repression was a major establishment institution, the repression was condemned. Thus, when the government tried to censor the *New York Times* in 1971, almost the entire media establishment rose to defend freedom of the press. And the Nixon administration's attempt to burgle the national headquarters of the Democratic Party—and the ensuing cover-up—brought virtually unanimous condemnation and ultimately the President's resignation.

But when the federal government targeted minority and progressive organizations, the repression—although much more severe than that against establishment institutions—went unnoticed and unprotested by mainstream institutions. During this era:

- The U.S. government launched a comprehensive program to silence the underground papers; anti-war editors were jailed, presses were bombed, reporters were harassed, news vendors were arrested for distributing newspapers, newsrooms were infiltrated by government spies and businesses were intimidated from advertising in the opposition papers;
- Police illegally broke into the headquarters of the Socialist Workers Party on the average of once every three weeks during the early-1960s;
- National Guard and local police shot and killed unarmed, innocent and non-violent protestors;
- Conspiracy trials—often no more than kangaroo courts—were organized to remove the leaders of anti-war and minority peoples' movements;
- Agents provocateurs—undercover police—infiltrated peaceful organizations and then encouraged and led anti-war and civil rights protestors in bombings and other violent activities;

* The FBI engaged in a concerted program to destroy the New Left and the black movement, a program that included infiltrations, agents provocateurs, disinformation, manipulation of the media, bombings and assassinations;
* Local police spied on churches, unions and organizations engaged in peaceful protest activity;
* Every federal intelligence agency—the FBI, CIA, NSA, and military intelligence units—spied on U.S. citizens.

The repression was great enough to compel Amnesty International to adopt at least thirty-nine U.S. Prisoners of Conscience during this era. Amnesty International stated at that time that the true number of political prisoners in the United States was "impossible to estimate." [11]

Treatment of Anti-war Demonstrators

In July 1959, the first U.S. soldier was killed in Vietnam, marking the beginning of a U.S. war that would last fifteen years—the bloodiest and most divisive since the Civil War, the longest and one of the least justified in U.S. history.

The first campus demonstrations against the War took place during the fall of 1963, during a U.S. visit of Ngo Dinh Nhu, the wife of the chief of South Vietnam's secret police and sister-in-law of President Diem. During the next decade, well in excess of 20,000,000 people would publicly protest the war; tens of thousands would be arrested; thousands of young men would flee the country to escape the draft; martial law would be declared numerous times; and at least six unarmed students would be shot dead by the National Guard. In reaction to generally peaceful political protest, the government bugged phones, prepared spurious indictments, infiltrated peaceful organizations and provoked violence.

As the anti-war protests increased, trials for draft evasion, draft card burning and destruction of draft records became more and more common. During the Vietnam War, 26.8 million men came of draft age. It is estimated that 10,000 draft-age men burned their draft-registration cards in protest of the war. Some 150,000 young men chose to leave the country of their birth rather than fight in a war they found immoral.[12] Over 2,000 young men received prison sentences for draft resistance or refusal.[13]

As the courts had been confronted by religious abolitionists, suffragists and civil rights workers, so now they began to be confronted by a new breed of non-violent protestor: citizens who felt morally compelled to disrupt the operations of their local draft board.

> On a warm spring day in 1966, a nineteen year old Minnesotan by the name of Barry Bondhus broke into his local draft board and dumped two large bucketfuls of human feces into a filing cabinet, mutilating several hundred I-A draft records in protest against the Vietnam draft.
>
> This primordial deed is known in the annals of the anti-war protest as the Big Lake One action, in honor of Barry Bondhus's hometown, Big Lake, Minnesota...Big Lake One was hardly mentioned in the press, but Bondhus's was "the movement that started the Movement." [14]

During the next three years, over one hundred people offered themselves up for arrest for destroying hundreds of thousands of draft records.[15] Not once were such defendants acquitted.

It was not uncommon for peaceful demonstrations to become violent—often at the instigation of police or agents provocateurs. The first major incident in which police attacked peaceful anti-war demonstrators occurred on June 23, 1967 in front of the Century Plaza Hotel in Los Angeles. Some 20,000 demonstrators of all ages—mostly white and middle-class—were protesting a dinner being given in honor of President Johnson. As night fell, 1,000 "club-swinging" police attacked the demonstrators;[16] hundreds were injured, sixty hospitalized. Several reporters were clubbed by police and one reporter's arm was broken.[17] Mayor Sam Yorty called the attack by the police a "superb job"; the police chief described the "crowd dispersal" activity as "a beautiful plan and well-executed." [18]

The Chicago Convention

While the 1968 Democratic Convention was convening in Chicago, 10-15,000 anti-war protestors demonstrated outside the Hilton Hotel to protest the policies of President Johnson and Vice President Hubert Humphrey. Confronting the demonstrators were 6,000 National Guardsmen, 7,500 U.S. Army troops and 1,000 FBI, CIA and army intelligence agents. The government claimed that one out of every six demonstrators was an undercover agent.[19]

The whole world watched on television as Mayor Daley's police, yelling "kill, kill, kill," attacked the anti-war protestors.[20] Some 668 people were arrested during the convention; hundreds were injured. Seventeen reporters and camera operators from three television networks were attacked by police.[21] Dan Rather was slugged while on camera; Mike Wallace was punched in the jaw and physically removed from the convention floor when he questioned the police attacks; Walter Cronkite talked about Mayor Daley's "thugs."[22] In all, sixty-three reporters—more than 20 percent of the journalists covering the convention—were arrested or attacked by the police.[23]

Writer Norman Mailer described the police attacking demonstrators with billy clubs, tear gas and Mace:

> They attacked like a chain saw cutting into wood...lines of twenty and thirty policemen striking in an arc...seen from overhead, from the nineteenth floor [of the Hilton Hotel], it was like a wind blowing dust..."[24]

At 5 a.m. on August 30, the police broke into the headquarters of Eugene McCarthy, the Democratic anti-war candidate. McCarthy staffers were dragged from their beds and beaten by the cops.[25]

Three months later, the National Commission on the Causes and Prevention of Violence released their report, finding that although the police had been provoked by obscenities and stones, their response had been an indiscriminate "police riot." Three days later, Mayor Daley reacted to the report by giving his police a 22 percent salary increase. Polling revealed that only 19 percent of the population thought the police had used "too much force."[26]

As a result of the police riot at the Chicago Democratic Convention, eight people were arrested and charged with conspiracy: Rennie Davis and David Dellinger (National Mobilization to End the War in Vietnam), John Froines (assistant professor of chemistry at the University of Oregon), Tom Hayden (Students for a Democratic Society), Abbie Hoffman and Jerry Rubin (Youth International Party, the Yippies), Lee Weiner (graduate student at Northwestern University) and Bobby Seale (Black Panther Party). Many of the eight defendants had never met prior to the Chicago demonstrations; some had never met until their joint indictment.

The trial of the Chicago Eight started on September 24, 1969 and lasted four months. In what appeared to be no more than a kangaroo court, Judge Julius Hoffman (no relation to the defendant, Abbie Hoffman) constantly mocked the defense, admitted hearsay from the prosecution and refused to allow the defendants their choice of witnesses. When Judge Hoffman prevented former Attorney General Ramsey Clark from testifying for the defense, the *New York Times* called the Judge's action "the ultimate outrage in a trial which has become a shame of American justice." [27]

The only African American among the Chicago Eight was Bobby Seale, the last national leader of the Black Panther Party who was not in jail or exile. During the conspiracy trial, Seale demanded that he either be allowed an attorney of his own choosing or the right to defend himself. The Judge denied his request. On October 29, after the trial had been underway for five weeks, Seale again demanded the right to choose his own counsel. Judge Hoffman had Seale bound, gagged and chained to his courtroom chair in leg irons. As one participant in the trial wrote:

> Surrounded by marshals, [Bobby Seale] was sitting in a high chair with his wrists and ankles strapped under clanking chains. Wrapped around his mouth and the back of his head was a thick white cloth. His eyes and the veins in his neck and temples were bulging with the strain of maintaining his breath. [28]

On November 5, Seale's case was severed from that of the other seven defendants. The Judge ordered Seale to serve forty-eight months in jail on contempt charges arising from his just-aborted trial. Seale was never retried on conspiracy charges, nor did he serve time on the contempt citations. [29]

The jury ultimately acquitted all seven of the remaining defendants on the conspiracy charges. Two defendants, John Froines and Lee Weiner were found not guilty on all counts; the other five were found guilty of the lesser offense of crossing state lines to incite a riot.

FBI documents uncovered after the trial indicate that Judge Julius Hoffman was in continual contact with both prosecutors and FBI, discussing strategy and tactics for convicting the defendants.[30] Judge Hoffman handed down 175 contempt citations against the defendants and their lawyers, totaling nineteen years of jail time. Attorney William Kunstler and Bobby Seale both received a jail sentence of four years for contempt; Leonard Weinglass, the other defense lawyer, received two years. Over 160 of the 175 contempt citations were eventually overturned by the appeals court.[31]

Shootings of Demonstrators

Coinciding with the U.S. bombing of Cambodia in the spring of 1970, governmental repression at home reached its peak. On May 4, four students were gunned down, one crippled for life and many wounded by the National Guard at Kent State University, Ohio. Within a few days of the killings, 448 colleges and universities were either closed or on strike;[32] four million students protested the war and the killings.[33] ROTC buildings in Utah, Idaho and Wisconsin were bombed. Police at the University of Buffalo shot and wounded a dozen students. At the University of New Mexico, ten students were bayonetted;[34] the National Guard was sent to twenty-one campuses.[35]

No member of the National Guard was ever indicted for any of these deaths. However, twenty-five Kent State students—all politically opposed to the war—were indicted. Three were ultimately convicted of minor misdemeanors; the others were acquitted or had the charges against them dropped.[36] A *Newsweek* poll conducted shortly after the shootings showed that 58 percent of the country blamed the students, only 11 percent blamed the National Guard.[37] In 1979, nine years after killings, and at a time when the Vietnam War was fading into history, the State of Ohio paid the families of the slain students $675,000 and apologized for the events at Kent State.[38]

On May 5, 1970, martial law was declared at the University of Alabama at Tuscaloosa following a peaceful 1,500 person memorial march in honor of the Kent state students.[39] On May 13, the Mayor of Jackson, Mississippi called in the National Guard and ordered blockades around a thirty block area in response to a demonstration of 300 black students. The next evening, the National Guard fired into a women's dormitory at Jackson State, killing two black students.[40]

Unlike the killing of the four white students at Kent State, the shootings at Jackson State aroused little public outrage. Nor was there much outcry the year before when police fired upon students protesting segregated facilities at South Carolina State University in Orangeburg, killing two and wounding forty.[41]

Three months after Kent State, two students were killed by police in Lawrence, Kansas, and another killed at the University of Wisconsin. In November 1972, two students were killed by deputy sheriffs at Southern University in New Orleans. A special commission convened by Louisiana's attorney general found there was "no justification for the shootings."[42] The establishment media paid little attention to these political killings.

In numerical terms, the largest repressive actions by the government occurred during the 1971 May Day protest in Washington, D.C. Some 12,000 demonstrators gathered at the Capital to protest the war. They were met by 5,000 police, 2,000 National Guard and 8,000 soldiers and marines. The police did not even make a pretense of following constitutional procedures. Instead, they arrested over 7,000 people in huge sweeps. Innocent bystanders were caught up in the arrests, including a *Washington Star* reporter, several businesspeople, an army lieutenant, an off-duty cop, a law professor and a couple on their way to get married.[43] Detainees were herded into the Stadium and Coliseum, and left without food or sanitary facilities for many hours. Conditions in some of the police stations were worse:

> They packed seventeen of us in one small holding-cell for forty-eight hours. It was dirty with no water in the toilet. We had to organize rotation to lie down. It was so tight one person at all times had to stand on the toilet, or sit on it if they could bear it. The Red Cross sent us sandwiches the first day, but the jailers didn't give them to us until the next day and they were loaded with mayonnaise. A lot of us got very sick from it. I still think the cops did that deliberately.[44]

Of the thousands of people arrested that day, fewer than one hundred were convicted. An ACLU suit resulted in $12 million in damages being awarded to some of those arrested.[45]

Repression Against Minority Groups

Governmental repression during the Vietnam War era against minority leaders was even greater than that against the predominantly middle-class and white anti-war protestors.

During the first half of the 1960s, southern police and vigilantes harassed, attacked, tortured and murdered both white and black civil rights workers. Andrew Goodman, Michael Schwerner, James Chaney, and Medger Evers were only the most noted of the several dozen political murders of civil rights workers in the South during the early 1960s.[46] Those who survived were generally convicted by southern juries who ignored basic due process guarantees in their effort to enforce segregation. In a throwback to the governmental practices of the World War I era, civil rights demonstrators of the 1960s were at times arrested and charged with criminal syndicalism, criminal anarchy and insurrection.[47]

J. Edgar Hoover had a long-standing vendetta against Martin Luther King, Jr. After King criticized the FBI for not being more vigorous in protecting the civil rights of black citizens, the Bureau began

> putting a "trash cover" on the SCLC office, investigating King's bank and charge accounts, instituting electronic surveillance on an Atlanta hideaway apartment often used by King; installing a bug in King's office; looking for personal weaknesses among SCLC employees that could be used to win their cooperation with the Bureau; sending a forged letter in King's name to SCLC contributors warning them that an IRS investigation was about to begin; and attempting to intensify a well-known mutual dislike of King and NAACP head Roy Wilkins.[48]

At the urging of J. Edgar Hoover, Attorney General Nicholas Katzenbach approved the illegal bugging of King's Washington, D.C. hotel room in July 1965. Highlights of these tapes, purportedly evidence of King consorting with prostitutes, were sent by the FBI to his wife, Coretta Scott King. Another letter, along with edited audio tapes, was sent to Dr. King thirty-four days before he was to receive the Nobel Peace Prize. The letter urged King to commit suicide as the only method of preventing the release of the tapes. Had the FBI's crude attempt to convince King to commit suicide been successful, Hoover was ready to replace him with another black "leader" who had the approval of the FBI.[49]* The Bureau also sent copies of these tapes to reporters at *Newsweek,* the *New York Times,* the *Los Angeles Times,* the *Atlanta Constitution* and other papers. The FBI smear campaign failed, and these papers refused to print the FBI story.[50]

Racial tensions flared during "the long, hot summers" of the 1960s. There were twenty riots in 1964 and eighty-two during the summer of 1967.[51] During the week of July 12th, twenty-six people were killed and over 1,000 arrested in Newark, New Jersey. During the week of July 23rd, 4,700 paratroopers and 8,000 National Guard occupied a smoldering Detroit.[52]

Probably the largest single instance of the use of martial law in the 1960s was during the riots following the assassination of Dr. Martin Luther King, Jr. on April 4, 1968. Riots occurred in 110 cities.[53] Twenty thousand army troops and 34,000 National Guard were called out to reinforce tens of thousands of local police in scores of cities; 15,000 people were arrested, thirty-eight were killed, and 2,500 injured.[54] As a result of these riots, Congress passed an amendment, sponsored by Senator Strom Thurmond, which made it a felony to cross state lines with the "intent" to cause a "riot." The only people ever indicted under the law were the Chicago Eight.[55]

By the summer of 1969, over 200 black people had died in urban riots and uprisings, more than seventy cities had been occupied by the National Guard and major demonstrations had taken place on over 200 college campuses.[56]

---

* This "more malleable and less troublesome" black "leader" was Samuel R. Pierce, Jr. Pierce was later appointed by President Reagan as Secretary of Housing and Urban Development. After serving longer than any other member of Reagan's Cabinet, Pierce became embroiled in the corruption and influence-peddling scandals at HUD. (See, e.g., Ostrow and Frantz, "FBI Once Planned to Push Pierce as Rival to King," *L.A. Times,* August 29, 1989, p. 4.)

Between January 1968 and May 1970, the National Guard was mobilized to suppress civil disorders on 324 different occasions.[57] Curfews were often imposed in conjunction with the deployment of the National Guard.[58] Most were night-time curfews, but at least one, in Milwaukee in 1967, was a continuous twenty-six-hour curfew. The Supreme Court never ruled on the constitutionality of riot curfews;[59] state courts differed on their validity.[60]

In at least one instance, an emergency municipal ordinance banning peaceful demonstrations was upheld.[61]

The Campaign to Eliminate the Black Panthers

As the decade progressed, the optimism that "We Shall Overcome" gave way to a realization that equality for blacks in this country was a long way off. Many in the black community turned to more militant black nationalist organizations to lead the struggle for freedom.

During the latter half of the 1960s, the Black Panthers and other Black Power advocates—some of whom openly carried rifles as a means of showing their opposition to the government and defending themselves—bore the brunt of governmental repression.

J. Edgar Hoover urged his Special Agents in Charge to:

> prevent the coalition of militant black nationalist groups...prevent militant black national groups and leaders from gaining respectability...Prevent the *rise of a black "messiah" who would unify and electrify the militant black nationalist movement. Malcomb X [sic] might have been such a "messiah;" he is a martyr of the movement today. Martin Luther King, Stokely Carmichael and Elijah Muhammed all aspire to his position. Elijah Muhammed is less of a threat because of his age. King could be a very real contender for this position should he abandon his supposed "obedience" to "white, liberal doctrines" (nonviolence) and embrace black nationalism. Carmichael has the necessary charisma to be a real threat in this way.* [original emphasis][62]

Elijah Muhammed and Stokely Carmichael were the victims of assorted FBI COINTELPRO (Counter-Intelligence Program) dirty tricks; Malcolm X and Dr. King were eventually assassinated.

The FBI considered the Black Panther Party (BPP) the most dangerous of the black nationalist movements in the 1960s, even though the BPP had less than 2,000 members nationwide.[63]

One effort of the FBI's COINTELPRO[64] was to turn one segment of the black community against the other. This is detailed in the congressional report, *The FBI's Covert Action Program to Destroy the Black Panther Party,* under a sub-heading, "The Effort to Promote Violence Between the Black Panther Party and Other, Well-Armed, Potentially Violent Organizations." The FBI used all of its "black propaganda" arts—including fabricated evidence, bogus letters sent to the leadership of various organizations and "bad-jacketing" (the leaking of false rumors that an organization's leader was an FBI undercover agent)—to create dissension and division between the various black nationalist organizations. Of the 295 authorized FBI COINTELPRO operations against black groups, 233 were directed against the Black Panthers.[65]

A rift between the Black Panther Party and Ron Karenga's US Organization was created and exacerbated by the FBI, in part by the use of phony cartoons and caricatures purporting to be from the Panthers attacking US, or from US attacking the BPP. On January 17, 1969, two Los Angeles Black Panther leaders, Jon Huggins and Alprentice "Bunchy" Carter, were gunned down by US members on the UCLA campus. In internal memoranda, the FBI took credit for this incident. Seven months later, when two Black Panthers were wounded and a third, Sylvester Bell, was killed by US members in San Diego, the FBI again congratulated itself for its "success," and stated, "In view of the recent killing of BPP member Sylvester Bell, a new cartoon is being considered in hopes that it will assist in the continuance of the rift between the BPP and US." [66]

Other Black Panther Party leaders were murdered, with the apparent involvement of the FBI. In 1968, the FBI gave William O'Neal the assignment to infiltrate the Chicago BPP. O'Neal quickly rose through the ranks, becoming head of Panther security in Chicago and the personal bodyguard for Fred Hampton, leader of the Chicago chapter and one of the Panther's most promising national leaders.[67]

As an agent provocateur, O'Neal urged that the Black Panther headquarters be equipped with nerve gas and wired to electrocute interlopers, that they construct an "electric chair" for informers, that they acquire mortars to bomb city hall and that the Panthers engage in armed robbery to raise funds. All of these "suggestions" were rejected by Fred Hampton and the Black Panther Party.[68]

O'Neal supplied the Chicago police with a detailed floor diagram of Hampton's apartment, used by the police in the 4 a.m. December 4, 1969 raid in which Hampton and another Black Panther were murdered. The police burst into Hampton's apartment and fired at least eighty rounds of ammunition, almost all directed at the head of Hampton's bed as marked on O'Neal's diagram. Only one bullet was fired in the direction of the police. The Panthers that survived the police raid were arraigned the next day and held on $100,000 bail. Five months later, after a grand jury concluded that the police investigation into the killings was "so seriously deficient that it suggests purposeful malfeasance," the charges against the surviving Panthers were dropped.[69]

The FBI, again in internal memoranda, took partial credit for the "success" of the raid. Cook County District Attorney Edward Hanhrahan announced that the police had shown "good judgement, considerable restraint [and] professional discipline." [70]

Shortly after the assassinations, the survivors and families of the deceased filed a $47.7 million suit against the Chicago Police and the FBI. Fourteen years later, in 1983, after numerous trials and appeals, the police and the FBI defendants were found guilty of conspiracy to deny Fred Hampton and the other Black Panthers their civil rights. Sanctions were imposed on the FBI for their role in the cover-up and the survivors of the raid and the families of the deceased recovered $1.85 million in damages.[71]

Twenty-eight Panthers were killed during an eighteen-month period during the late-1960s, "some direct victims of aggressive intelligence actions and others traceable to [FBI]-assisted feuds." [72]

Other Black Panther leaders, although not targeted for elimination, were victims of continual harassment and arrest. During the late-1960s, the Oakland, California police bulletin board listed twenty "known Panther vehicles." These cars were routinely stopped, their drivers and occupants searched and harassed.[73] The fact of this "petty" police harassment was vividly illustrated by a sociology experiment conducted in the summer of 1969. Fifteen students at California State College, Los Angeles volunteered to put bumper stickers bearing the picture of a panther and the words "Black Panther" on their cars. During the prior year, none of the fifteen students had received even one moving violation. Within seventeen days, however, the fifteen students received thirty-three moving violations, and in five instances were subjected to thorough police searches.[74]

Such harassment often turned violent. On October 28, 1967, police stopped Huey Newton as he was driving in a "known Panther vehicle." What happened next is disputed; what is certain is that one officer was shot in the arm, another officer was killed by a bullet fired from his own gun and Newton was shot four times in the abdomen and once in the thigh. The surviving officer couldn't recall seeing Newton with a gun in his hand, and Newton claimed to be only carrying his lawbook. Nonetheless, Newton was charged with murder.

At his first trial, Newton was found guilty of voluntary manslaughter and served twenty-two months before the verdict was overturned due to judicial error at the trial. He was denied bail while California appealed the ruling of the higher court. Both a second and third trial ended in hung juries. The slogan "Free Huey" became a rallying cry in black ghettos.[75]

Similar trials of Bobby Seale, Erica Huggins, Elmer Pratt, Angela Davis and virtually the entire Panther leadership continued into the early-1970s.

One Black Panther leader, Richard (Dhoruba) Moore was convicted on April 26, 1973 on charges of machine-gunning two policemen. He is still in prison, serving a twenty-five-year-to-life term. It has recently come to light that the prosecution concealed evidence during Moore's trial that might have led to his acquittal.[76]

The New York Panther 21 were arrested for allegedly conspiring to blow up department stores, railroad facilities, a police station and the Bronx Botanical Gardens(!). In order to raise defense funds, Leonard Bernstein held his now-famous "radical chic" party for the Black Panthers.[77] The Panther 21 withstood an eight-month trial, including six months of evidence, only to be found not guilty of all 156 counts after three hours of jury deliberation. As a juror on that case later said, "[a]fter hearing all the evidence and everything, I came to the conclusion myself that the whole thing was a conspiracy to eliminate the Panthers as a whole." [78]

In an August 25, 1967 memo from J. Edgar Hoover to the Albany field office entitled "Counterintelligence Program Black Nationalist-Hate Groups Internal Security," Hoover advised that

> [t]he purpose of this new counterintelligence endeavor is to expose, disrupt, misdirect, discredit, or otherwise neutralize the activities of black nationalist, hate-type organizations and groupings, their leadership, spokesmen, membership and supporters...No opportunity should be missed to exploit...the organizational and personal conflicts of the leaderships of the groups...When an opportunity is apparent to disrupt or neutralize black nationalist, hate-type organizations through the cooperation of established local news media contacts or through such contact with sources available to the Seat of Government, in every instance careful attention must be given to the proposal to insure the targeted group is disrupted, ridiculed or discredited...
>
> Intensified attention under this program should be afforded to the activities of such groups as the Student Nonviolent Coordinating Committee, the Southern Christian Leadership Conference...Congress of Racial Equality, and the Nation of Islam.[79]

One such campaign was used to virtually destroy a black nationalist group known as the Revolutionary Action Movement (RAM). According to an FBI memorandum from the Special Agent in Charge of the Bureau's Philadelphia office, dated August 30, 1967:

> Cars stopping at [name deleted] residence were checked as to license numbers. When they left the residence area, they were subject to car stops by uniformed police. The occupants were identified. They then became the target for harassment...
>
> Any excuse for arrest was promptly implemented by arrest. Any possibility of neutralizing a RAM activist was exercised.
>
> [Name deleted] was arrested for defacing private property when he painted "Black Guard" on a private building. His companion was also arrested. A charge of carrying a concealed deadly weapon, a switch-blade knife [actually a pen-knife with a blade less than three inches long], was pushed against the companion. His probation

officer was contacted, his parole revoked, and he was returned to prison for several years.

Legal searches of the home of [name deleted] and other RAM members produced a volume of literature of such nature that the District Attorney authorized arrest of [name deleted] and five other RAM members. They are still in prison.

Other RAM people were arrested and released on bail, but they were re-arrested several times until they could no longer make bail.

The above activities appear for the present to have curtailed the activities of this [deleted] group. It was apparently a highly frustrating experience for the person involved...[80]

Non-black supporters of the Panthers were also subjects of FBI and police operations. The FBI targeted actress Jean Seberg, in order to discredit her support for the Black Panthers and "cheapen her image with the general public." The FBI planted a story in the *Los Angeles Times* that Seberg (who was married) was pregnant by a prominent Black Panther leader. The story was later picked up by *Newsweek*. She and her husband successfully sued for libel. Her husband later charged that the publicity resulted in a stillborn delivery of their child, a psychotic breakdown and Seberg's ultimate suicide.[81]

Besides its campaign against the Black Panther Party and the black civil rights and liberation movement, the FBI also targeted other militant minority organizations. Their campaign against the American Indian Movement (AIM) employed assassinations, infiltrators, informers, agents provocateurs, illegal surveillance and break-ins, forgery, fabrication of evidence, perjury and other abuses of the judicial system—virtually every "dirty trick" in the FBI's black bag.[82] Similarly, Chicano, Latino and Asian-American organizations also experienced violations of civil liberties at the hands of local police departments and the FBI.[83]

Prisoners of Conscience

Amnesty International began adopting Prisoners of Conscience in the United States in 1966. Defining the term " 'prisoner of

conscience' [to] include any person who refuses, on grounds of conscience, to fight in or train for all wars or any particular war," [84]
Amnesty International began an investigation of some 200 cases of
young men imprisoned for refusing to register or cooperate with the
draft. In 1966, Amnesty International adopted eighteen prisoners of
conscience, including sixteen who were imprisoned for conscientious
objection to the Vietnam War.

Between 1966 and 1979, Amnesty International adopted at least
thirty-nine Prisoners of Conscience in the United States. [85] These
political prisoners were either people who opposed the Vietnam War
or were members of ethnic minorities struggling against discrimination. Two of the prisoners of conscience, Wilbert Lee and Freddie Lee
Pitts, served twelve years in jail, while another, Martin Sostre, was
imprisoned nearly nine years. [86]

During this time Amnesty stated that even though there is no
overt political imprisonment in the United States, "it is impossible to
estimate the number of political prisoners in the United States," [87]
because "it is suspected that many people may be 'framed' on criminal
charges because of their political activities or ethnic origin." [88]

As late as 1979, six years after the last U.S. soldier left Vietnam,
Amnesty still counted eleven Prisoners of Conscience in U.S. jails; that
year they adopted another Prisoner of Conscience, Imari Obadele, a
black nationalist leader. [89]

States of Emergency

The Espionage Act of 1917 was never repealed following World
War I and remained in force through two decades of peace and
throughout World War II.

In 1939, the Attorney General compiled a list of ninety-nine
statutes passed by Congress, still in effect, which expressly granted
emergency powers to the President in times of war or national emergency. [90] Among these were laws allowing the President to prohibit
foreign exchange transactions and hoarding of gold or currency; [91]
allowing the government to nationalize power stations, dams and
reservoirs; [92] authorizing the arrest, detention and deportation of any
citizen of a hostile nation over the age of fourteen; [93] and permitting the

President to designate places to which U.S. citizens could be prohibited access.[94]

In 1948 Congress enacted a new Espionage Act.[95] Under this act, any person who delivered any "information related to the national defense" to a foreign nation with the intent that it be used "to the injury of the United States or the advantage of a foreign nation" was liable for twenty years imprisonment.[96] If done during time of war, such action was punishable by death.[97]

Two years later, the United States was involved in a police action, not a war, in Korea. To meet the perceived threat, President Truman proclaimed a state of emergency,[98] the first since President Franklin Roosevelt's state of emergency to deal with the Great Depression. Truman relied on the state of emergency to attempt executive actions that could not have been made in peace-time.[99] Like other states of emergency, this one was not rescinded by the President and it served as the basis for at least two Vietnam-era prosecutions of anti-war protesters.[100]

Since the Korean conflict was not an officially declared war, the provisions of the Espionage Act of 1948, applying the death penalty for communication of defense information, was not applicable. As war-time paranoia increased, Congress felt a need to rectify this situation, passing a law to extend the provisions of the Espionage Act until "six months after the termination of the national emergency proclaimed by the President on December 16, 1950." [101] Since the state of emergency was not repealed by the President, this statute by Congress is arguably still in effect.

Before the Watergate spying and cover-up forced President Nixon to resign, his Attorney General, Richard Kleindienst, commented that a declaration of a state of emergency:

> could not happen here under any circumstances. We wouldn't suspend the Bill of Rights even if the whole Cabinet, the Chief Justice and the Speaker of the House were kidnapped...We wouldn't have to because our existing laws—together with our surveillance and intelligence apparatus, which is the best in the world—are sufficient to cope with any situation...There is enough play at the joints of our...law, enough flexibility, so that if we really felt we had to pick up leaders of a violent uprising, we could. We

would find something to charge them with and we would
hold them that way for a while.[102]

Despite the Attorney General's comments, the United States actually
experienced as many as four simultaneous national states of emergency from the Depression through the Vietnam War.

In 1976 Congress reported that "our Constitutional government
has been weakened by 41 consecutive years of emergency rule" [103] and
listed four presidentially declared states of national emergency to be
still in existence. These four were declared by:

- President Roosevelt in 1933 to fight the Great Depression;
- President Truman in 1950 during the Korean War;
- President Nixon in 1970 to handle the Post Office strike; and
- President Nixon in 1971 to meet balance of payment problems.

The report stated, "A majority of the American people have lived
all their lives under emergency government." [104] Over 470 statutes
gave the President extra-constitutional powers in times of national
emergency. Under these four states of emergencies, the President had
the power

> to seize property and commodities, organize and control the
> means of production, call to active duty 2.5 million reser-
> vists, assign military forces abroad, seize and control all
> means of transportation and communication, restrict
> travel, and institute martial law, and in many other ways,
> manage every aspect of the lives of all American citizens.[105]

Congress reacted by passing the National Emergencies Act in
1976,[106] presumably terminating all existing states of emergency and
setting guidelines for their future determination by the President.
However, while Congress can certainly repeal statutes that give
emergency powers to the President, it is not clear that Congress has
the authority to terminate a state of emergency declared by the
President. Whether these four states of emergency are still in existence
has never been tested in court.

The Use of the Secret Police

"A Cancer in our Body Politic"

By 1968, at the height of the anti-war movement, every intelligence agency in the United States was spying on non-violent domestic protest by U.S. citizens.

Even before the exposure of Nixon's burglars, it had already become clear that the Army itself had been engaged in a "massive and comprehensive" surveillance of civilians for the past thirty years involving 1,000 investigators and 300 officers.[107] The Army spied on such organizations as the Southern Christian Leadership Conference, the American Civil Liberties Union and the National Association for the Advancement of Colored People, by means which included "staking out teams of agents, infiltrating undercover agents, creating command posts inside meetings, posing as press photographers and newsmen, posing as TV newsmen, posing as students and shadowing public figures."[108] Army agents posed as newspaper reporters to interview leaders of the demonstration at the 1968 Chicago Democratic Convention; infiltrated the anti-war Moratorium marches in October and November 1969; and posed as students to monitor Black Studies classes at New York University.[109] The Army's "subversive file" contained more than 210,000 dossiers on organizations and 80,000 biographical files.[110] In 1968 more Army Counter-Intelligence Analysis Branch personnel monitored domestic protests than were assigned to any other counter-intelligence operation, including that of Southeast Asia and Vietnam.[111]

The Supreme Court refused to declare that domestic political spying by the Army violated the First Amendment. The majority side-stepped the legality of the Army's surveillance program, holding that "respondents have not presented a case for resolution by the courts."[112] The two dissenting justices, however, noted that this was not the first time that "[a]rmy intelligence had been maintaining an unauthorized watch over civilian political activity" and termed such surveillance "a cancer in our body politic."[113]

The National Security Agency (NSA) electronically intercepted messages of anti-war activists and other people opposed to United States government policies. During World War II, all electronic and cable communications had been censored in compliance with war-time restrictions. However, government spying on domestic cable and radio transmission continued after the war. Under Project SHAMROCK, initiated in 1945, the NSA intercepted messages sent overseas by U.S. citizens. As part of SHAMROCK, Western Union, RCA and ITT continued to give NSA and other intelligence personnel unrestricted access to the private communications of U.S. citizens. RCA, for instance, allowed Army intelligence officers to set up an office inside the RCA facilities, requiring only that the soldiers wear civilian clothing.[114]

With the advent of computers, "watch lists" could be automated. A computer could be instructed to pick out every communication that mentioned a particular word, or a particular person's name. By 1967, under instructions from President Johnson, NSA had developed a sophisticated watch list of prominent people in the anti-war movement. Every communication of almost 1,200 prominent opponents of the administration was read. This project became known as MINARET. As part of Project MINARET, NSA maintained files on some 75,000 U.S. citizens, including members of Congress.[115]

In the late-1960s and early-1970s, the National Security Agency intercepted over 150,000 messages a month, dwarfing the CIA's mail-opening program.[116] No links to foreign agents were ever found; nonetheless, some 2,000 reports containing personal information were disseminated by the NSA to various intelligence agencies.

An attempt to challenge the constitutionality of these warrantless intercepts failed when the court ruled that national security prevented the subpoenaing of information to prove whether or not such communications had in fact been intercepted.[117]

CIA Domestic Spying

While the National Security Agency and the Army intelligence programs escaped Court sanction, the CIA's illegal activities came under fire from Congress. By the mid-1960s, it became known that the CIA had covertly funded and infiltrated many organizations, including the National Student Association, the American Newspaper Guild, and the National Council of Churches.[118] In an attempt to head off a broad-based congressional investigation of the CIA, President Ford appointed the Commission on CIA Activities in January 1975. The

Commission's report[119] documented massive illegal domestic spying
activities by the CIA, including:

- A letter opening program, begun at the end of the Korean War
  in 1953, under which the CIA opened and read letters being sent
  to and from the Soviet Union. By 1973, when the program was
  halted, some 2,300,000 letters had been photographed by the
  CIA, including letters to Senators Church and Kennedy;[120]
- Operation CHAOS, started in 1967, to gather information on
  political protestors. CHAOS compiled some 13,000 different
  files, spied on over 7,000 individuals and 1,000 organizations,
  and entered into a computerized index the names of more than
  300,000 persons and organizations;[121]
- Operation RESISTANCE, originally developed to protect CIA
  recruiters on college campuses, maintained files on some 500-
  800 dissenters, indexed thousands of names of campus radicals,
  and spied on the student press;[122]
- Project MERRIMAC, which infiltrated CIA agents into at least
  ten major peace and civil rights organizations, including the
  Black Panthers, the Congress of Racial Equality, the War
  Resisters League and Women Strike for Peace;[123] and
- Project MUDHEN, which used seventeen CIA operatives to spy
  on syndicated columnist Jack Anderson.[124]

In 1973, the *Washington Star-News* reported that the CIA had
placed thirty-six journalists on its payroll. The U.S. Senate committee
chaired by Senator Church discovered that some 200 newspapers,
magazines, wire services and publishing companies were owned outright by the CIA.[125]

The Church Committee also learned that the CIA had several
hundred professors and academics to front for them on university
campuses around the country. As late as 1985, Nadav Safran, director
of Harvard's Center for Middle Eastern Studies, resigned after it was
reported that the CIA had secretly funded a conference he had ar-
ranged on Islamic fundamentalism.[126]

FBI Spying

The most infamous domestic spying program, begun in 1956 and
continuing into the early 1970s, was known as COINTELPRO
(*Counter Intelligence Program*). The purpose of this FBI program, in

the words of one court, was to "expose, disrupt, misdirect, discredit, or otherwise neutralize the activities" of New Left and other progressive organizations, "including those involved in legitimate, non-violent activities." [127] Under the guise of preventing national and civil disorder:

> the FBI planted stories about "subversives" in the media, wrote scurrilous letters from fictional sources, opened mail, forged public documents, pressured universities and employers to dismiss targeted workers, encouraged "friendly" organizations and local police to harass dissidents, exploited IRS tax records, and infiltrated legal organizations.[128]

COINTELPRO consisted of numerous illegal tactics by the FBI, including:

- Eavesdropping: illegally bugging a person's home or office;
- Bogus mail: forging and sending (usually) anonymous letters, ranging from letters to the editor to death threats;
- "Black propaganda": creating false documents, purporting to come from the target organization;
- Infiltration: sending undercover spies into an organization, some of whom rose to positions of power and helped set policy for the organization;
- Agents provocateurs: undercover agents who urged others to violent activity, trained others in violent methods, and consciously provoked violence;
- Bad-jacketing: creating the impression, through false documents, rumors, bogus mail, etc., that the leader of an organization was actually a police informer;

as well as disinformation, harassment arrests, fabrication of evidence, and complicity in assassinations.[129]

The FBI was fully aware that COINTELPRO was highly illegal. COINTELPRO documents were marked "do not file," and were prepared without the FBI's sequential filing system serial numbers. Thus, anyone looking through the files would find documents in perfect sequential order. Since there would be no missing serial numbers, the investigator would not be aware that documents had not been filed. In addition, this system allowed an FBI official to honestly testify that a thorough review of the files had yielded no COINTELPRO documents.[130]

In 1959, 400 agents in the New York FBI office were assigned to "communism," while only four were assigned to organized crime.[131] This preoccupation with political dissidents continued for at least the next fifteen years. In 1976, the FBI allocated $7,401,000 for its political informers, more than twice that allocated for organized crime informers.[132]

For at least thirty years, the FBI engaged in a major campaign to harass and neutralize the Socialist Workers Party (SWP). During a sixteen-year period beginning in 1960, the FBI employed some 1,600 informers at an estimated cost of $26 million to infiltrate or monitor the SWP.[133] Its New York headquarters was burglarized by the FBI at least ninety-two times between 1960 and 1966. This is approximately one FBI burglary of the headquarters every three weeks. The illegal burglaries yielded over 10,000 photographs of SWP documents, correspondence and other material.[134] The FBI also infiltrated and even helped set policy for the Socialist Workers Party. Between 1960 and 1976, forty-two FBI undercover agents held office in the SWP or Young Socialist Alliance (the SWP youth organization).[135]

A similar campaign was directed at the Communist Party, USA, also a legal political party. In the mid-1960s more than one out of every six members of the Communist Party USA was an FBI agent.[136]

The FBI proposed 3,247 illegal, repressive and disruptive actions throughout the course of COINTELPRO; 2,370 were carried out:[137] false documents were planted on movement leaders to make it appear as if they were FBI informers;[138] FBI agents established dummy chapters of the Communist Party which then "deviated" from the party line;[139] undercover agents blew up cars with molotov cocktails to make it appear as if one faction of the Left were attacking another;[140] at least one FBI agent provocateur organized and led a draft board raid that resulted in arrest and prosecution by the FBI of the participants;[141] and agents beat up anti-war activists to frighten them and disrupt political rallies.[142]

In the 1960s, the FBI established a Security Index and a Rabble Rouser Index. Every sixty days, the person's file was supposed to be updated, so that the Bureau would be in a position to round up the person in the event of an emergency. The FBI's Security Index—containing the names of people to be summarily arrested and detained in the event of a war—listed 200,000 persons, including writer Norman

Mailer and Democratic Senator Paul Douglas.[143] In 1965, the same year that both Cuba and Czechoslovakia expelled poet Allen Ginsberg for chanting slogans against the communist police, Ginsberg was put on the Dangerous Subversive Internal Security List by the FBI.[144]

The FBI was not alone in developing a list of people to be summarily arrested and incarcerated in the event of a national emergency. The CIA and the National Security Agency had their own Watch Lists of dissident Americans.

In 1970, Tom Huston, advisor to President Nixon, developed the infamous Huston Plan which advocated surreptitious opening of mail, electronic surveillance, illegal break-ins and campus infiltrations.[145] As late as 1975, the FBI was conducting surveillance on 1,100 political organizations.[146]

A July 5, 1968 memo from J. Edgar Hoover to the Albany field office detailed a twelve-point program for disrupting the New Left. Among the recommendations were:

2. The instigation...of personal conflicts or animosities existing between New Left leaders...

3. The creating of the impression that certain New Left leaders are informants...

6. The drawing up of anonymous letters regarding individuals active in the New Left...[to] be sent to their parents, neighbors and the parents' employers...

7. Anonymous letters or leaflets describing faculty members and graduate assistants...Anonymous mailings should be made to university officials, members of the state legislature, Board of Regents, and to the press. Such letters could be signed "A Concerned Alumni"[sic] or "A Concerned Taxpayer"...

11. Consider the use of cartoons, photographs, and anonymous letter which will have the effect of ridiculing the New Left...

12. Be alert for opportunities to confuse and disrupt New Left activities by misinformation...[147]

Over 500,000 secret investigations of "subversives" were conducted.

The Bureau maintained informants at virtually every major newspaper and media outlet.[148] The Chicago Field Office of the FBI, for instance, had sources at the *Chicago Tribune, Chicago American,*

Chicago Daily News, Chicago Sun-Times, Chicago Defender, Joliet Herald, Rockford Register Republic, Rockford Morning Star, and the *Waukegan News Star;* at the local affiliates of ABC, CBS and NBC; at radio station WGN; and at the City News Bureau.

While undercover agents were illegally and surreptitiously making policy for the Socialist Workers Party, the FBI was openly helping to make policy for the entire United States. Seventy former FBI agents were elected to Congress during these two decades.[149]

Numerous incidents of provocation were reported throughout the decade. One of the most militant members of the Weather Underground, "widely known for his skill in making bombs and fuses," had often criticized his comrades for limiting their bombing to property. He berated them, stating that "[t]rue revolutionaries had to be ready and anxious to kill people." It turned out that he was a paid informer and agent provocateur for the FBI.[150]

During the final ten years of COINTELPRO, the FBI spent $80 million annually on domestic spying. Yet despite this massive expenditure, there has not been a single prosecution since 1957 under laws which prevent the overthrow of the U.S. government.[151]

The information gleaned from spying on citizens was used not only by the FBI to harass, disrupt, discredit and control left-leaning political groups, but was also transmitted to administration officials for their own political use. Information from illegal FBI break-ins and spying was continually fed to both the Dies Committee and the House Un-American Activities Committee. FBI Director J. Edgar Hoover kept dossiers on politically prominent individuals, including members of Congress. Presidents used FBI-obtained information against their political opponents: President Johnson, for instance, received FBI political intelligence reports on the strategies that members of Congress, Robert F. Kennedy and various civil rights leaders planned to use at the 1964 Democratic National Convention;[152] Vice-President Hubert Humphrey was given access to similar FBI reports on anti-war advocates at the 1968 Democratic Convention in Chicago.[153]

During this era, the FBI used its power both to influence the sympathetic media and harass journalists critical of the FBI. The FBI helped produce several television shows. For instance, the 1960s series "The FBI," although nominally produced by Quinn Martin (selected by the FBI for this job), was practically an FBI propaganda series. All scripts for the show were submitted for FBI approval before the episode was filmed.[154]

In 1970, columnist Jack Nelson of the *Los Angeles Times* wrote an article stating that the FBI had provoked a Ku Klux Klan firebombing directed at a civil rights activist in Mississippi. The article was accurate. After the article appeared, J. Edgar Hoover exerted pressure on Otis Chandler, publisher of the *Los Angeles Times*, to fire Nelson. The FBI targeted numerous other columnists and reporters who dared write articles critical of Hoover or the Bureau.[155]

COINTELPRO was uncovered in the early 1970s. A year after the Vietnam War, under the spotlight of the Church Committee's criticism, reforms were adopted by President Carter that presumably reined in the unconstitutional activities of the FBI by restricting their ability to engage in "surveillance, wiretaps, mail interception, break-ins and undercover work in the absence of an official criminal investigation." [156]

Spying by Local Police

Local police departments throughout the nation also engaged in illegal surveillance against progressives. In 1967, Chicago police broke into the offices of the Chicago Peace Council, Women for Peace and the Fellowship of Reconciliation, stealing files, correspondence and membership lists for the purpose of "destroy[ing] the left." [157] Seven years later, the Chicago police infiltrated the Alliance to End Repression, an organization planning to file suit against police spying.[158]

In 1975, the Los Angeles Board of Police Commissioners stated that the Public Disorder Intelligence Division (PDID) had destroyed two million(!) outdated intelligence files on various political groups and individuals. One of the organizations formed to oppose police spying, the Citizens Commission on Police Repression, was itself infiltrated by the police. It was revealed that the PDID had kept dossiers on various political organizations and churches, politicians, and a judge, as well as on the President of the Board of Police Commissioners, its own oversight body.[159]

These illegal police actions were not unusual. Police in numerous other cities, including New York, Detroit, Seattle and Memphis, had illegally spied and kept dossiers on peaceful political organizations throughout the Vietnam War era.[160]

Perhaps the most notorious agent provocateur of the decade was Tommy Tongyai, better known as "Tommy-the-Traveler." In 1968, Tommy-the-Traveler infiltrated the Students for a Democratic Society and traveled from campus to campus as their representative in the Finger Lakes District of upstate New York. He constantly urged students to undertake violent actions against the university, condemned blacks on campus because they "hadn't burned any [buildings] down," [161] and urged non-violent protestors to kidnap university officials and a visiting member of Congress. He showed students at Hobart College how to use guns and make bombs, and told the students he could supply them with explosives. Tommy-the-Traveler was an undercover agent (code-name, Maxwell Smart) hired by County Sheriff Ray Morrow. He may also have worked undercover for the FBI during this time.[162]

Hobart College was relatively conservative, and the students became so fed up with Tommy-the-Traveler's provocation that the Hobart Student Association banned him from campus, and even the radical student leadership had him expelled from their demonstrations.[163]

Nonetheless, Tommy-the-Traveler persisted and was eventually able to convince two nineteen-year-old students to fire-bomb the local ROTC building; he thereupon had the students arrested.

When students at Hobart College finally realized that Tommy-the-Traveler was a police agent, a campus riot ensued. As a result of the riot and the college's grant of amnesty to the arrested students, Hobart College was indicted—the only time in U.S. history when a college itself was the subject of criminal charges in connection with a campus disorder.[164]

Although exposed as a provocateur, Tommy-the-Traveler was never indicted for his role in these incidents. (He later pled guilty to another charge—illegally accepting unemployment checks while working for the Sheriff's department.) A year later, he was hired as an officer on the New Britain Township police force in upstate New York.[165]

Censorship of the Press

The Establishment Press

In past wars, the military combined accreditation—giving reporters semi-official status and access to the front lines—with censorship. During the beginning stages of the Vietnam War, the armed forces had considered imposing military censorship, and Associated Press, at least, indicated a willingness to abide by such formal restrictions.[166]

Ultimately, the military decided that censorship would not be feasible. They felt that censorship in Vietnam would be ineffective unless it could also be imposed in the United States. Otherwise, instead of filing from Saigon, correspondents would simply dispatch their reports from Bangkok, Tokyo or Hong Kong. Further, military censorship in Vietnam would not plug the leaks emanating from Washington, D.C. Secretary of State Dean Rusk told reporters in 1968,

> Unless we are in a formal state of war, with censorship here [in Washington], there is no point in having censorship [in Vietnam]…Here is where most of the leaks come from.[167]

Instead of censorship, the Pentagon decided to accredit reporters and devised a list of fifteen types of information that could not be reported without military approval. Among the proscribed topics were unannounced troop movements or casualty figures. Violations of these rules could result in loss of accreditation. Out of over 2,000 correspondents in Vietnam, only six security violations were deemed serious enough by the Defense Department to warrant revocation of accreditation.[168]

The other reason that there was no official censorship during the Vietnam War was that censorship was not necessary: the establishment papers accurately reflected the opinions and beliefs of the major governmental and business institutions of the nation. When the United States began its massive military intervention in Vietnam in 1965, this build-up enjoyed virtually total editorial support from the establishment press.[169] Studies have shown that during the first several years of the war, the large majority of television coverage spoke favorably of the administration and its allies in South Vietnam, and extremely negatively of the opposition.[170] Only after major U.S. institutions were themselves divided over the wisdom of continuing the war did the mainstream press begin to reflect this split through editorial and reporting policies.

While there was no official censorship, the military did have a policy of preventing reporters from learning about military activities "that are likely to result in undesirable stories." [171] For instance, reporters were prevented from flying to see a downed U.S. airplane in Vietnam, since, at that time, "a crashed plane...contradicts the [military's] optimistic line." [172]

The Pentagon Papers

In early 1971, the *New York Times* was notified by its Washington Bureau that they were in possession of some highly-classified documents relating to the Vietnam War. These documents turned out to be an extremely detailed study of the history of U.S. involvement in Vietnam. Forty-seven volumes, formally titled "History of U.S. Decision-Making Process on Vietnam Policy," containing over 7,000 pages of material, were written between 1967 and 1969 by a special Defense Department task force and were classified Secret, Top Secret or Top Secret-Sensitive.

Popularly known as the *Pentagon Papers,* the study detailed two decades of manipulation, deception and deceit by four succeeding administrations regarding the U.S. role in Vietnam. Although it provided informed critics of the war with little new information, the *New York Times* decided after much internal debate to publish a series of articles based on the *Pentagon Papers.*

On Sunday, June 13, 1971, the first of a series of lengthy articles appeared,[173] but it provoked almost no official reaction. The next day's installment was headlined "Vietnam Archive: A Consensus to Bomb Developed Before '64 Election, Study Says." Before the day was over, Attorney General John Mitchell sent a telegram to the *New York Times* stating that the series of articles was prohibited by the espionage laws and that continued publication "will cause irreparable injury to the defense interests of the United States." [174]

The *New York Times* refused to accede to governmental pressure. The next morning's edition contained a five-column headline

"Mitchell Seeks to Halt Series on Vietnam but Times Refuses." To defend themselves against the expected government restraining order, the *Times* sought help from their law firm, Lord, Day & Lord. However, the law firm disagreed with the decision to print the articles and refused to represent the *New York Times* on this issue.

The next day, the government was in court to prevent the *New York Times* from printing any more articles derived from the *Pentagon Papers*. While the government's attempt to censor the *Times* continued in New York, the *Washington Post* had independently obtained copies of the *Pentagon Papers* and, on June 18, published the first of their own series. The government immediately moved to stop the *Washington Post* from printing these articles.

All told, the U.S. government succeeded in getting six injunctions issued against the *New York Times*, which prevented the newspaper from publishing the *Pentagon Papers* for fifteen days.[175] Both the *New York Times* and the *Washington Post* cases were appealed to the Supreme Court. The Government rested its case on the assertion that publication of the *Pentagon Papers* would "irreparably damage" the ability of our "free government to endure."[176] Solicitor General of the United States Erwin N. Griswold maintained that publication would pose a "grave and immediate danger to the security of the United States." In oral argument before the Supreme Court, he stated that

> Publication will...materially affect the security of the United States. It will affect lives. It will affect the process of the termination of the war. It will affect the process of recovering prisoners of war.[177]

After an expedited hearing, the Supreme Court, in a 6-3 decision, ruled that the prior restraints against the *New York Times* and the *Washington Post* violated the First Amendment's guarantee of a free press.[178] Three justices ruled that pre-publication censorship of a paper was never justified, three believed that such prior restraint was constitutional in the case of the *Pentagon Papers*, and the deciding three justices held that prior restraint might sometimes be justified, but not in this case.

A few weeks after the ruling, Senator Mike Gravel had the entire forty-seven volumes of the *Pentagon Papers* published. Almost two decades later, former Solicitor General Griswold, contradicting the statements he had made when arguing before the Supreme Court, admitted that he had "never seen any trace of a threat to the national security from the publication" of the *Pentagon Papers.*[179]

The *Pentagon Papers* case was unusual on two counts: first, that disagreement existed between the government and the media, making governmental censorship "necessary"; and second, the lack of subtlety that governmental pressure took. Other Vietnam War-related incidents of disagreement were resolved through media self-censorship or pressure that fell short of censorship by the government.

During the Kennedy administration, for example, NBC News planned to broadcast a clip which showed a U.S. Army captain standing-by while South Vietnamese soldiers abused Viet-Cong prisoners. Under pressure from the Pentagon, NBC withdrew this film.[180]

Most of the time such pressure was not needed as the media, especially television, favored the government's version of the war and cooperated in a form of self-censorship.[181] All three television networks had internal guidelines which prevented the showing of disturbing footage of wounded U.S. soldiers or U.S. atrocities in Vietnam. The evening news editors at both NBC and ABC were ordered by their superiors to delete shots that appeared excessively detailed.[182]

Perhaps the most famous exception to television's "sanitizing" of the War occurred on CBS on August 5, 1965 when Morley Safer showed U.S. Marines burning huts in the village of Cam Ne with cigarette lighters. President Johnson ordered a background investigation of Safer and the Pentagon responded with a campaign "to discredit the television story and vilify the correspondent as 'unpatriotic.' "[183]

In 1966, the Pentagon publicly castigated CBS reporters Martin Agronsky and Peter Fromson for airing accurate but unflattering accounts of the Vietnam War. Television newscasters reported that they could not voice their concerns about the government's handling of the War on TV. Both Mike Wallace and David Brinkley had to confine their criticisms to printed articles.[184]

In 1967, the Smothers Brothers comedy show was taken off of network TV because of their political satire against the Vietnam War.[185] Even the FCC's guidelines for applying the Fairness Doctrine— which holds that both sides of an issue should get equal air time—were slanted towards censorship. The guidelines stated that "it is not the

Commission's intention to make time available to Communists or to the Communist viewpoints." [186]

Television's self-censorship was evident not only in what was shown on the news, but also in what television refused to cover. The November 16, 1969 Mobilization Against the War was the largest anti-war demonstration up to that time, bringing over 500,000 people to the Washington Monument. Yet there was no live television coverage of the march and rally, perhaps because the media had recently been attacked by Vice President Agnew for supposed anti-war bias. [187]

The Campaign Against the Underground Press

It is the accepted wisdom that during the Vietnam War the press was free from governmental censorship. As we have seen, this is not completely true. However, the censorship and harassment that establishment media faced were minor when compared with the repression directed against the opposition and alternative press—generally known as the "underground press."

The term "underground press" is used to denote a large range of independent papers whose common bond was both an opposition to the administration's domestic and foreign policies (the papers tended to be pro-civil rights and anti-war) and an affinity with the counter-culture of the 1960s and early-1970s. Unlike the establishment press, the underground press combined reporting with advocacy, urging people to oppose the War—an advocacy that infuriated the government. These papers ranged in size from small local papers to major weeklies with press runs approaching 100,000.

In the late-1960s and early-1970s, between 200 and 500 opposition papers operated in the United States. [188] In 1969, *Newsweek* estimated the readership of the underground press at 2 million; other estimates have put their readership as high as 4.6 million. [189] By the late-1960s, many of the underground papers were major enterprises: the *Los Angeles Free Press* boasted a paid circulation of over 90,000, making it the second largest weekly newspaper in the United States; Berkeley's *Barb* and the *Black Panther Paper* both had a circulation of over 85,000; the *East Village Other,* 65,000. [190]

The underground papers during the Vietnam War faced the same type of governmental repression as did the opposition press during the Alien and Sedition Acts 160 years earlier—editors were jailed, presses were bombed, reporters were harassed, news vendors were arrested, newsrooms were infiltrated by government spies, businesses were intimidated from advertising in the papers and numerous publications were forced to close due to government harassment.

As the underground papers started to publish investigative journalism and became more active in opposition politics, they were targeted by the government.[191] The government rarely made a frontal attack on the papers' political statements, and never obtained a conviction against any paper on a political charge. Nonetheless,

> Faced with the prospect of trials on petty charges, and unable to meet court costs, underground papers were ruined. Fourth Amendment rights were violated in searches and seizures of equipment by police agents. Records were lost, typewriters destroyed, and staffs disbanded as a result of police raids. When they failed to find drugs, agents nevertheless ransacked equipment and files. In other cases, where drugs were found, police brought publication to a halt by arresting an entire staff rather than charging an individual offender.[192]

The level of official government harassment and repression of the underground press can be understood by looking at the cases of a few major opposition papers.

In 1964, a thirty-seven-year-old named Arthur Kunkin distributed an eight-page mimeographed paper at the KPFK Renaissance Faire, a fund-raising event for the non-profit Pacifica radio station in Los Angeles. This was the first edition of what was to become the *Los Angeles Free Press* (commonly known as FREEP), one of the largest and most influential of the underground papers. Within six years, the *Los Angeles Free Press* was publishing a sixty-four-page newspaper employing 150 people and earning revenues of $2 million/year.[193] One measure of its importance is the fact that Daniel Ellsberg had considered giving the *Pentagon Papers* to the *Los Angeles Free Press* before his ultimate decision to give them to the *New York Times*.[194]

In July 1969, Jerry Resnick, a clerk in the California State Attorney General's office, walked into the *Los Angeles Free Press* office with a photocopy of a report alleging serious misconduct on the part of the UCLA Police Department. The *Los Angeles Free Press* printed a front-page article based on this report.[195]

The next week, Resnick returned to the *Los Angeles Free Press* offices with a list of eighty undercover narcotics officers. The names came from a Christmas-card mailing list of the State Bureau of Narcotics employees. The *Los Angeles Free Press* printed an article based on this information, accompanied by a front-page editorial headlined, "There Should Be No Secret Police."

The State of California launched a vendetta against the *Los Angeles Free Press*. First, the state filed a $10 million obstruction of justice civil suit against the paper. Since the printing of the list of names was not illegal, the state also charged the owner and publisher of FREEP with receiving stolen property (the report and list of names from the Attorney General's office)—a felony.* After six days of deliberation, the jury found the *Los Angeles Free Press* guilty. The court imposed a light sentence, fining the owner and publisher of the *Los Angeles Free Press* $1,000 and $5,000 respectively, and fining the *Los Angeles Free Press* itself just $500.

The paper appealed and the criminal charges were eventually overturned. The obstruction of justice case was settled for $10,000, payable in twenty monthly installments of $500.[196]

Compared with other underground papers, FREEP got off easy. Its size and large financial base enabled the paper to pay the court costs and continue publishing. Other papers did not fare as well.

In the late 1960s, the main underground paper in San Diego was the *Street Journal*. At the time, it had a circulation of just 8,000 and,

---

* This almost exactly parallels the situation of the *New York Times* in the *Pentagon Papers* case. In both cases, the documents were government property, copied by a government employee, and brought, unsolicited, to the newspaper's offices. Of course, the *New York Times* was never indicted for receiving stolen property. One wonders what would have happened if Daniel Ellsberg had actually given the *Pentagon Papers* to FREEP instead of to the *New York Times*.

unbeknownst to the *Journal,* an undercover cop on staff.[197] In October 1969, the paper ran an exposé of C. Arnholt Smith, a multimillionaire Republican banker, leading San Diego citizen, and friend and confidant of President Richard Nixon. The next month, the San Diego power structure struck back:

> On November 18, bullets from a 38-caliber weapon shot through the [*Street Journal*] office window. On November 23, five patrol cars surrounded the offices, entered, and searched the premises without a search warrant. On November 29, the office's glass front door was smashed and 2,500 copies of the *Street Journal* were stolen—with little police investigation. In that November more than twenty street vendors were arrested by the police for "obstructing the sidewalk," were handcuffed, searched and jailed under an ordinance subsequently declared unconstitutional by the municipal court. On December 11, police without a search warrant entered the [editors'] residence and arrested a guest on "suspicion of burglary," handcuffed him, and later let him go without taking him to jail. On Christmas Eve someone broke into the offices and destroyed over four thousand dollars' worth of typesetting equipment—with little police investigation. On January 3, [1970] a *Street Journal* car was firebombed, with little police investigation. On January 18 and 25, vendors were arrested, handcuffed, searched, and booked for littering.[198]

The constant harassment finally forced the *Street Journal* to close in 1970. Nine years later C. Arnholt Smith was convicted and sentenced to prison on charges of grand theft and tax fraud.[199]

After the closing of the *Street Journal,* the *Free Door* became the main underground paper in San Diego. Local police continued to arrest *Free Door* vendors long after the law under which they were arrested had been declared unconstitutional. The *Free Door* offices were also vandalized and sprayed with bullets.[200]

Had the *New York Times* or any other establishment paper been subject to such attacks, the media would have united in its support and editorialized about the importance of freedom of the press. However, San Diego's establishment media rarely even covered the attacks.[201]

In Jackson, Mississippi, people could read "Subterranean News from the Heart of Ole Dixie," as printed in *Kudzu,* the local underground paper. Its first issue in September 1968 contained stories about Eugene McCarthy and the NAACP, Bob Dylan and the Jefferson Airplane, the 1968 Chicago Democratic Convention and the FBI.[202] Like other opposition papers, *Kudzu* also faced a campaign of official and semi-official harassment. Street vendors were arrested for "obstructing traffic." Staff members of *Kudzu* were arrested for vagrancy, staff and editors were harassed with parking tickets and were physically attacked by local citizens. On October 8, 1968, eighteen staff members were attacked and beaten by Jackson police. In 1970, police and FBI set up round-the-clock surveillance of the *Kudzu* house, ostensibly to investigate alleged drug use. During the course of two months, the FBI made daily, warrantless searches of the paper's office. On June 12, 1970, one of the paper's editors was arrested on charges of using abusive language, resisting arrest, assaulting an officer and failure to yield to an emergency vehicle. He was severely beaten by the five arresting police officers. All charges, except for using abusive language, were ultimately dropped.[203]

Other underground presses throughout the country were attacked and bombed. In July 1969, the Houston *Space City!* offices were bombed and later burglarized. In April 1970, someone shot a heavy steel arrow from a cross-bow through the front door. *Space City!* staffers said that the police did not respond to their telephone calls for help.[204]

Because many of the opposition presses were operating on a shoe-string budget and could not afford the legal fees necessary to defend themselves, obscenity or drug charges were often successful in closing them down. The rate of arrest of underground journalists on drug charges was one hundred times the rate of narcotics arrests in the general population.[205]

The *Open City*, Los Angeles' second largest underground paper, ceased publishing in March 1969 after a $1,000 fine on an obscenity conviction. Although the conviction was later overturned by the appeals court, the paper was unable to reopen.[206]

The editor of the Miami *Daily Planet* was arrested twenty-nine times on obscenity charges. Although acquitted twenty-eight times, bail bonds cost him over $92,000.[207] When poet Allen Ginsberg came to Miami to do a benefit for the newspaper, the police broke up his poetry reading. Only after an appeal to the federal court was Ginsberg allowed to complete his reading.[208]

By the end of the 1960s, local police, the FBI and the CIA were mounting a full-scale effort to disrupt and silence the opposition and underground press. In 1969, the Underground Press Service reported that 60 percent of the alternative newspapers were facing harassment and serious repression.[209]

The CIA's Operation CHAOS developed out of an investigation of *Ramparts* Magazine in 1967. Upon learning that *Ramparts* was preparing an exposé of the ties between the CIA and the National Student Association, the CIA pressured the IRS to begin an investigation of the magazine.[210] Again at the CIA's request, the IRS audited Victor Marchetti in 1972, while he was writing a critique of the CIA.[211]

Based on information compiled by another CIA operation known as Project Resistance, the FBI began to pressure businesses not to advertise in the underground press. In January 1969, the San Francisco FBI office sent a memo to Washington, D.C. noting that Columbia Records was a major advertiser in many underground papers. The memo "suggested that the FBI should use its contacts to persuade Columbia Records to stop advertising in the underground press."

CBS, which at the time owned Columbia Records, had many ties to the U.S. government and intelligence agencies. CBS President Frank Stanton headed a committee that had oversight responsibilities for the CIA-funded United States Information Agency; CBS Board Chairman William S. Paley had used his own foundation to help funnel CIA money to research scholarships in the 1950s; until 1961, the CIA had from time to time debriefed correspondents and screened CBS news broadcasts.

Four months after the FBI Columbia Records memo, CBS ceased advertising in the underground papers.[212] Several alternative newspapers folded when this source of revenue dried up.[213]

The FBI conducted similar campaigns against businesses advertising in the *South End*, Wayne State University's paper; the *State News*, the Michigan State University alternative paper; and the *Tech*, the student paper at MIT.[214]

Because of FBI and local police harassment, many underground papers could not hire printers to print their papers. One of the few printers in the Midwest who resisted such intimidation was William

Schanen of Port Washington, Wisconsin. Schanen had been publishing the local *Ozaukee Press* since 1940. In 1970, he also published *Kaleido-scope*, the main Milwaukee underground paper, with a circulation of 15,000, as well as other alternative papers from as far away as Omaha, Nebraska. In fact, Schanen's was the only shop between Iowa and Michigan that would print underground papers. Because of his association with *Kaleidoscope*, the FBI urged local businesses to boycott the *Ozaukee Press*. In June 1970, the very week that the *Ozaukee Press* was awarded first prize for general excellence by the National Newspaper Association, twenty-five businesses canceled their ads. Although Schanen refused to cave in to this political pressure, he lost over $200,000 in 1970 due to the boycott. The next year Schanen died of a heart attack.[215]

The FBI pressured landlords to evict people who wrote or worked for underground papers. In 1968, the FBI convinced the landlord of the New York *Rat* to double the paper's rent, forcing the newspaper to relocate. The same year, the Bureau got two New Left papers in Los Angeles evicted.[216]

After being visited by the FBI, the regular printer of the *Los Angeles Free Press* refused to continue printing the paper[217] and the distributer of the *Rat* refused to do any more business with that newspaper.[218]

The FBI proposed a plan to disrupt the distribution of the Black Panther Party paper by spraying the paper with Skatole, an offensive-smelling chemical. The Detroit FBI office made a similar request for "a solution capable of duplicating the scent of the most foul-smelling feces available." [219] Although these two plans were not implemented, the FBI carried out a program to forge and send anonymous letters to school officials protesting the fact that the Black Panther paper was in the school library.[220]

The Army was also involved in domestic surveillance and harassment of the press. On January 14, 1969, shortly before Nixon's inauguration, Army intelligence participated with the FBI in a break-in of the offices of the *Free Press,* a Washington, D.C. underground newspaper.[221]

In many instances, it did not become known until years after the fact that the troubles encountered by underground papers were caused by police or FBI tactics. "The sudden refusal of a printer to continue printing a paper, an overnight doubling of a journal's office rent, advertising cancellations, or shipping losses" [222] were often attributed to bad luck or poor planning, rather than the results of a concerted governmental effort to silence the opposition press.

In addition to harassment, arrests, jailings and beatings, local police and government intelligence agencies engaged in a covert effort to infiltrate the legitimate underground press and to establish bogus "opposition" papers.

The editorial offices of many local papers were infiltrated by undercover police agents; in 1968, the FBI had assigned three agents to infiltrate the Liberation News Service, one of the two major news services serving the underground presses. [223]

When the editor of the *Spectator,* Bloomington, Indiana's first underground paper, was being tried for draft evasion, a second "alternative" paper appeared on newstands. Unbeknownst to its readers, the entire staff of *Armageddon News* consisted of FBI agents, operating out of their Indianapolis Bureau office. [224] At least two other phony underground papers were published by the FBI: the *Longhorn Tale* at the University of Texas at Austin, and the *Rational Observer* at American University in Washington, D.C. [225]

In addition to creating bogus "underground" papers, the FBI established three phony news services, the Pacific International News Service in San Francisco, the Midwest News in Chicago, and the New York Press Service on the East Coast. The New York Press Service advertised its services to left-wing publications and organizations in a letter stating:

> The next time your organization schedules a demonstration, march, picket or office party, let us know in advance. We'll cover it like a blanket and deliver a cost-free sample of our work to your office...We will photograph any single individual during any type of demonstration...[!] [226]

Looking back on this era, Bob Woodward of the *Washington Post* said in 1974:

> The underground press was largely right about government sabotage, but the country didn't get upset because it was the left that was being sabotaged. The country got upset when the broad political center, with its established political institutions, came under attack. [227]

By 1978, there were only sixty-five underground papers left—a tribute to the success of the government's policy of harassment against the opposition press.[228]

Freedom of Speech

In 1965, Julian Bond was elected to the Georgia House of Representatives. By a vote of 184 to 12, the Georgia House refused to seat Bond because of his past political statements. Bond's seat was declared vacant and a special election was called. While Bond was appealing the denial of his seat, he was overwhelmingly re-elected to the Georgia legislature. This time, unlike the Court's previous tolerance for the expulsion of socialists from the New York Assembly and the House of Representatives in the 1920s,[229] the Supreme Court held that Georgia's action violated Bond's First Amendment rights and that Bond must be seated.[230]

During this era, the Court was willing to uphold free speech rights if they were connected with the civil rights movement. In sharp contrast to the 1930s, the Court upheld the right of blacks to violate Southern laws that made it a virtual crime to picket or parade;[231] however, when it came to violating equally unconstitutional court injunctions, the Supreme Court, fearing an erosion of its own power, drew the line, confirming the lower courts' sentences.[232]

But as the anti-war movement began to gain strength and the civil rights movement began to question the distribution of wealth and power in society, the Court started to retreat from this broad reading of constitutional protections for civil liberties.

In 1966, on the steps of the Boston Courthouse, David O'Brien and three friends burned their draft cards in a symbolic protest against the escalating war in Vietnam—the first four of some 10,000 draft-age men to burn their draft cards during the course of the war. Two years later, when the case reached the Supreme Court at the height of the anti-war demonstrations, the Court upheld O'Brien's conviction, ruling that such symbolic speech was not protected by the First Amendment.[233]

In 1968, Congress passed legislation to allow the federal government to prosecute political "agitators."[234] Although the measure was billed as an anti-riot act, its definitions—reminiscent of the criminal anarchy and syndicalism statutes of thirty years before—were so broad as to allow federal prosecution of virtually anyone. The law was commonly known as the Rap Brown Act, as it was designed to allow federal prosecution of Hubert Giroid "Rap" Brown, a black militant. It made incitement to riot illegal, defining a riot as a disturbance, or threat of disturbance, involving "one or more persons part of an assemblage of three or more persons" as long as there was a "clear and present danger" of injury to property or persons. The penalty for such incitement to riot—whether or not such riot actually occurred—was five years in jail.[235]

The only trial for alleged violation of the Rap Brown Act was that of the Chicago Eight, who were tried and ultimately acquitted on conspiracy charges stemming from the violence at the Democratic National Convention in Chicago during August 1968.[236]

In 1968, 28,000 people signed a petition, known as the "Call to Resist Illegitimate Authority," urging active opposition to the Vietnam War. Five people, some of whom hadn't known each other previously, were indicted for conspiracy. The Boston Five included William Sloane Coffin, Benjamin Spock and Mitchell Goodman, prominent anti-war activists who had participated in the press conference announcing the petition; Marcus Raskin, who had authored the petition; and Harvard graduate student Michael Ferber.[237] The jury found four of the five guilty, including Ferber who had not even signed the petition. The appeals court overturned the convictions because the trial judge's instructions were biased. As one of the jurors said later, "I knew they were guilty when we were charged by the judge. I did not know prior to that time—I was in full agreement with the defendants until we were charged by the judge. That was the kiss of death!" [238]

On at least one occasion, such individual and collective actions brought forth a more institutional response against the war. In 1970, the Massachusetts legislature enacted a statute to protect its citizens from military service in any war not authorized by Congress. The legislature hoped to challenge the constitutionality of the undeclared war in Vietnam through Court review of the act. The Supreme Court refused to examine the issues of the War's constitutionality.[239]

Although never ruling on the legality of the War, and continuing to uphold the convictions of people engaged in non-violent protest of the War, the Supreme Court, in the late-1960s and early-1970s, became more attuned to preserving the free speech rights inherent in symbolic speech and protest.

In 1969, the Court upheld the right of high school students to silently protest the War by wearing armbands in class,[240] and two years later upheld the right of a draft protester to use vulgarity to protest the War.[241] Finally, one year after U.S. troops were evacuated from South Vietnam, the Supreme Court struck down the conviction of an anti-war protestor who had sewn an American flag to the seat of his pants.[242]

Prosecutions of anti-war speech more or less ended with this decision—whether due to the decision or because the war itself was ending is not clear.

Freedom of Travel

In 1964, the Supreme Court, in *Aptheker v. Secretary of State,* struck down Section 6 of the Subversive Activities Control Act of 1950 which had prohibited the granting of passports to members of the Communist Party.[243] Although agreeing that the government could not restrict a citizen's freedom to travel during peace-time, Justice Douglas (who himself had been denied a passport during the previous decade) indicated that in times of war such restrictions might constitutionally be imposed.[244]

The ability of the government to restrict the right to travel was greatly limited by the ruling. But the government, unable to prevent some of the people from traveling to all countries, adopted a policy to prevent all people from traveling to some countries. Just one year after *Aptheker,* the Court re-legitimized travel restrictions by upholding the government's declaration of entire countries as off-limits to travel.[245] U.S. passports issued throughout this era warned citizens that they could not freely travel to North Vietnam, North Korea, China or Cuba. It was not until 1977 that President Carter finally lifted the last of the travel restrictions on U.S. citizens.

Nonetheless, the courts still made a sharp distinction between the right to speak and travel, and the right to hear the views of others. In 1972, the Supreme Court ruled that the State Department's refusal to let a journalist enter the country to speak at a symposium at Stanford University did not violate the First Amendment rights of U.S. citizens.[246]

Buoyed by this decision, the government continued to deny visas to foreigners who held opinions in opposition to that of the administration. The list of notable people denied entry visas to visit, tour or speak in the United States during this era includes such literary figures as Graham Greene, Gabriel García Márquez, Pablo Neruda, Julio Cortázar, Dario Fo and Simone de Beauvoir.

In 1983, Hortensia Allende, widow of assassinated Chilean President Salvador Allende, was invited to speak before the Northern California Ecumenical Council and other religious forums on the contemporary situation in Latin America. The State Department denied her an entry visa. This denial was challenged in court as a violation of the First Amendment. Reversing forty years of war-time restrictions, the First Circuit Court of Appeals ruled in April 1988 that the "government [may not] exclud[e] an alien from the United States based upon that individual's beliefs, associations or speech-related activities." [247] Despite this ruling, politically motivated denials of visas continue to prevent "dangerous" foreigners from entering the United States.

Chapter VII

The "Low-Intensity" Conflict Era

Unfortunately, governmental restrictions of our basic constitutional and civil liberties are not confined to wars of the past. There are frightening indications that the government plans to impose even more severe restrictions during future wars.

Since the Vietnam War, both the U.S. government and public have been loath to engage in a major commitment of troops overseas. Instead, military planners are now advocating that the United States exert its military might through what has come to be known as "low-intensity" conflicts (LICs).[1] According to the Pentagon doctrine of "low-intensity conflict," probable future scenarios do not include a major military conflict with the Soviet Union, but rather "a continuous succession of hostage crises, peacekeeping operations, rescue missions and counterinsurgency efforts."[2] Recognizing this, President Reagan created a "Board for Low Intensity Conflict" within the National Security Council in 1987.

"Low-intensity" conflicts are not new; counter-insurgency has been a part of U.S. foreign policy at least since World War II. During the past three decades, when the United States has nominally been at peace, we have used military force "on an average of once every eighteen months either to prevent a government deemed undesirable from coming to power or to overthrow a revolutionary or reformist government considered inimical to America's interests."[3] "Low-intensity" conflicts have included: the 1953 overthrow of the Mossedegh government in Iran, and the 1954 bombing of Guatemala City to overthrow the democratically-elected government of Jacobo Arbenz in Guatemala; the 1962 invasion of Cuba and the 1965 landing of Marines in the Dominican Republic; the overthrow of the democratically-elected socialist President of Chile in 1973; and, in the 1980s, the 1983 invasion of Grenada, the 1986 air strikes against Libya, the 1989 invasion of Panama, counter-insurgency in El Salvador, and the contra war in Nicaragua.[4]

This type of warfare—usually viewed as an occasional skirmish in the East-West conflict—has in fact become a permanent state of affairs. We have entered an era of perpetual "semi-war." The line between peace and "low-intensity" conflicts is even more blurry than that between peace and conventional warfare. Military planners foresee a continual series of military operations as the norm; peace as we know it, much less as the dictionary or common sense defines it, would be a thing of the past.

Based on our experience in these "low-intensity" conflicts, the prospect for the maintenance of our constitutional liberties during a renewed era of warfare—albeit "low-intensity" warfare—does not appear good.

Post-Vietnam Era Press Censorship

One recent example of press censorship during a "minor" war involved the invasion of the tiny island of Grenada on October 25, 1983. Censorship was total. Rather than requiring that reporters on site submit copy for approval, the United States banned all reporters from traveling to Grenada during the first days of the invasion. Reporters were kept 150 miles away on Barbados and were forced to rely completely on second-hand reports and information hand-fed by the military.[5]

From the government's viewpoint, the blanket denial of access to the press was successful since it prevented questioning of administration propaganda and policy. Then-White House Chief of Staff James A. Baker said that he would adopt the same policy in a similar situation and Secretary of State George Shultz stated that "it was possible that reporters would be banned from other military actions in the future." [6]

After the Grenada invasion, the Pentagon created a media pool to cover, on a rotating basis, future military actions. The military decides when such a pool will be mobilized and the qualifications and ground rules for participation in the pool.

Such a pool was activated to cover the invasion of Panama in December 1989, but reporters in the pool were "kept under such tight control that journalistic initiative was all but impossible." During the first crucial hours of the invasion, the pool reporters were confined to a windowless room at Fort Clayton; instead of being allowed to cover the war, they were subjected to Army propaganda briefings. Retired Major General Winant Sidle, who headed the Pentagon commission that recommended the pool system, stated after the Panama invasion that pools "just don't work."[7]

Even in calmer times, the specter of national security continues to infringe upon First Amendment rights. In 1979, in the first case of its kind in modern history, a court in peace-time imposed prior restraint on a publication in the name of protecting national security.[8] The *Progressive* magazine had planned to publish an article entitled "The H-Bomb Secret: How We Got It; Why We're Telling It." The information in the article was taken exclusively from non-classified public sources.

The district court, without holding evidentiary hearings, forbade the *Progressive* from printing the article. Referring to *Near v. Minnesota*,[9] Judge Robert Warren stated:

> [P]ublication of technical information on the hydrogen bomb contained in [the *Progressive*'s] article is analogous to publication of troop movements or locations in time of war and falls within the extremely narrow exception to the rule against prior restraints.[10]

The *Progressive* appealed, but the issue became moot before the appeal was heard, when another reporter, after spending a week in his local public library, wrote and published essentially the same article in another newspaper. When the information contained in the banned article became public, the government dropped its case.

Judge Warren's doctrine greatly expands the original and quite limited *Near* exception which has been assumed to mean that the government could censor the printing of information about troop movements or locations during times of war on the grounds of national security. But the *Progressive* ruling expands this limited exception from times of war to times of peace because of the supposed reality of the nuclear age.[11] If this singular ruling were to be accepted as precedent, a large exception will have been gouged out of the First Amendment.

The government has made sporadic attempts to censor other works, mostly by former employees of U.S. intelligence agencies. In one such case, the government obtained an injunction against publication of Victor Marchetti's book *The CIA and the Cult of Intelligence*.[12] The injunction allowed the CIA to review the book prior to publication, censoring 339 items. One of the "sensitive" items that was censored was a reference to CIA Director Richard Helm's mispronunciation of "Malagasy" (previously Madagascar), when referring to that nation in a NSC meeting. After three years of litigation, the book was allowed to be published with 168 deletions.[13]

Another such case involved Frank Snepp, who began working for the CIA in 1968. After leaving the Agency, he wrote *Decent Interval*, a highly critical account of the corruption and deceit involved in the U.S. evacuation from South Vietnam in 1975. Snepp's book revealed no classified information. Without allowing for the submission of briefs or oral argument, the Supreme Court upheld a ruling that, among other things, prohibited Snepp from speaking or writing about the CIA without the Agency's permission for the rest of his life.[14]

Even more startling, Snepp is permanently prohibited from publishing *anything,* even poetry or fiction, without first having the items approved by the CIA. Snepp has had to submit to CIA censors a novel based on the assassination of President Kennedy and a motion picture script he wrote for actor Marlon Brando.[15] The Snepp case is "the first time in the nation's history [in] which...a book and a publisher have been officially censored by the United States under authority of an injunction."[16]

Based on the precedent of *Snepp v. United States,*[17] the Reagan administration issued National Security Decision Directive (NSDD) 84 in 1983, requiring all federal employees with access to "sensitive compartmented information" to sign a nondisclosure agreement which prevents them from publishing anything for the rest of their lives without prior approval of the federal government. The agreement not only covers classified material, but any potentially classifiable material—that is, anything that the government might wish to keep secret.[18]

Four years later, after the filing of a lawsuit challenging the nondisclosure contracts, Congress prohibited the expenditure of money for the enforcement of NSDD 84.

The Right to Travel

By 1977, two years after the evacuation of the last U.S. soldier from Vietnam, President Carter lifted the remaining Vietnam-era travel restrictions on U.S. citizens. Unrestricted freedom to travel was to be short-lived however. In 1982, the Reagan administration, while not declaring travel to Cuba off-limits *per se*, accomplished virtually the same objective by issuing regulations preventing U.S. citizens from spending money while traveling to Cuba. These economic restrictions were held constitutional by the Court in 1984.[19]

Despite the general lifting of travel restrictions during the Reagan administration, the U.S. Information Agency kept a "blacklist" of people who, because of their political views, should not participate in overseas speaking tours. Among those blacklisted were Walter Cronkite, Coretta Scott King and former presidential candidate Gary Hart.[20]

The government has moved to deport at least one former citizen because of her political beliefs. U.S.-born writer Margaret Randall gave up her citizenship (in order to acquire working papers and employment to support her family in Mexico) and lived abroad for many years. In 1984, she returned to the United States to teach at the University of New Mexico and be near her aging parents. The Immigration and Naturalization Service (INS), using the McCarran Act, moved to deport her, as she had lived in Cuba and had written extensively in support of the Cuban revolution.[21]

There is currently one citizen who is being denied a passport for "national security" reasons. After leaving the CIA, Philip Agee began an international campaign to expose crimes committed by the CIA. Unlike Frank Snepp,[22] Agee was able to evade the CIA censors by traveling and publishing abroad. Even though he had broken no laws through his disclosures, the Secretary of State revoked his passport on the grounds that his "activities...have caused serious damage to the national security and foreign policy of the United States."[23] Both the trial and appellate courts ruled for Agee and ordered the Secretary of State to reinstate his passport.[24] The Supreme Court overturned the lower courts in *Haig v. Agee*,[25] admitting that Agee's passport was being revoked, at least in part, due to the content of his speech. Nonetheless, quoting *Near v. Minnesota*[26] and echoing the reasoning in *United States v. Progressive*,[27] the Court ruled:

> Agee's First Amendment claim has no foundation...Long ago,...this Court recognized that "[n]o one would question but that a government might prevent actual obstruction to its recruiting service or the publication of the sailing dates of transports or the number and location of troops."[28]

By a critical, and presumably conscious omission, the Supreme Court seriously misinterprets the holding of the above quotation taken from *Near v. Minnesota*. While *Near* does state that it would be permissible to prevent the publication of the sailing dates of transports, it holds that such prior restraint is permissible "only in exceptional cases," that is, only "when a nation is at war."[29] The Supreme Court in *Haig v. Agee* omits this all-important qualifier and, like the district court two years before in *United States v. Progressive*, seems to have expanded this war-time exception into a low-intensity war exception—that is, an exception that swallows the rule.

The government has continued to prevent some foreign visitors from entering the United States. In October 1988, the Reagan administration issued an order barring Sandinista officials and Nicaraguan diplomats from entering the United States. The decree prevents Nicaraguan officials from entering the United States to talk to members of Congress. Among others, Father Ernesto Cardenal, reknowned poet and former Minister of Culture, was prevented from speaking in a nationwide tour of college campuses. Similar restrictions have prevented Tomás Borge, Nicaragua's Minister of the Interior, from obtaining a visa.[30]

Due Process, Political Spying and the Suspension of *Habeas Corpus*

Some 2,500 people who are not even accused of any crime are currently being held in U.S. prisons. Although they face no criminal charges, they are being held in 23-hour lockdowns: "they can't mix with other prisoners, they can't take a prison job, they can't leave their cells without handcuffs and shackles." [31] They are being detained indefinitely; some may never leave prison.

The 2,500 are Cuban refugees who arrived in the United States on the Mariel boat-lift in 1980. Considered to be "excludable aliens," these refugees have less rights than citizens, immigrants or undocumented aliens. Many of the detainees were originally arrested on petty offenses such as shoplifting or drunk driving and, as one judge said, "should never have been in jail to begin with." [32] But instead of being released after serving their original sentences, they were turned over to the INS for permanent detention.

The courts have ruled that the INS may hold these detainees in jail forever. As was the case with the Japanese-American internment during World War II, "the government is again detaining people who face no criminal charges;" [33] and once again, not surprisingly, these detainees happen to be people of color.

During the early-1980s, a mass movement arose in the United States to challenge both the Cold War and the nuclear arms race. The Nuclear Freeze movement mobilized tens of millions of people to challenge the administration's arms policy. In 1982, referenda in several states urging a nuclear freeze won large majorities of the electorate.

One of the concerns of the Freeze movement was the imminent arming and deployment of Trident nuclear submarines. The first anti-Trident demonstration was held in 1982 in Bangor, Washington, where the submarine was to be launched. Immediately prior to the planned demonstration, President Reagan declared a temporary emergency in the area, even though there was no threat of violence from the largely middle-class, middle-aged demonstrators. With the emergency declaration, penalties for demonstrating rose from $1,000 and one year in jail, to $10,000 and ten years. Numerous people were arrested at the Trident launch facility; however, charges were dropped when the government discovered that one of those arrested was Ruth Youngdahl Nelson, who was seventy-eight years old and had been named American Mother of the Year in 1973.[34]

On July 19, 1979, the Nicaraguan people overthrew the Somoza dynasty—a dictatorship installed and backed by the U.S. government and one of the most brutal in Latin America. Within two years, the Reagan administration secretly approved $19 million to fund a force of 500 mercenaries to engage in guerilla attacks against Nicaragua. A year later, the counter-revolutionary or "contra" army, had grown, under U.S. sponsorship, to over 5,000 soldiers.[35]

On February 14, 1982, the first press reports about the covert war in Nicaragua began to appear in the U.S. press. Soon it became common knowledge that the Reagan administration was violating both domestic and international law by funding the contras. As reports of contra atrocities against Nicaraguan civilians became known, demonstrations and other expressions of opposition to the U.S.-funded attack on Nicaragua were organized.

Throughout the early-1980s, public opinion polls consistently showed a substantial majority of the population opposed to U.S. support for the contras. Protests organized by the Central America solidarity movement, a loose collection of hundreds of grass-roots organizations across the nation, began to attract more and more support. Many North Americans and many Nicaraguans felt that an all-out U.S. invasion was imminent.

Government officials and peace movement activists alike were afraid that our involvement in Nicaragua would become "another Vietnam," with illegal and covert actions, a growing military commitment to forces that had no popular support and major domestic opposition to U.S. involvement.

As the "low-intensity" war in Nicaragua heated up, the government, as it had done during all previous times of war, began to spy on opposition organizations, harass dissidents and develop a plan for the imposition of press censorship and martial law.

Less than half a decade after the Senate hearings that supposedly reigned-in the domestic spying of our national intelligence agencies, President Reagan issued Executive Order 12333, allowing the FBI to again engage in warrantless wiretaps, break-ins, surveillance and undercover work. In a pattern reminiscent of the Vietnam War era, the FBI engaged in a nationwide campaign to harass and surveil 138 organizations opposed to U.S. foreign policy in Central America. Fifty-two of the FBI's fifty-nine field offices were involved in the campaign to infiltrate peaceful anti-intervention organizations and religious groups, wiretap political activists and surveil students and professors on college campuses. It is also suspected that the FBI may have been involved in as many as eighty-five Watergate-style break-ins of political organizations and churches working to oppose Reagan administration policies.[36]

Just as the civil rights movement of the 1960s was led in large part by religious leaders, much of the anti-intervention movement of the 1980s was based in the churches. The government, in an attempt to silence its critics, infiltrated undercover agents into churches and synagogues and targeted religious activists for harassment. In 1984 and 1985, the INS hired informants to infiltrate and tape religious services and Bible-study meetings.[37] On January 29, 1987, Stacey Lynn Merkt, a pregnant volunteer church worker, was sentenced to serve 179 days in jail for her work on behalf of Central American refugees in the United States. Amnesty International viewed this as a clear attempt by the government to imprison someone for her non-violent expression of belief. Amnesty International adopted Merkt as a Prisoner of Conscience—the first U.S. prisoner of conscience since the end of the Vietnam era.

Much of the opposition to U.S. policies was conducted by individuals acting out of their own conscience, apart from any organization or movement. This was particularly true of opposition to the military registration. After the Vietnam War, the United States abolished the military draft, instituting an all-volunteer army. However, in 1980, the government re-instituted mandatory registration for all eighteen-year-old men.

From 1980-84, approximately 500,000 young men refused to register for the draft, twice as many as had refused to register during the ten years of the Vietnam War.[38] The government began selective prosecutions against those who not only refused to register, but whose conscience or religion required them to speak out against registration. In 1982, Enten Eiler, twenty years old, became the first person convicted of refusing to register; the Supreme Court upheld these selective prosecutions three years later.[39]

As public protest against U.S. involvement in Central America increased, Lt. Col. Oliver North met with the Federal Emergency Management Agency (FEMA), the federal government's crisis-management agency, to formulate secret plans for dealing with domestic protests in the event of a U.S. invasion of Nicaragua. Out of these meetings in 1982, FEMA developed a contingency plan to suspend the Constitution in the event that a U.S. invasion of Nicaragua provoked widespread domestic opposition.[40] The plans called for:

- Suspension of the Constitution;
- Declaration of martial law;
- Abolition of state and local legislatures and their replacement with military commanders;
- The round-up and detention in relocation camps of U.S. citizens opposed to the invasion.

FEMA's plans would put the Department of Defense in charge of a military government. Although the documents contain detailed plans for military commanders to impose martial law, none of the documents describe how the government would be returned to civilian hands once the "crisis" was past.[41]

Other FEMA plans called for the censorship of all telecommunications and the seizure of private property, ranging all the way from personal computers and modems to factories. They also spoke of having the government solicit and possibly impress people to work in critical industries. Under FEMA's plan, even such relatively "low-level" workers such as data processing managers, programmers and circuit board assemblers might be conscripted into the work force by the government.[42]

These plans were developed under the guidance of then-director Louis Giuffrida, a former general of the National Guard and an expert on "counter-terrorism." [43]

During the Iran-contra hearings, Representative Jack Brooks (D-TX) was prevented from delving into this area in his questioning of Lt. Col. North. On July 13, 1987, Rep. Brooks asked,

> Colonel North, in your work at NSC, were you not assigned at one time to work on plans for the continuity of government [i.e., plans for the establishment of martial law] in the event of a major disaster?

Before North could answer, Committee Chair Daniel Inouye (D-HI) refused to allow this line of questioning in public, stating:

> I believe the question touches upon a highly sensitive and classified area. So may I request that you not touch upon that, sir?

The next day, Senate Intelligence Committee Chair David Boren (D-OK) indicated that the "question of the so-called Martial Law Plan" had been discussed in Executive Session and that the Intelligence Committee would be briefed on the matter.[44]

FEMA's martial law plan, entailing a dismemberment of democratic rights far more severe than any previous war-time violations of civil liberties, was written to be part of an executive order that President Reagan was to sign and keep secret until "necessary." If either Presidents Reagan or Bush have signed such an executive order, the suspension of the Constitution, the replacement of elected officials by military commanders, the declaration of martial law and the incarceration of millions of innocent people could begin at the outset of the next war, U.S. military invasion of another country or presidential declaration of a state of national emergency. To this day, the exact provisions written into the executive order —and whether or not the order was ever signed—remain unknown.

Chapter VIII

Conclusion

During times of war, violations of civil liberties have been the norm: from the first censorship laws in the thirteen colonies to the attempts of the FBI and police to muzzle the opposition press during the Vietnam War; from people's tribunals and loyalty oaths during the Revolution to the "show trials" of HUAC during the Korean War; from the unconstitutional suspension of *habeas corpus* during the Civil War and the internment of 110,000 Japanese-Americans during World War II, to the government's plan in the 1980s to impose martial law on the United States.

The stated justification for virtually every violation of civil liberties has been "national security." But as Supreme Court Justice Brennan observed:

> The perceived threats to national security that have motivated the sacrifice of civil liberties during times of crisis are often overblown and factually unfounded. The rumors of French intrigue during the 1790s, the claims that civilian courts were unable to adjudicate the allegedly treasonous actions of Northerners during the Civil War, the hysterical belief that criticism of conscription and the war effort might lead droves of soldiers to desert the Army or resist the draft during World War I, the wild assertions of sabotage and espionage by Japanese-Americans during World War II, and the paranoid fear that the American Communist Party stood ready to overthrow the government, were all so baseless that they would be comical were it not for the serious hardship that they caused during the times of crisis.[1]

Many politicians have learned that by fanning fears of subversion, a people's freedom can be curtailed. The cry of "national security"

169

has been used by politicians to further their own political careers, to eliminate their domestic opponents, to break unions and disrupt social protest movements, and to promote a reactionary political agenda.

Few people would say that war-time restrictions on civil liberties are never justified. Most would agree that, for instance, the abolishment of the elected state legislatures in the South and their replacement by a military government after the Civil War was necessary, and indeed appropriate, to prevent southern whites from re-imposing racist laws upon the newly emancipated black populations. In a similar manner, many civil libertarians who lived through World War II still believe that censorship restrictions imposed at the time were needed to protect the troops, maintain home-front morale and build the consensus needed to prevail over fascism.

In a small handful of exceptional situations, such restrictions may have been necessary. But the history recounted in this book shows that:

1) The government and the more conservative elements of society have repeatedly used claims of foreign or domestic subversion to justify the violation of civil liberties. In almost all cases, these claims were gross exaggerations if not outright fabrications.

2) In those few cases where our nation did confront a threat to its national security, the violations of civil liberties were far more severe and indiscriminate than necessary, and the restrictions lasted long after any possible danger to the nation had ceased to exist.

3) Our government's violations of civil liberties during times of war or crisis have not been confined to the historical past but continue through the present day.

Despite a lessening of Cold War hostilities, we remain mired in an era of quasi-permanent war. "Low-intensity" warfare—be it the contra war in Nicaragua or the "war on drugs"—blurs the boundary line between war and peace. Engaged in these "little" wars, our society teeters precariously between peace-time tolerance and war-time repression.

For two centuries, the dominant forces in U.S. society have been those whose myopic definition of national security has time after time taken precedence over the Constitution. Yet there are encouraging signs that the people of the United States believe that true national security rests not on military might, domestic censorship or internal repression, but on a full realization of the freedoms guaranteed in the Constitution.[2]

Building upon these beliefs and strengthening these freedoms can be the only basis for a meaningful celebration of the 200th anniversary of the Bill of Rights.

A. Freedom of Expression in Nicaragua

Background

The Nicaraguan constitution contains guarantees similar to our own First Amendment.[1] Article 30 of the Nicaraguan constitution states:

> Nicaraguans have the right to freely express their beliefs in public or private, individually or collectively, in oral, written or any other form...[2]

And Article 66 guarantees:

> Nicaraguans have the right to truthful information. This right comprises the freedom to seek, receive and disseminate information and ideas, be they spoken or written, in graphic or any other form.[3]

Article 67 proclaims that there shall be no censorship, but immediately follows this with a limitation clause:

> The right to inform is a social responsibility and shall be exercised with strict respect for the principles established in the Constitution...[4]

and Article 68 proclaims that "[t]he means of mass communication are in the service of national interests."[5]

Other articles of the Nicaraguan constitution guarantee freedom of religion and the right to assemble and petition the government.[6]

However all of these guarantees are subject to Articles 185 and 186, which state:

The President of the Republic may suspend, within part or all of the national territory, the rights and guarantees consecrated in this Constitution in case of war or when demanded by the security of the nation, economic conditions or a national catastrophe.[7]

The constitution was passed by the National Assembly on January 9, 1987. The next day, in accordance with Articles 185 and 186, President Daniel Ortega declared a state of emergency, suspending, among others, the above rights relating to freedom of speech, press and assembly.

Censorship of the Press

La Prensa

The most publicized and politicized case of press censorship in Nicaragua concerns La Prensa, the newspaper of the Chamorros, one of the wealthiest and most influential families in the country.[8] In the latter 1970s, under the editorship of Pedro Joaquín Chamorro, La Prensa became a center of opposition to the Somoza government.[9] The fame and stature of both the paper and its editor rested not on the paper's quality, which was always fairly low, but on Chamorro as a symbol of opposition to the Somoza regime.[10] During this era, the paper had relatively close ties with the Sandinista front. Just prior to Chamorro's assassination by Somoza's forces in 1978, there was talk of Chamorro becoming part of "The Group of Twelve"—prominent upper-class Nicaraguans who were supporting the Sandinista guerrillas.[11]

After Chamorro's murder, the paper was taken over by his brother Xavier. La Prensa was originally supportive of the revolution; Violeta de Chamorro, the widow of Pedro Joaquín, was a member of the original five-member governing junta following the Sandinista victory.

Following Violeta de Chamorro's resignation from the junta in April 1980, a split occurred within the Chamorro family regarding the editorial direction of La Prensa. The editor, Xavier, was outvoted four-to-one by other family members who favored an anti-Sandinista line. The result was that the editor, and some 80 percent of the editorial and technical staff of *La Prensa* left the paper, moving two buildings down the block to start their own opposition daily, *El Nuevo Diario*.[12] Although the rest of the Chamorro family was left with little more than a shell of a paper, they retained what would become their most important asset: the name *La Prensa*.[13]

In 1982, *La Prensa* printed stories about a plaster statue of the Virgin Mary sweating like a person in apparent disapproval of the Sandinista Revolution. (The promotor of that story capitalized on the publicity by selling swabs of cotton which he claimed had been dampened from the brow of the Virgin.) In 1984, *La Prensa* published an article on a woman giving birth to a chicken.[14]

La Prensa exclusively followed the U.S. line on foreign policy.[15] It refused to allow opposition parties to purchase space in its paper for electoral ads during the campaign of 1984.[16] (The official Sandinista daily, *Barricada,* and the pro-Sandinista independent, *El Nuevo Diario,* did sell space to opposition candidates; in addition, thirty to forty-five minutes of free time was daily given on radio and TV for opposition party ads.[17]) The Central American Historical Institute recently performed a content analysis of *La Prensa* articles during October 1987, the first month of its republication.[18] The study found that only 0.3 percent of the articles dealing with domestic issues were pro-government and only 10.9 percent were neutral in content, the remainder being pro-opposition and anti-government. On foreign news, the majority of the paper's articles were taken from AP, UPI or Agence France Presse news services and were pro-U.S.

Not only was the paper not "independent" in its politics, it was not an independent paper. Within six months of the Sandinista victory, President Carter signed a top-secret finding authorizing the CIA to provide funds to opposition elements within Nicaragua, including *La Prensa*.[19] The National Endowment for Democracy (NED), an agency set up by Congress, funneled money to *La Prensa,* both directly and through PRODEMCA, a pro-contra lobbying organization.[20] Violeta de Chamorro told this author that *La Prensa* has never received any money from the NED or from any private U.S. source,[21] but the *New York Times* has reported that *La Prensa* received approximately $100,000 yearly from NED.[22] U.S. embassy staff have reportedly sat in on editorial meetings of the paper,[23] although this too was denied by Violeta de Chamorro.[24]

In 1980, the government issued Decrees 511 and 512 prohibiting publication of information damaging to national security or giving alarmist or misleading information regarding economic shortages.[25] Despite *La Prensa*'s clear tilt to the right, it continued to publish without prior censorship until 1982, although it was closed on five separate occasions for one or two days during this era.[26]

From the declaration of the state of emergency in 1982 through the closing of the paper in 1986, *La Prensa* was continually censored by the Dirección de Medios de Comunicación of the Ministry of Interior, although the level of censorship was greatly reduced during the 1984 election period.[27] Varying with the external and internal political situation, and depending on who was doing the counting, it is estimated that between 10 and 60 percent of the paper was censored at any given time.[28] Although many of the censored items concerned military conscription,[29] the censor's pen was applied to a wide variety of matters. Despite the censorship, however, *La Prensa* published "the harshest criticism of its own government that could be read in any newspaper in Central America during 1985." [30]

As *La Prensa* became more and more anti-Sandinista during the early 1980s, it began to publish "articles aimed at bringing down the government by any means possible." [31] Stories were published about the shortages of various basic goods, stories which caused panic buying and thus created shortages that otherwise might not have existed.[32]

In addition to censoring items regarding the war, economic shortages (real or imagined) and military conscription, seemingly innocuous digs at the government were often forbidden.[33] In July 1981, *La Prensa* suggested that a suitable wedding gift from Nicaragua to Prince Charles and Lady Diana Spencer would be the complete works of Carlos Fonseca, the hero of the Sandinista revolution, since the books would be sure to put the newlyweds to sleep at night. This joke resulted in a suspension of the paper.

Not only was censorship applied unevenly and capriciously, it was ultimately ineffective. *La Prensa* was allowed to xerox censored articles for distribution to foreign journalists and all embassies in Managua. Copies of censored articles were posted on the fence in front of the paper's building for any passerby to read.[34]

The censorship minuet between the government and *La Prensa* continued for four years: *La Prensa* had the dual goals of printing as much as possible and simultaneously provoking the censors in order to prove that Sandinista freedom of the press was a myth; the government, concerned about internal morale and an ever escalating war, felt the need to censor anything considered sensitive, yet at the same time wished to avoid closing the paper so they could point to the existence of *La Prensa* as proof that freedom of the press existed in post-revolutionary Nicaragua.

The final steps in this censorship dance came in mid-1986. On April 3, 1986, the day before the U.S. Congress was to vote on a $100 million aid package to the contras, Jaime Chamorro, editor of *La Prensa*, wrote an article for *The Washington Post* urging the $100 million funding be approved. The House voted down the aid, and nothing was done to *La Prensa*. Three months later the House reconsidered the contra aid issue. The day after the House of Representatives approved the appropriation, the Nicaraguan government closed *La Prensa*. The Nicaraguan government claimed that the closing of the paper was in direct response to the vote in Washington.[35]

Although *La Prensa* was closed indefinitely on July 27, 1986, the government made no attempt to take over its building or confiscate its presses. Vice-President Ramirez stated that the paper could reopen as soon as it disassociated itself from the contras.[36] President Ortega made a similar offer on August 2, 1986 in Chicago.[37]

The paper remained closed throughout 1986, with neither side budging from its previous position. With the signing of the Arias peace plan in Esquipulas on August 7, 1987, the government promised to allow the paper to reopen. On September 21, 1987, the government lifted press restrictions that had been in effect for the past five years,[38] and on October 1, 1987, *La Prensa* reopened with the agreement that there would be no further censorship of the paper. The first issue of the re-opened *La Prensa* was headlined, "La Prensa Uncensored: The People Triumph!" [39] Three months later, Violeta de Chamorro affirmed that there had been no attempt by the Sandinistas to censor the paper, nor had *La Prensa* engaged in any self-censorship.[40]

Within the next year, however, censorship, although on a smaller scale, was re-imposed. On July 10, 1988, a protest march of about 2,500 was held in the town of Nandaime. Demonstrators taunted and threw rocks at the police and the police attacked the marchers. Seven organizers were arrested and sentenced to six months in prison by police courts. These sentences were overturned five days later. On July 18, the government announced that those arrested would be tried in the regular courts for incitement to riot, criminal association and acting as an apologist for crime.[41] On July 11, *La Prensa* was closed for fifteen days in response to its reporting of the Nandaime protest.[42]

Other Press

Only one publication other than *La Prensa* has been banned. On October 12, 1985, the Catholic Church printed a new monthly titled *Iglesia*. Whether to court government sanction or through inadvertent error, *Iglesia* failed to register as a paper prior to publication. After the first edition was printed, but before distribution, it was seized by the government; none of the copies were ever publicly distributed. Even had the periodical registered, it is doubtful that the government would have allowed *Iglesia* to be published. The first, and only, edition of *Iglesia* contained articles on government raids on Radio Catolica,[43] a letter from Nicaraguan bishops protesting government attacks on the church, and three articles protesting military conscription and the draft of seminarians into the army.[44] According to CNPPDH, the pro-Sandinista Human Rights Organization, this edition of *Iglesia* "contained 7 articles encouraging draft evasion." [45] No subsequent edition has ever been printed.

Other smaller publications are printed and distributed without censorship. Each political party publishes its own weekly or monthly magazine uncensored.[46] Both of the human rights organizations in Nicaragua publish monthly reports uncensored.[47]

The anti-government human rights organization, the CPDH, has indicated an understanding of the necessity for occasional censorship during the war situation confronting Nicaragua.

> Our Commission understands that restrictions on liberty of expression are imposed when a country is facing a serious military threat. However, under no circumstances can we accept that these restrictions be used as a pretext for eliminating the independent media.[48]

Newspapers and magazines entering the country are not censored. Several U.S. papers, including the *New York Times* and *The Miami Herald,* as well as *Time* and *Newsweek,* are available.[49] Foreign books are scarce, but this seems due to the lack of hard currency in the Nicaraguan economy. There is no censorship of domestic or foreign books.[50]

In late July 1987, Nicaragua held its first annual international book fair. Thousands of books published in over forty countries were on display and were quickly bought by Managuans. The United States was represented at the book fair by two booths: one for the independent presses, and an official U.S. Information Service (USIS) booth. At the USIS booth, U.S. embassy personnel handed out free copies of two anti-Sandinista books to any Nicaraguan who wanted them.[51] The books, in Spanish, were stamped "Donated by the USIS, American Embassy, Managua, Nicaragua." Hundreds of Managuans queued up to get the free books. The next morning, a four-column front page photo in *Barricada,* the official Sandinista daily, showed President Daniel Ortega and Vice-President Sergio Ramirez, standing in front of the American Eagle, admiring the books in the USIS booth.[52]

In addition to this openness regarding most printed media, a visitor to Nicaragua will instantly be confronted with numerous billboards for all political parties represented in the National Assembly, as well as graffiti and political slogans for all political persuasions on virtually every wall.

Censorship of Radio and TV

La Prensa has been the focus of U.S. concern regarding freedom of expression in Nicaragua. At the time of its closing, *La Prensa* was the third largest of the three daily newspapers in the country,[53] with a circulation of 60,000.[54]

But in Nicaragua, as in most of the third world, the press is not the predominant source of news for the majority of the people; most get their news from radio and TV.

Approximately half of the radio stations in Nicaragua are privately owned. The conservative "Freedom House" found that the "radio stations are private and diverse." [55] Of the approximately thirty news programs on these stations, only one is state-run.[56]

When the State of Emergency was declared in 1982, the government closed twenty-two radio news programs. Since that time, there has been no prior censorship of radio, although a station is liable to post-broadcast sanctions if it oversteps the bounds of "acceptable" reporting. Depending on whom one talks to, this has led either to relatively free reporting or massive self-censorship.[57]

On the government station, the most popular program is an uncensored, daily, open-mike call-in program. Known as "Contacto 6-20" (for the AM frequency on which it airs), this is by far the most popular show in Nicaragua, listened to by some 600,000 Nicaraguans daily.[58] The show broadcasts four hours daily, is devoted to airing the complaints and concerns of the callers and has subjected the government to strenuous criticism.[59]

In contrast to the relative freedom given most radio stations, the Catholic radio station, Radio Catolica, was shut down on January 1, 1986, ostensibly for refusing to broadcast the New Year's message of President Daniel Ortega.[60] The shutdown appeared to be part of an ongoing dispute between the Sandinista administration and the hierarchy of the Catholic Church. The government claims the station's license was revoked after numerous "previous warnings and violations, including a temporary shut down of two days after the station carried an appeal to evade the military draft in October." [61]

With the Esquipulas agreements and the lifting of press censorship by the government, Radio Catolica re-opened uncensored on October 2, 1987.[62] The majority of the twenty-two news programs closed in 1982 were allowed to resume broadcasting in January 1988. According to Americas Watch,

> it appears that those [stations] that did not receive permission [to began broadcasting again] did not request it; some of the owners and/or reporters were living in exile.[63]

During the next year, however, radio broadcasts were suspended on at least three occasions for reporting false news or news favorable to the contras. A Radio Catolica news program was suspended for ten days for broadcasting a contra military communique that had not been cleared by the Ministry of Defense. Another suspension, in April,

involved a false report of the death of a hunger striker. On July 11,
1988, Radio Catolica reported on the Nandaime protest. The radio
station stated that demonstrators had been attacked by Sandinista
mobs carrying military arms and bayonets, that mustard gas had been
used on the demonstrators and that the Sandinista attack had been
worse than the genocide of the Somoza National Guard. None of this
was true.[64] The station was closed for ten days as punishment for false
reporting.

The government even closed down one of its own news programs
for violating the media law. In late July 1988, the morning news
program on Radio Sandino was closed for two days for broadcasting
an obscene insult to Cristiana Chamorro of *La Prensa*.[65]

Although it is still forbidden for news programs to discuss
military recruitment campaigns, they often broadcast reports about
economic conditions and the scarcity of goods, all without sanction.[66]

Nicaragua has two TV stations; both are government-owned.
However, nine TV stations from Costa Rica, Honduras and El Salvador, and 74 foreign radio stations can be received without censorship
by Nicaraguans.[67] The government has made no attempt to jam
U.S./CIA-sponsored broadcasts from these countries.[68]

Despite the long-term state of emergency, Nicaraguans discuss
politics openly; criticizing the government seems to be a national
pastime. Observers of the 1984 elections noted wide-ranging debate,
fostered by the availability of free air time for all opposition candidates.
All parties participating in the November 4, 1984 elections "were free
to be as strident as they chose in attacking the Sandinista Party and
its leaders, and frequently exercised this right on television and radio
time provided to them without cost [by the government]." [69] In 1987
and again in 1988, this observer saw no inhibitions on citizens openly
discussing, arguing and criticizing, whether alone or in the presence
of soldiers, police or government officials.[70]

Freedom of Travel

The Nicaraguan constitution guarantees to all Nicaraguans the
right to travel freely throughout the country,[71] although this right can
be derogated during times of war or national emergency.[72]

Nicaraguans do not carry identity cards or internal passports, nor are they stopped and required to identify themselves on the streets.

Travel is sometimes restricted upon entering a war zone for security purposes.

Denial of Passports

In general, Nicaraguans can freely enter and leave the country. Exit visas are required to leave the country but are granted *pro-forma*. The only requirement is that the citizen does not owe back taxes and is not subject to be called for the military draft. There is much travel (by upper-class Nicaraguans) to and from the United States.

Although Nicaraguans have the right to freely enter and leave the country without restrictions, these rights have, on occasion, been ignored for political reasons.

On November 4, 1984, Nicaragua held its first free elections in over fifty years. The Sandinistas received 67 percent of the valid votes cast, gaining sixty-one out of ninety-six seats in the National Assembly. President Daniel Ortega and Vice-President Sergio Ramirez were elected for a six-year term of office. Two days later, President Reagan was re-elected to a second term as President of the United States with 59 percent of the popular vote.

The day after the election, the Reagan administration announced that Soviet MiGs were being shipped to Nicaragua. For the rest of the week, U.S. newspapers followed the progress of the alleged shipment of Soviet arms.[73] Nicaragua denied that MiGs were being sent.[74] A few days later, the Soviet boat unloaded its weaponless cargo in Nicaragua.[75]

The Nicaraguan government, however, felt that the Reagan administration's focus on the "arrival" of MiGs was going to be used as a pretext for a U.S. invasion. Various defensive strategies were undertaken in preparation for the expected invasion.

During this crisis, several right-wing members of the Nicaraguan Conservative Democratic Party wanted to leave on a trip to Miami. Their passports were withheld by the government and they were prevented from leaving; the government feared that they wanted to cheer the U.S. invasion from a safe distance and then return in the footsteps of the Marines. They were apparently told that they would have to watch any planned U.S. invasion from Managua, not from Miami.

A similar incident, also in November 1984, involved Enrique Bolaños, the president of COSEP, the organization of chambers of commerce in Nicaragua, and a prominent opponent of the Sandinistas. A page in his passport was torn out by immigration authorities in Managua to prevent him from attending a conference of Latin American employer organizations in Mexico.[76]

Such travel restrictions against suspected "fifth columnists" are the exception. In general, Nicaraguans are allowed to leave the country to meet with U.S. government officials, even when it is known that they will lobby for contra aid.

In November 1985, Juan Manuel Gutierrez, a leader of the right-wing faction of Partido Liberal Independiente (PLI), one of the opposition parties in the National Assembly, travelled with a delegation to Washington, D.C. In speaking with Representative Don Bonker of Washington, he stated, "We are in your hands. We can't do anything. Why are you waiting to invade?" 77 The Nicaraguan government neither tried Gutierrez for treason, expelled him from the National Assembly, nor revoked his passport. Rather, he returned to take his seat again in the National Assembly and later ran for president of the PLI.

Another such incident involved Mario Rappaccioli, a member of the right-wing Partido Cristiano Democratica (PCD). In January 1984, Geraldine Ferraro was in Central America as part of a Congressional fact-finding delegation. During a meeting, Rappaccioli urged Ferraro to send Marines to Nicaragua since, under the new government, he was unable to send his sons to school in America. (Ferraro responded that she would not have American boys dying in the jungles of Nicaragua so that his son could attend an Ivy League school in the United States.) Again, no action was taken to restrict Rappaccioli.

Denial of Entry Visas

Aliens who wish to visit Nicaragua have not been denied visas for political reasons. U.S. citizens are free to enter at any time and scores fly into Augusto Sandino airport in Managua every day. Before mid-1989, U.S. citizens did not even need to obtain a visa from the Sandinista government prior to entering Nicaragua. Foreign visitors, the largest number from the United States, are ubiquitous in Managua and travel virtually without restrictions.[78] The foreign press travels and reports without censorship or restriction.

U.S. politicians routinely enter Managua for visits with opposition leaders; they too enter without restrictions. A pilgrimage to the offices of *La Prensa* has become *de rigueur* for conservative politicians visiting the region. On October 11, 1987, Jeanne Kirkpatrick, former U.S. Ambassador to the United Nations and one of the most vocal anti-Sandinista members of the Reagan administration, addressed opposition members at the U.S. embassy in Managua and, to the applause of her audience, praised the contras.[79]

The contra leadership was offered amnesty and permission to return to Nicaragua if they would lay down their guns. However, they have been told they would be arrested if they returned to Nicaragua while still conducting a war against the country. There are no reported cases of foreign visitors being denied entry due to their political affiliation.

Deportations

In 1984, ten foreign priests critical of government policies participated in a demonstration protesting the government's treatment of Father Amado Peña.[80] The government claimed that the demonstration was illegal, and even though some of the priests had been living in Nicaragua for thirty years, they were summarily deported.[81]

In March 1986, Bishop Pablo Vega traveled to Washington, D.C. to address the right-wing Heritage Foundation. During the trip, he appeared publicly with three of the top contra leaders. He returned to the United States in June, stating that the armed struggle of the contras was a "human right."[82] President Reagan, in his last public appearance before the June 25th Congressional vote on $100 million aid to the contras, referred to Bishop Vega: "Reverend Father, we have listened to you, because we in the United States believe, like you, that even the most humble peasant has a right to be free."[83]

On July 2, Bishop Vega held a press conference in Managua, offering justification for U.S. aid to the contras and an invasion by the United States. On July 3, thirty-two civilians, including several children, were killed when their truck detonated a mine planted by the contras. The next morning, the government expelled Bishop Vega from the country, physically escorting him from his office to the Honduran border.[84]

Six days earlier, Father Bismarck Carballo was returning from a trip to Europe and the United States, during which he had made numerous anti-government statements. When he attempted to board the return flight from Miami to Managua, he was informed that the airline had been ordered by the Nicaraguan government not to let him deplane in Managua. It was later explained that his right to return had been "temporarily suspended." [85]

There was no legal justification, under either Nicaraguan or international law, for either the expulsion of Bishop Vega or the refusal to allow Father Carballo to return.[86] On August 20, 1987, with the signing of the Esquipulas Peace Accords, President Ortega announced that Bishop Vega, Father Carballo and Father Benito Pitito (one of the ten foreign priests expelled in 1984) would be allowed to return to Nicaragua. Father Carballo and Father Pitito returned on September 13. Bishop Vega chose not to return to Nicaragua, stating that he had more contact with Nicaraguans outside the country than inside.[87]

B. Due Process in Nicaragua

Background

Under the U.S. Constitution, the protections of personal and physical integrity and guarantees of due process are found in the 4th,[88] 5th,[89] 6th,[90] 8th[91] and 14th Amendments,[92] as well as in Article I, Section 9 Clauses 2[93] and 3.[94] The Nicaraguan constitution has nine articles which guarantee similar protections for all Nicaraguans. Various articles of Title IV[95] of the Nicaraguan constitution guarantee: the right of privacy, the inviolability of the home, the need for search warrants prior to entering a home, and the exclusion of illegally-obtained evidence from trial;[96] the right to a speedy trial;[97] the presumption of innocence;[98] the right to an adequate defense;[99] the right against self-incrimination;[100] the right to *habeas corpus*;[101] the right of appeal and against double jeopardy[102] and *ex post facto* laws;[103] that there shall be no death penalty;[104] that there shall be no arbitrary arrest or detention;[105] that there shall be no cruel, inhumane or degrading punishment;[106] and that all Nicaraguans enjoy the protections of various international treaties and covenants on human rights.[107]

At the same time, the constitution gives the president the power to declare a state of emergency and suspend many of these rights in time of war.[108] However, even in a state of emergency, fifty-five of the constitution's articles cannot be suspended, including those abolishing the death penalty, the exclusion of illegally-seized evidence, the right to be considered innocent until proven guilty, the guarantees of an adequate defense and against self-incrimination, the right of appeal and to be free from *ex post facto* laws, and the right to be free from cruel, inhumane or degrading punishment.[109]

Fundamental Human Rights

Human rights organizations agree that the Nicaraguan government does not violate fundamental human rights.[110] There are no verified accounts of government-sponsored murder, torture or disappearances in Nicaragua today.[111]

In 1981, Amnesty International stated that they had "received no convincing accounts alleging systematic ill-treatment or torture of prisoners under the [Sandinista] government." [112] In 1982, Americas Watch stated that "the Nicaraguan Government does not engage in a practice of torturing, murdering or abducting its citizens," [113] and in 1987, they reaffirmed that "the government of Nicaragua do[es] not have a policy of violating the laws of war with regard to the treatment of civilians." [114]

Although there is no *policy* of human rights abuses by the government, there have been isolated *incidents* of human rights abuses. The major such incident occurred in Leimus, in the Atlantic Coast region. On December 20, 1981, seven Sandinista soldiers had been tortured, mutilated and killed in the region. On December 22, about thirty-six Miskito Indians, returning to their villages from work, were arrested by Sandinista soldiers.

The 36 were taken to a *bodega,* at first to protect them. Later it became clear that they were being held prisoner. The next night at 6 p.m. approximately 7 people from the group were taken away and did not return. Later that night [the witness], his brother and two others were also taken out of the *bodega.* They walked about 10 minutes and came to the place where the 7 had been executed by being shot in the head. They lay in a shallow grave. One was a Moravian minister. The witness and his three companions were given the task of burying these 7 people.

...The witness reports that six more persons from the original 36 kept captive were taken away. They were tied hand and foot and thrown into a well by the Sandinista soldiers...When the remaining captives were being taken away from the *bodega,* many made a break for it. [The witness] escaped by jumping into the Rio Coco and swimming to the other side. He was shot at and his left arm was amputated as a result of the wound...His brother was killed in the escape attempt.[115]

Between fourteen and seventeen civilians were killed in the Leimus incident.[116] The government has claimed that the soldiers involved in the massacre have been tried, sentenced and imprisoned; information on the prosecutions, however, has never been made public.[117] This is the only case of the Sandinista military murdering civilians that has been documented by the OAS Inter-American Commission on Human Rights,[118] and Amnesty has stated that "no cases similar to that of Leimus have come to [their] attention." [119]

With the exception of the Leimus incident, human rights organizations have been satisfied that when such abuses have occurred, the government has taken steps to punish those responsible. Further, there is no indication that such human rights violations are part of any systematic governmental policy.[120]

One other verified incident involving the killing of civilians by Nicaraguan soldiers occurred in 1982. In the Atlantic Coast town of Walpa Siksa, seven Miskito youths were killed by a soldier. The officer in command of the unit then summarily executed the soldier responsible for the murders.[121] According to Americas Watch, "[b]oth [the Leimus and Walpa Siksa] incidents occurred in remote, conflicted areas, and there is no evidence that what took place was directed or condoned by the central Government." [122]

However, as the contra war began to wind down, there have been reports of summary executions by Sandinista soldiers. Although the reports remain unverified, Americas Watch cautioned "if the reports we have obtained prove to be substantiated, the cases are numerous enough to suggest tolerance or complicity by higher authorities." [123]

The Reagan administration and the Comisión Permanente de Derechos Humanos (CPDH), the anti-Sandinista human rights organization, have made continual allegations that the Nicaraguan government uses torture against political prisoners. Perhaps the most widely circulated allegation is that of Mr. Sofonias Cisneros Leiva, an outspoken critic of the Sandinista government. This incident was reported in a special brochure by the CPDH[124] and prominently repeated by the U.S. State Department.[125]

According to Mr. Cisneros,[126] he was arrested on May 14, 1985 and taken to El Chipote prison in Managua. He was stripped naked and taken before Mr. Lenin Cerna, Nicaragua's Chief of Security. Cerna asked, "Do you know who I am? Well, I am Commander Lenin Cerna, and you are a son-of-a-bitch who is going to die right here," and held a gun to Cisneros' temple. Cisneros reported to the CPDH that:

> Commander Cerna attacked me, punching and kicking me all over my body...Cerna ordered that I be handcuffed with my arms behind my back; I realized that the handcuff had a cutting edge on the side closer to my body that resembled a smooth spur, and as they made me kneel in front of him and they pushed me backwards, this cutting edge cut my back in several places. As I reclined thus on the handcuffs, Commander Cerna delat [sic] me a series of kicks, and then placing his boot on my ribs, he stood on me with the intention of breaking them... Then he made me get up and, grabbing my hair, he pounded my head against the wall repeatedly; his auxiliaries did the same thing...I received heavy blows in the face, on my ears, the back of my head, my chest, abdomen and the wounds in my back [from Cerna].[127]

Cisneros claims he was released, naked, about five blocks from his home and was told that if he said anything about the incident, he would be killed. A few days later he went to a doctor for X-rays and two weeks later, he reported the incident to the CPDH.

Subsequent investigation by a Scottish lawyer, Paul Laverty, raises serious doubts about the veracity of Mr. Cisneros' account of torture. In a subsequent interview with Mr. Laverty, Cisneros' description of the beatings and torture differed in several important aspects from the account given the CPDH.[128] Mr. Cisneros claims to have had his head hit against a brick wall fifteen to seventeen times by Cerna and the guards, yet he stated that the skin was not broken, nor was there any blood.[129] Cisneros claims that the X-rays taken after the incident have been lost, and although he stated that his family and friends were in his home when he returned from the interrogation and torture, he has refused to supply any corroborating testimony from them. Mr. Cisneros says he did not take any photographs of his bruises. More surprising, perhaps, when Cisneros reported this incident to the CPDH, the Commission, which is trained to document human rights abuses, did not ask for the X-rays or for corroborating statements from his family. Nor did the CPDH take any photographs of the alleged injuries on Mr. Cisneros' body.[130] Mr. Laverty, concluded:

> To date...there is not one single piece of reliable evidence to corroborate his version of events...I think that if Mr. Cisneros had given the same information in court...he would not have appeared as a reliable witness.[131]

Most allegations of Sandinista torture and abuse of prisoners are either not credible or not verified. As Americas Watch, Helsinki Watch and the Lawyers Committee for International Human Rights pointed out, the Nicaraguan government may use "harsh interrogation tactics, perhaps at times cruel and degrading treatment, but not the systematic and perverse infliction of bodily harm generally associated with the word torture..."[132]

Although torture is not used by the Nicaraguan government, there seems ample evidence of the use of harsh interrogation techniques, sometimes called "white torture" or what was known in the United States as the "third degree." This includes threatening the accused with indefinite detention or the arrest of family members if the detainee doesn't cooperate with interrogators.[133] "Psychological abuse is 'commonly' used; torture is not." [134]

Similarly, incommunicado detention of suspected contras seems to be practiced routinely in conjunction with the above-mentioned interrogation techniques. Cells used for isolation are small and lighting is poor. "Ventilation is typically through a dark and unlit ceiling airshaft; sanitary and sleeping facilities in many cells are said to be extremely primitive, though at least some cells apparently have toilets, wash basins, beds and ceiling lights." [135] Tomás Borge, Minister of Interior, admitted that such detentions occur but attempted to defend the practice by noting that such detention rarely lasts more than thirty days, and in most cases not more than ten days.[136]

The Revolutionary Era

On July 19, 1979, a popular revolution under the leadership of the Sandinista National Liberation Front (Frente Sandinista de Liberación Nacional, or FSLN) established a new government in Nicaragua, ending fifty years of corrupt, brutal and tyrannical rule by the Somoza dynasty. The last years of the revolution were particularly disastrous for the Nicaraguan people. From 1977-79, as the FSLN gained more and more support, Somoza's troops increasingly resorted to murder, disappearances, mutilations and torture against the civilian population.[137] Fifty thousand Nicaraguans, from a population of only 3.5 million, were killed by Somoza's troops during the civil war.[138]

Two days after Somoza fled the country, the FSLN declared victory and attempted to establish civilian rule over what was left of the country and economy.[139] Despite the length of dictatorship and the brutality of Somoza's National Guard, the new government did not accede to popular sentiment and begin mass executions of the old guard. Rather, within 72 hours of coming to power, the new ruling junta abolished the death penalty.[140] Some executions of National Guardsmen by civilians did take place, but the new government put a stop to such killings as soon as order was restored throughout the country and arrested many of their own supporters who were suspected of the killings.[141]

With public sentiment running strongly against the Somocistas, the new government felt the need to establish special tribunals for the speedy trials of former National Guardsmen who were accused of committing crimes under the former regime. Nine such tribunals were established, each consisting of three members: one lawyer (or graduating law student) and two lay judges. Trials were public; defendants were allowed counsel. Within a few weeks, 7,000-8,000 former National Guardsmen were arrested: 6,310 were tried by the special tribunals; 1,760 were acquitted; and 4,331 received prison sentences. Prison sentences ranged up to thirty years, the longest possible sentence under post-revolutionary Nicaraguan law.[142]

The procedures of the special tribunals have been criticized by many human rights organizations for relaxing the standard of proof necessary for convictions, for having lay judges and for not providing enough time for the accused to mount an adequate defense.[143] The law establishing these tribunals made association with the National Guard a criminal act in itself.[144] Some former National Guardsmen were convicted of murder even though the prosecution was unable to identify a specific victim.[145] Other National Guardsmen were held liable for human rights abuses committed by their unit.[146]

The abuses of due process that occurred have been justified by some jurists and investigators alike in light of the political circumstances facing Nicaragua in the immediate post-revolutionary period. The Catholic Institute for International Relations wrote:

> The special courts...faced great difficulties. One court president complained that it was impossible to prove the guilt of someone who tortured and killed a hooded victim and then disposed of all the witnesses. Defendant after defendant claimed that they had only innocuous responsibilities within the National Guard. If he believed them all, the court president said, the National Guard was a body composed exclusively of cooks, gardeners and bricklayers. All the accused claimed that they had deserted during the last two months of the previous regime, when some of the worst atrocities took place. One driver, a member of the National Guard since 1978, claimed that he had no idea of what was going on because he was illiterate and did not read the papers, was too tired to listen to the radio when he got home and could not hear what the occupants of the bus were talking about...A sergeant-major with ten years'

service said that he was in the band and never left the barracks.[147]

The relative newness of the judicial apparatus and lack of resources and experience of the judicial branch were also cited as reasons for the creation of special tribunals to try National Guardsmen. A former Supreme Court Justice and leader of the second largest opposition party in Nicaragua stated:

> Immediately after the triumph of the Revolution... the organization of the judicial branch was deficient, and could not do all of the work that would have been necessary with the trials of so many people who had committed crimes under the protection of the previous regime. The creation of the special tribunals was justified.[148]

The special tribunals finished their work and disbanded in February 1981.[149] A year later, 2,400 of the original 4,331 sentenced remained in jail; as of July 1986, approximately 2,100 were still in detention.[150]

Recognizing that abuses had occurred, the government instructed the newly-created, government-funded human rights organization, the CNPPDH,[151] to review cases tried before the special tribunals and to recommend pardons or reductions of sentences in appropriate cases.[152]

The Recent Judicial Situation

From 1983 through January 19, 1988, there were three parallel judicial systems operating in the country: 1) the regular judicial system, with its system of district and appellate courts, culminating in the Supreme Court; 2) the Popular Anti-Somocista Tribunals or TPAs (Tribunales Populares Anti-Somocistas), special tribunals used for trying suspected contras; and 3) the Auditoría Militar, or Military Court system, for the trials of members of the military.[153] Almost all of the concerns expressed by human rights organizations regarding due process violations during the past five years have involved the establishment and functioning of the TPAs.

The Regular Judicial System

Supreme Court Justices in Nicaragua serve for terms of six years. The President submits to the National Assembly a slate of three nominees for each of the seven positions on the Court. The National Assembly elects the Justices from these lists.[154] The Supreme Court appoints all of the lower court justices.

In 1987, of the seven Supreme Court Justices, three were affiliated with the Sandinista Party, and three with opposition parties.[155] During two trips to Nicaragua, I interviewed eight of the eleven Justices serving on, or immediately retired from, the Court;[156] all eight Justices, be they members of the FSLN or of opposition parties, assured me that they were totally independent of their political parties and that their parties did not try to influence their decisions on the Court.[157] Most of the decisions of the court are unanimous; very few decisions split along four-to-three lines.

One of the main concerns of the judiciary during the first years of the revolution was its ability to maintain independence and to enforce its rulings. Since the judiciary has no police powers, compliance with the rulings of the Court could not be an issue of force, but rather one of concern for a rule of law and institutional loyalty.

As explained by Chief Justice Alejandro Serrano of Nicaragua:

> There was a lack of compliance at the beginning of the Revolution, but this of course was understandable, because this is a process of legal re-adjustment of those who have just taken power through arms, struggling against a dictatorial system of 50 years when the law served as an instrument of oppression.[158]

The Court, however, feels that this problem is being overcome:

> When I came to the Supreme Court [in 1985] there were 114 verdicts that had not been complied with. Today, there are 6. It is a problem, but seen in its historical context, we see a positive change towards institutionalizing the full rule of law."[159]

According to the then-Chief Justice of the Nicaraguan Supreme Court, "in 95 percent of Amparo[160] cases, the verdicts have been against the Executive Branch," yet there has been "almost 100 percent compliance" by the Executive with these decisions.[161]

The TPAs: The Popular
Anti-Somocista Tribunals

In December 1981, the Reagan adminstration secretly approved $19 million to develop a 500-man army to engage in guerilla attacks against Nicaragua.[162] Six months later, as the U.S.-funded counter-revolutionary war against Nicaragua intensified, the Nicaraguan government passed a newer version of a previously-enacted emergency statute known as the Law for the Maintenance of Order and Public Security.[163] The law had four main provisions:

Article I concerns crimes against national security. The law makes it a crime to submit the country to foreign domination, reveal national security secrets, damage defense-related installations, take up arms against the government, prevent the authorities from doing their job, or conspire to do any of the above.

Article II deals with sabotage and conducting attacks while wearing uniforms or using arms.

Article III punishes economic crimes, including the publication of false proclamations to provoke panic buying or induce changes in prices and salaries.

Article IV criminalizes seditious libel, punishing speech 1) against the security and integrity of the nation, 2) against the health, morals, dignity or reputation of another, or 3) against the legitimately constituted authorities.

Violations of the law were punishable by imprisonment of from ten days to two years.

A year after the law's enactment—at a time when the contra army had grown to over 5,000 soldiers[164]—special tribunals were established, having jurisdiction over suspected contras charged with violations of Articles I or II.[165] The tribunals were known as the TPAs (Tribunales Populares Anti-Somocistas, or Popular Anti-Somocista Tribunals).

Each Tribunal consisted of three judges: one lawyer, who acted as president of the tribunal, and two lay judges. All of the judges were appointed by the executive, and the two lay judges came from the popular mass organizations run by the Sandinista party.[166]

Expedited trial procedures were used by the TPAs. If the accused could not afford counsel, a public defender was appointed. The trial lasted no more than eight days, and a verdict was to be delivered within three days of the completion of the trial.[167]

Convictions from the trial-level TPA were appealable to a second level TPA, also composed of one lawyer and two lay judges. The appellate TPA could either increase or decrease the sentences of the appellant. Convictions under the TPA were not appealable to the Supreme Court.

From their inception in June 1983 through May 1986, 1,215 people were tried before the TPAs. 846 were convicted.*

Numerous problems of due process have been noted under the TPAs. A conviction rate of 70-88 percent has caused some human rights organizations to express concern.[168] The fact that the judges were appointed by the executive branch, and often returned to the executive branch after serving their term of office on the TPA, put the executive in the position of prosecutor, judge and jury, making a fair trial all the more difficult.[169] Human rights organizations have criticized the use of lay judges on the TPAs, and their ties with the Sandinista Defense Committees.[170]

Although each accused was guaranteed a public defender at no cost, the defenders did little good. Accusations that court-appointed defenders were under political pressure not to press for acquittals[171] have been denied by both the former dean of the Central American University Law School in Managua (and current Supreme Court Justice) and the head of the Law School's public defender program, whose students often took such cases.[172] Nonetheless, the system militated against the possibility of success.

Under the law, the defense had only two days to prepare its case.[173] Since many of the accused were from remote war zones, it would take more than two days simply to travel and interview witnesses.[174] Further, public defenders were not paid by the state, but were required

---

* Probably the most famous of the defendants was Eugene Hasenfus, a U.S. mercenary shot down over Nicaragua on October 5,1986. He was tried and given the maximum possible sentence, 30 years, by the TPA. Shortly thereafter, Hasenfus was pardoned and released by the government.

to represent indigent accused on a *pro bono* basis,[175] expending their own money for travel, interviews, etc.[176] This system made for neither an enthusiastic nor an adequate defense.[177]

The TPAs were established to create an expedited legal system in response to the exigencies of the war. But by the final years of their existence, the large backlog of cases created a time lag under the TPAs equal to that of the traditional court system.[178]

This may stem from three different causes: 1) Nicaragua's civil law system, in which the prosecutorial investigation begins in earnest after the accused is arrested;[179] 2) the almost total lack of resources that hampers the entire judicial system;[180] or 3) a deliberate effort on the part of the government to harass and/or incarcerate suspected contras.

Regardless of the reason, clear deprivations of liberty occurred. When visiting one TPA on July 20, 1987, I observed the arraignments in three cases against five suspected contras. While it appeared that none of the suspects had been abused—all looked healthy and well-fed—all five had been arrested two years previously and had been in jail the entire two years awaiting this first opportunity to have charges read and an attorney appointed.

Members of the Supreme Court were unanimous in their concerns regarding the TPAs. None supported a separate judicial system outside the Court's jurisdiction.[181] Most agreed that due process violations occurred under the TPAs.[182] Yet every Justice except one believed the TPAs were justified by: 1) the extremely grave war situation faced by the country, and 2) the inexperience and lack of resources of the judicial system.[183] This was echoed by other members of the legal community.[184]

The government had stated repeatedly that both the TPAs and the Law of Public Order were temporary measures that would be abolished as soon as aggression against the country ended.[185] On January 19, 1988, as a result of the peace discussions of Esquipulas III, President Daniel Ortega lifted the State of Emergency and suspended the TPAs.[186] All pending cases were transferred to the regular court system. Any person sentenced by a TPA can now appeal to the Supreme Court.[187] Virtually all jurists with whom I spoke believed that even if a state of emergency were to be reimposed, the TPAs should not be reestablished.

Auditoría Militar: The Military Justice System

The army has its own judicial system, the *auditoría militar,* for trying members of the military accused of both common crimes and human rights abuses. Many of the cases are highly publicized on state-run media as evidence of the government's effort to prevent abuses by the military.

In July 1983, three suspected contra collaborators were taken from their homes in Rio San Juan by Nicaraguan security forces. Secretly executed, their mutilated bodies were discovered several days later. Seven soldiers were sentenced by a military court to thirty years in prison for the murders.[188]

In January 1984, some forty Nicaraguan civilians in Pantasma, near the Honduran border, were killed by contra forces.

> Nicaraguan army officers at Pantasma responded with a wave of human rights violations directed at individuals suspected to be supporters of the [contras]. Abuses reported included the torture of detainees, at least six extrajudicial executions, and the apparent "disappearance" of four local people.[189]

The government immediately appointed a special prosecutor to investigate charges against the military personnel; forty-one military personnel were detained. A March 1984 court-martial sentenced the regional army commander to forty-four years imprisonment on two counts of murder and the torture of four captives.[190] Twelve subordinates were sentenced to up to fourteen years in prison.[191]

In May 1984, an Army sublieutenant was sentenced to eighteen years for the rape of a Miskito woman in Lapan, on the Atlantic Coast.[192]

During the first six months of 1987, 1,091 members of the army, including 276 officers, as well as 837 members of the police and State Security organizations, were tried for crimes ranging from desertion and abuse of authority to homicide and assault.[193] Officers tried and convicted received somewhat longer sentences than did draftees.[194] These figures, provided by the *Auditoría Militar,* are consistent with those published by Americas Watch, which indicate that 3,470 soldiers, including 791 officers, were tried during the first eleven months of 1987. The crimes they were charged with resulted in 248 dead, 423 wounded and property damage of approximately $50,000.[195]

Amnesty International has concluded that allegations of abuses by the army "have been investigated and the police and military forces alleged to be responsible for such abuses have been brought to justice."[196]

Recent events tend to confirm Amnesty's conclusion. On March 6, 1988, the Communist-affiliated trade union CAUS organized a march of some fifty-nine people. The army and police shot and killed two demonstrators when the marchers disobeyed an army order to turn back. The government arrested and charged five soldiers with homicide. The government also apologized to the demonstrators and offered to pay transportation and burial expenses, an offer that was refused.[197]

More recently, the Nicaraguan government brought murder charges against thirteen Sandinista soldiers for killing seven unarmed civilians. In August 1989, the soldiers were publicly tried and sentenced to prison terms of six to thirty years.[198]

Prisoners of Conscience

Amnesty International has expressed concern during the past nine years regarding due process violations, arbitrary arrest and harassment of individuals for the expression of political views. Amnesty observed a systematic policy of harassment of certain opposition members, consisting of questioning, arrests and short-term detention.[199]

When Amnesty uncovers cases of people who have been convicted for non-violent expression of views, the organization labels the person a "prisoner of conscience." In 1981, Amnesty International adopted eight Prisoners of Conscience in Nicaragua. Four were leaders of the Communist Party, arrested for inciting strikes and claiming that the government was "diverting the revolutionary process to a capitalist line."[200] The other four, arrested the same day, were business leaders of Nicaragua's association of Chambers of Commerce, arrested for accusing the government of creating economic disaster by following "a Marxist-Leninist adventure."[201] All eight were convicted of violations of the Law for the Maintenance of Order and Public Security: the four business leaders were sentenced to terms of seven months, while the four Communist Party leaders were sentenced for terms of twenty-nine months.[202] All eight were released within five months and pardoned by the Council of State.[203] This is the only case of a prosecution under Article IV of the Law for the Maintenance of Public Order, which criminalizes seditious libel.[204]

In 1984, Amnesty identified another prisoner of conscience, Father Amado Peña, who appears to have been the victim of a frame-up by the State Security Service. Although charges were brought against Father Peña, he was not brought to trial and the charges were dismissed by a legislative pardon three months later.[205]

In 1987, Amnesty identified several new "prisoners of conscience" in Nicaragua. One was Mario Baldizón Aviles, sentenced to ten years for treason. Mario Baldizón's brother, Alvaro Baldizón Aviles, a former Minister of Interior employee, left Nicaragua and sought asylum in the United States. Upon his arrival, Alvaro Baldizón accused the Nicaraguan government of human rights abuses, charges that were prominently publicized by the U.S. State Department. Mario Baldizón was convicted of helping his brother, although Amnesty International believes that Mario Baldizón was actually imprisoned solely because of his family relation with his brother.[206]

Political Prisoners

There has been an ongoing debate over the number of "political prisoners" in Nicaragua, with the Sandinista government, backed by such organizations as the International Red Cross, citing one set of figures and the United States and the pro-U.S. Nicaraguan Human Rights Organization citing substantially higher figures.

According to the International Red Cross, as of the end of February 1988, there were 1,822 former National Guardsmen and 1,532 accused contras in Nicaraguan prisons for a total of 3,354 "political prisoners." [207] The Nicaraguan government announced at the end of 1987 that there were 3,434 prisoners who had been charged with politically-motivated offenses. Of these, 924 had been convicted of violations of the Law of Public Order; 1,800 were former Somoza National Guardsmen.[208]

The pro-U.S. human rights organization, the CPDH, on the other hand, claims that there are 8,000-9,000 political prisoners in Nicaragua, at least 4,000 more than the International Red Cross counted. However, Americas Watch noted:

> While the ICRC [Red Cross] might not have found *some* prisoners, or the government might have hidden *some* prisoners from them, neither the CPDH or the U.S. State Department which repeats its figures has any explanation of how the government could hide more than 4,000 prisoners from so experienced a body as the ICRC. In effect, the government is being charged with "disappearing" more than four thousand prisoners whose names, addresses, ages and last known locations and circumstances of detention have not been supplied. We do not find such charges credible. [emphasis in original] [209]

It should be remembered, when analyzing these figures, that after the Sandinista victory in 1979, there was no bloodbath. Former Somoza National Guardsmen were not executed, but were instead arrested, tried and imprisoned. Thus, one of the reasons the number of political prisoners is high is precisely because the Sandinistas did *not* violate fundamental human rights during the revolution.

During the past several years, the Nicaraguan government has slowly been releasing political prisoners. As part of the Esquipulas Peace Agreement, the Nicaraguan government agreed to an unconditional amnesty for the approximately 1,600 people accused of contra activity, an amnesty to be implemented as soon as a permanent cease-fire was reached.[210] In November 1987, the Nicaraguan government released 985 prisoners accused or convicted of security-related offenses.[211] Four months later, the government, complying with another promise made during the Sapoa peace discussions, released one hundred prisoners whose names had been submitted by the contra leadership.[212]

Finally, on March 17, 1989, the Nicaraguan government released virtually all of the former members of Somoza's National Guard who had been imprisoned since the revolution. The Sandinista government granted unconditional liberty to 1,894 former Guardsmen; thirty-nine

Appendix 201

who had been convicted of particularly "atrocious" crimes remain imprisoned.[213]

Habeas Corpus

The constitution guarantees Nicaraguans the right of *habeas corpus*.[214] However, both under the Nicaraguan constitution[215] and various international human rights instruments,[216] *habeas corpus* can be suspended in times of emergency.

Under the states of emergencies that had been in effect virtually since the founding of the Nicaraguan republic on July 19, 1979, this right has been restricted. The state of emergency promulgated immediately after ratification of the constitution in 1987 (and lifted on January 19, 1988), continued to suspend *habeas corpus*.

However, as interpreted by the Nicaraguan Court of Appeals and enforced by the Supreme Court,[217] *habeas corpus* has existed in full for all common crimes. Even for crimes against national security, there was only a partial suspension of *habeas corpus*. Former Chief Justice Alejandro Serrano of the Nicaraguan Supreme Court explained:

Although the State of Emergency suspended *habeas corpus* for crimes against the national security, the Courts interpreted that the State of Emergency only made reference to derogation of *habeas corpus* in regards to a speedy trial. They ruled that *habeas corpus* was not suspended in regards to personal integrity. *Habeas corpus* always existed in spite of the State of Emergency.[218]

Figures presented to the author by Justice Humberto Obregón, Court of Appeals for the District of Managua, show the Court received 4,502 *habeas corpus* petitions from January 1 through December 5, 1987, up from 986 *habeas corpus* petitions the year before. Justice Obregón described this as "undoubtedly a cause for concern" since these figures show that the "index of repression has increased tremendously" during 1987.[219] "What is going on here is unheard of, unbelievable. The volume of work doesn't allow us to improve the quality of our decisions," he stated.[220]

Police Detentions

Since 1936 under Somoza, and continuing under post-revolutionary Nicaraguan law,[221] the police have had the power to detain, try and convict a person for up to six months for certain violations of the law. Violations punishable by police courts include drug trafficking, cattle rustling, disrespect for authority and the economic crimes of hoarding and speculation.

There is no judicial review of sentences handed down by the police courts.[222] Although *habeas corpus* is technically available, in practice it is of no use; by the time a *habeas corpus* petition is acted upon, the defendants would normally have already served their term.[223] Defendants are not guaranteed counsel, nor do they have the right to confront their accusers. Such police detentions have been used as a method of political harassment.[224]

Current Supreme Court Justices believe that such police detentions should not be continued and that the decree authorizing such actions should be repealed. The Supreme Court is currently working on a draft proposal to reform the Penal Code and abolish police detention.[225]

Forced Relocation of Civilian Populations

In early January and February 1982, the government evacuated some thirty-five villages and relocated approximately 8,000 Miskito Indians from their homes. Although the OAS Inter-American Commission on Human Rights and Americas Watch have both said that the decision to relocate the Miskitos was justified due to the war conditions prevalent in the area,[226] the manner in which the relocation was carried out has been criticized.

The Miskitos were not involved in the decision to relocate and were given little, if any, prior notice. There were no confirmed allegations of abuse or harsh treatment during the relocation effort;[227] however, even though the elderly and sick were evacuated by helicopter,[228] many Miskitos had to walk to the settlement camps, a journey which lasted up to seven days.[229]

Other forced evacuations of Miskito Indians from war zones and border areas have occurred. In one such evacuation in November 1982, 6,000 Miskito and Sumu Indians were evacuated from an area on the Honduran border to a resettlement camp in Wiwili, Jinotega. Other smaller evacuations have involved hundreds or thousands of people.

Many Miskito Indians are still living in resettlement camps. Although conditions were primitive during the 1982 resettlement, by 1985:

> international visitors to the camps...report that housing, health services, work opportunities, education and welfare assistance are adequate in all settlements except in Jinotega, where some of the 3,000 Miskitos relocated to several areas of that department still live in collective housing facilities.[230]

In many of the resettlement camps, the Miskitos were given title to their own single-family houses and small plots of land. This was little recompense, however, for a traditional community with strong ties to their own land.[231]

In the spring of 1987, the government evacuated some 9,000 peasants from an area known as Nueva Guinea. Evacuees were given no advance notice and did not have time to pack most of their belongings. They were forced to live in relocation camps for six months, but were allowed to return to their farms and towns in November 1987.[232]

Unlike relocations and resettlement camps in many other countries, the Miskito Indians were not forced to live in the camps. Although they were not allowed to return to the border areas, the Miskitos could leave the camps at will and travel or settle in any part of the country.[233] Recently, as part of an autonomy program passed by the National Assembly, Miskito Indians have been "repatriated" to areas of the Atlantic Coast from which they had previously been evacuated.[234]

According to the United Nations High Commissioner for Refugees:

> some 11,500 Nicaraguans of Indian origin have repatriated from Honduras and other countries of asylum since September 1987, when the [Nicaraguan] National Assembly

adopted legislation providing for autonomy in the Atlantic Coast Region.[235]

Prison Conditions

Conditions for the majority of prisoners serving sentences in Nicaragua are considered good by most standards.[236] Prisoners are encouraged to participate in work programs and receive 70 percent of the minimum wage for their work.[237] Visits of family members are allowed between one and four times a month, depending on whether the person is participating in the work program or not.[238] All prisoners may receive conjugal visits.[239] The prison system has five grades, from maximum security to open farms where the prisoner is furloughed every six weeks.[240] Prisoners advance through this system as they serve their term. Maximum sentence is thirty years. Political and common prisoners are treated the same.

Despite this generally humane approach, reports of degrading treatment of prisoners, including threats, verbal abuse, and sleep, food and water deprivation, continue to be registered. Americas Watch has concluded:

> Though the abuses we complain about do not, in most cases, rise to the level of torture, they nevertheless violate the prohibition in international law of cruel, inhumane or degrading treatment and the prohibition on the use of coerced confessions.[241]

In addition, reports from pretrial detention centers describe tiny cells, harsh interrogation techniques, the use of small isolation cells known as "chiquitas," [242] as well as food and light deprivation.[243]

Amnesty reports some allegations of cruel and inhumane treatment of prisoners in Nicaragua. One such report is that of Tomás Blandon Hernández, who claims he was held for five days in a cell which was too small to sit down or stand up. He further claims to have been beaten, threatened and forced to sign blank papers which were then submitted as his "confession." [244] Amnesty believes such treatment occurs, but has not been able to independently confirm the allegations.

Reports of abuse at Las Tejas detention center prompted the removal, trial and sentencing of four officers to three months in jail for abuse of authority. Americas Watch noted:

it is rare indeed in Central America (as in most other parts of the world) for police interrogators to be punished in any way for torturing prisoners.[245]

State Security has refused to allow the International Red Cross access to their detention centers, although they finally allowed a delegation from Americas Watch to inspect the Managua El Chipote detention center in November 1987 and again in June 1988.[246] The prior refusal of the government to allow such access had been universally criticized by all human rights organizations, including the pro-Sandinista human rights organization, CNPPDH.[247]

Lack of Judicial Resources

Some of the reported problems, including long pre-trial delays, stem from the almost complete lack of resources available to the judicial system. This lack of material goods is due to two causes: poverty and the U.S.-funded contra war.

Nicaragua is an extremely poor third world country. Half of the approximately three million people living in Nicaragua are fifteen years of age or younger.[248] Average per capita Gross National Product is under $700.[249] During the last two years of the revolution, the Gross National Product dropped by one-third and much of the country's resources was destroyed.[250] In 1979, optimistic observers predicted that it would take the economy ten years to recover to pre-revolution levels.[251]

Within the first three years of the revolution, the government made impressive gains in improving the life of the average citizen. A massive literacy campaign in 1980-81 raised the adult literacy rate from under 50 percent to 87 percent.[252] The infant mortality rate was halved. A third of the urban population got access to housing and over half the peasants received land through the agrarian reform programs.[253]

Since 1982, however, the country has been defending itself against a counter-revolution supported, financed and directed by the

United States. The counter-revolutionary forces have targeted the civilian infrastructure, attacking farms, coffee collectives, health centers, etc. (The contras' first attack was against literacy workers teaching the peasants.[254] Three different contra groups took "credit" for this massacre.) "Government health volunteers, who are trained in administering vaccinations and often assist poor families with transportation to clinics and hospitals, have become targets for kidnap and murder by Contras." [255]

At the peak of contra violence in 1984, 1,500 armed encounters caused material damage equal to 70 percent of Nicaragua's exports.[256] As a result of the counter-revolution, production has fallen. The inflation rate in 1987 was running at well over 1,000 percent per year; by 1988, inflation was over 20,000 percent. The economy is in shambles.[257]

Much of what remains has been diverted for defense needs. On the eighth anniversary of the revolution, the government was spending 46 percent of its GNP for defense.[258] The 1988 budget for Nicaragua's entire judicial system, including all salaries, equipment, etc., was just 7.3 billion cordobas. At the official rate of exchange as of January 15, 1988, this equals $365,000—less than a single, well-paid lawyer in the United States might earn yearly.[259]

Material resources for judicial personnel are meager at best. There are judges in rural communities who do not have desks on which to work. Typewriters, even paper, are in short supply.

In 1986, the Supreme Court of Nicaragua embarked on an "ambitious project" of computerization.[260] The entire project consists of two Radio Shack Tandy-1000 personal computers (donated to the Court by French jurists). In the past, all records of convicts were kept by hand and sometimes, even though a prisoner's sentence was up, he or she would not be released because no one noticed that the release date had arrived. The two personal computers now keep track of all sentences, to ensure that no prisoner remains improperly incarcerated.

The Effect of the State of Emergency on Nicaraguans

The state of emergency in effect until 1988 did not affect the daily life of most Nicaraguans. It is the war, not the restrictions imposed by the government, that has most drastically affected the lives of the Nicaraguan people.

There is no curfew, and freedom of travel, except within the war zones, is not restricted. People come and go freely on the streets. The Chief Justice of the Nicaraguan Supreme Court explained:

> In the State of Emergency in our country, the ordinary citizen moved about with full freedom. He could come home at any time of the night that he wished...The State of Emergency, [could be viewed] not as a restrictive situation which encompassed the entire community, but rather as a bundle of legal instruments that the government grants itself...whose application is directed only at those who are endangering the life of the state...It does not operate against the entire community.[261]

People attend church openly. Catholics choose their church according to community and politics; anti-government and pro-government priests abound. Various Protestant and evangelical denominations coexist side-by-side with the dominant Catholic majority.

At no time during the past decade was there a feeling of living in a police state. Soldiers are everywhere, yet people discuss politics openly on the streets, often arguing with the soldiers themselves. Police and soldiers are surprisingly courteous.[262]

Although Nicaraguans have lived for most of the past ten years under a state of emergency, the restrictions were not visible in the lives of the average Nicaraguan.

Notes

Notes to Chapter I

1. Norman Thomas, *Is Conscience a Crime*, p. 74.
2. *Nebraska Press Association v. Stuart*, 427 U.S. 539, 589, (1976) quoting *Southeastern Promotions Ltd. v. Conrad*, 420 U.S. 546, 553 (1975).
3. Brief of the petitioner, *New York Times v. United States*, 403 U.S. 713 (1971), *New York Times*, June 26, 1971.
4. The first census of 1790 counted 757,000 blacks, 19.3 percent of the population.
5. See Bell, *And We Are Not Saved*, p. 34.
6. William Safire, "Tug-of-War," *New York Times Magazine*, September 13, 1987, pp. 61-66.
7. The European Convention on Human Rights states that "In times of war or other public emergency [that] threaten[s] the life of the nation," the nation "may take measures derogating from its obligations under this Convention to the extent strictly required by the exigencies of the situation." (Art. 15.)

Under the International Covenant on Civil and Political Rights, a country may derogate most human rights guarantees "in time of public emergency...[and] to the extent strictly required by the exigencies of the situation."

The American Convention on Human Rights (the San Jose Pact), allows for derogations from human rights treaties "In time of war, public danger, or other emergency that threatens the independence or security of a State Party," but only "to the extent and for the period of time strictly required by the exigencies of the situation, provided that such measures are not inconsistent with its other obligations under international law and do not involve discrimination on the ground of race, color, sex, language, religion, or social origin." (Art. 27(1).)
8. United States Constitution, Art. I, Sec. 9, Clause 2.

Notes to Chapter II

1. Levy, *Legacy of Suppression*, p. 176.
2. Constitution of the United States, Art. VII.
3. Christenson, *Political Trials*, p. 113.
4. *Ibid.*, pp. 113-115
5. Kohn, *Jailed for Peace*, pp. 6-10.
6. Calhoon, *The Loyalists in Revolutionary America*, p. 384.
7. *Ibid.*, pp. 404-405.

210   FREEDOM UNDER FIRE

8. *Ibid.*, p. 362.
9. *Ibid.*, p. 371.
10. Van Tyne, *The Loyalists in the American Revolution*, p. 183.
11. Calhoon, *The Loyalists in Revolutionary America*, pp. 295-312; Van Tyne, *The Loyalists in the American Revolution*, pp. 60-86.
12. E. Peck, *Tercentenary Commission of the State of Connecticut*, p. 15.
13. Van Tyne, *The Loyalists in the American Revolution*, p. 121.
14. Calhoon, *The Loyalists in Revolutionary America*, p. 303.
15. *Ibid.*, p. 306.
16. Van Tyne, *The Loyalists in the American Revolution*, p. 271.
17. Calhoon, *The Loyalists in Revolutionary America*, p. 401.
18. Van Tyne, *The Loyalists in the American Revolution*, pp. 193-194.
19. *Ibid.*, p. 318.
20. *Ibid.*, pp. 220-222.
21. *Ibid.*, pp. 331-333.
22. Nelson, *The American Tory*, p. 166.
23. Flick, Alexander Clarence, *Studies in History, Economics and Public Law*, Vol XIV, No. 1: "Loyalism in New York During the American Revolution," p. 137.
24. *Ibid.* See also *Disposition of Loyalist Estates in Southern New York*, p. 113. The Commission was not abolished until 1784, a year after the peace treaty with Britain was signed.
25. *Abstract of the Laws of the American States, Now in Force Relative to Debts Due to Loyalists, Subjects of Great Britain*, p. 36; see also Flick, *Studies in History, Economics and Public Law*, p. 146.
26. *Ibid.*, pp. 159-160; *Disposition of Loyalists Estates in Southern New York*, p. 116.
27. Harris, *Loyalism in Virginia*, p. 87. See also, *Martin v. Hunter's Lessee*, 14 U.S. (1 Wheat.) 304 (1816).
28. Myrick, *State Papers of Vermont: Sequestration, Confiscation and Sale of Estates*, p. 8.
29. Peck, *Tercentenary Commission of the State of Connecticut, Vol XXXI: Loyalists in Connecticut*, p. 22.
30. *Abstract of the Laws of the American States, Now in Force, Relative to Debts Due to Loyalists, Subjects of Great Britain*, pp. iii, 2.
31. Calhoon, *The Loyalists in Revolutionary America*, pp. 385-86, quoting Brock, *Pacifism in America*.
32. Act of October sessions, 1779. See *Abstract of the Laws of the American States, Now in Force, Relative to Debts Due to Loyalists, Subjects of Great Britain*.
33. Cf. *United States v. Brown*, 381 U.S. 437 (1965) (Warren, C.J., "During the American Revolution, the legislatures of all thirteen states passed statutes directed against the Tories; among these statutes were a large number of bills of attainder and bills of pains and penalties").
34. *Abstract of the Laws of the American States, Now in Force, Relative to Debts Due to Loyalists, Subjects of Great Britain.*
35. Act of 1782, Chap. 45, p. 182, Sec. 1. See *Abstract of the Laws of the American States, Now in Force, Relative to Debts Due to Loyalists, Subjects of Great Britain.*

36. New Jersey laws, Chap. 75, Sec. 3, April 18, 1778; Virginia laws, Chapt. 9, p. 65, 1777; Virginia laws, Chapt. 14, p. 96, Sec. 2, 1779.

37. Flick, *Studies in History, Economics and Public Law*, p. 164. By comparison, South Carolina was relatively lenient, allowing British subjects to recover one-fifth of their debts annually. *Ibid.*, p. iii.

38. Van Tyne, *The Loyalists in the American Revolution*, pp. 58-59.

39. Bradley, *Colonial Americans in Exile*, p. 121.

40. Kittrie and Wedlock, *The Tree of Liberty*, p. 71.

41. Flick, *Studies in History, Economics and Public Law*, pp. 179-80; see also Peck, *Tercentenary Commission of the State of Connecticut*, p. 78; Calhoon, *The Loyalists in Revolutionary America*, p. 499.

42. Calhoon, *The Loyalists in Revolutionary America*, p. 501.

43. Myrick, *State Papers of Vermont: Sequestration, Confiscation and Sale of Estates*, pp. 435-444.

44. Flick, *Studies in History, Economics and Public Law*, p. 158.

45. *Ibid.*, p. 10.

46. Stoler, *The War Against the Press*, p. 24; A. Peck, *Uncovering the Sixties: The Life and Times of the Underground Press*, p. 4.

47. Gottschalk, " 'Consistent with Security'…A History of American Military Press Censorship," 5 *Communications & Law*, 35 (1983).

48. Levy, *Legacy of Supression*, p. 178.

49. *Ibid.*, pp. 178-9.

50. Van Tyne, *The Loyalists in the American Revolution*, p. 199.

51. "An Act concerning Aliens," Statutes at Large, I, 570-572, June 25, 1798.

52. "An Act concerning Alien Enemies," Statutes at Large, I, 577-578, July 6, 1798.

53. Carroll, "Freedom of Speech and of the Press in the Federalist Period: The Sedition Act," 18 *Michigan Law Review* 615 (1920).

54. "An Act in addition to the act, entitled 'An act for the punishment of certain crimes against the United States'," Statutes at Large, I, 596-597, July 14, 1798.

55. Carroll, "Freedom of Speech and of the Press in the Federalist Period: The Sedition Act," 18 *Michigan Law Review* at 650, fn 71.

56. Smith, *Freedom's Fetters*, pp. 221-246.

57. *Ibid.*, pp. 390-398.

58. *Ibid.*, pp. 186-187.

59. *Ibid.*, pp. 188-204.

60. *Ibid.*, pp. 277-278.

61. *Ibid.*, pp. 247-257.

62. Volkman and Baggett, *Secret Intelligence*, p. xix.

63. Smith, *Freedom's Fetters*, pp. 270-275.

64. *Argus*, Oct. 15, 1799 and Nov. 15, 1799, as quoted in Smith, *Freedom's Fetters*, p. 274.

65. The sole possible exception was John Marshall, who stated in his election campaign of 1798 that he would not have voted for the Act had he been in Congress during its debate. Nonetheless, Marshall never questioned the Act's constitutionality. See, Smith, *Freedom's Fetters*, p. 151.

66. "Virginia Resolution of 1798, pronouncing the Alien and Sedition Laws to be Unconstitutional, and Defining the Rights of the States," Virginia House of Delegates, Dec. 21, 1798.

67. Kentucky Resolution, November 19, 1798, original draft written by Thomas Jefferson.

68. Resolution of the New Hampshire House of Representatives, June 14, 1799; Resolution of Massachusetts Senate, Feb. 9, 1799.

69. Letter to Mrs. Adams, July 22, 1804, 4 Jefferson's works, pp. 555-56.

70. "Seditious libel" is the doctrine that criticism of government officials and policy may be viewed as defamation of government and may be punished as a serious crime. [On] my view, the absence of seditious libel as a crime is the true programmatic test of freedom of speech." Kalven, *The Negro and the First Amendment,* as quoted in Lockhart, Kamisar, Choper, Shiffrin, *Constitutional Law,* p. 679.

71. See, Koffler and Gershman, "The New Seditious Libel," 69 *Cornell Law Review* 816, 827-28 (1984).

72. Levy, *Legacy of Supression,* pp. 299-307.

73. *Ibid.,* pp. 297-299.

74. *New York Times Co. v. Sullivan,* 376 U.S. 255, 276 (1964).

75. Chenery, *Freedom of the Press,* p. 155.

Notes to Chapter III

1. Chenery, *Freedom of the Press,* pp. 155-156.

2. Mock, *Censorship, 1917,* reprinted in *Wartime Censorship of Press and Radio,* p. 55.

3. *Ibid.*

4. *Ibid.*

5. Gottschalk, " 'Consistent with Security'...A History of American Military Press Censorship," 5 *Communications & Law,* at 36.

6. Stoler, *The War Against the Press,* p. 22.

7. *Ibid.,* p. 31.

8. See, "An Act for Enrolling and Calling out the National Forces, and for Other Purposes," 12 Stat. 731 (1863).

9. Kittrie and Wedlock, *The Tree of Liberty,* p. 190.

10. As quoted in Kittrie and Wedlock, *The Tree of Liberty,* p. 191.

11. Kittrie and Wedlock, *The Tree of Liberty,* p. 173.

12. U.S. Constitution, Art. I, Sec. 9.

13. Presidential Proclamations of April 27, 1861, June 20, 1861, and Sept. 24, 1862.

14. *Ex parte Merryman,* 17 F. Cas 144 (C.C.D., Md. 1861).

15. Letter to Erastus Corning, June 12, 1863.

16. Hyman, *To Try Men's Souls,* pp. 143-144.

17. Quoted in Brennan, J., "The Quest to Develop a Jurisprudence of Civil Liberties in Times of Security Crises," p. 4.

18. Reprinted in R.P. Basler, *The Collected Works of Abraham Lincoln*, Rutgers University Press, 1959, pp. 421-422.

19. Brennan, J., "The Quest to Develop a Jurisprudence of Civil Liberties in Times of Security Crises," p. 4, quoting Warren, Charles, *The Supreme Court in United States History*, Vol. 3, p. 91.

20. Inaugural Address of Jefferson Davis, Feb. 22, 1862.

21. *Ibid.*

22. Estimates vary; See, e.g., Kittrie and Wedlock, *The Tree of Liberty*, p. 178 ("over 10,000"); Koffler and Gershman, "The New Seditious Libel," fn. 53 ("War Department records indicated that 13,535 persons were arrested and confined"); Brennan, "The Quest to Develop a Jurisprudence of Civil Liberties in Times of Security Crises," p. 4 ("20-30,000"). This would be the per capita equivalent of having approximately 200,000 people behind bars today for political crimes.

23. *Ex Parte Milligan*, 71 U.S. (4 Wall.) 2 (1866).

24. Kittrie and Wedlock, *The Tree of Liberty*, p. 202.

25. *Ibid.*, p. 214; also see *Case of Davis*, 7 F. Cas. 63 (C.C.D. Va., 1867-71) (No. 3,621a).

26. Constitution of the United States, 14th Amendment, Sec. 3. This disability from holding office could be removed by a two-thirds vote of each House of Congress.

27. In 1868, a Congressional committee reported that during the prior two years, 373 freedmen had been killed by whites. See, Bell, *Race, Racism and American Law*, p. 131.

28. "An Act to Provide for More Efficient Government of the Rebel States," 14 Stat. 428 (1867).

29. *Ex parte McCardle*, 74 U.S. 506 (1869).

30. *Mitchell v. Harmony*, 13 How. 115, 133 (1852). ("There are without doubt, occasions in which private property may lawfully be taken possession of or destroyed to prevent it from falling into the hands of the public enemy...In such cases, the government is bound to make full compensation...")

31. Fleming, *The Civil War in Florida*, p. 238.

32. *Ibid.*, p. 239.

33. *Ibid.* See also, Kittrie and Wedlock, *The Tree of Liberty*, p. 189.

34. See "An Act to Suppress Insurrection, to Punish Treason and Rebellion and Confiscate the Property of Rebels," 12. Stat. 589 (1862).

35. *Youngstown Sheet and Tube Co. v. Sawyer*, 343 U.S. 579, 620 (Frankfurter, J., concurring, Appendix II).

36. 12. Stat. 820 (1863).

37. *Miller v. United States*, 78 U.S. (6 Wall.) 268 (1870). (The Confiscation Acts did not violate the Fifth and Sixth Amendments. "It would be absurd to hold that, while in a foreign war [the] enemy's property may be captured and confiscated...in a civil war of equal dimensions...the right to confiscate the property...does not exist...Every reason for the allowance of a right to confiscate in case of foreign wars exists in full force when the war is domestic or civil.") In *Juragua Iron Co. v. United States*, 212 U.S. 297, 306, the Court quoted approvingly of *Miller:* "It is sufficient that the right to confiscate the property of all public enemies is a conceded right." See also *United States v. Anderson*, 9 Wall. 56, which upheld the Abandoned Property Act ("all property obtained [by military force can be] appropriated to the necessities of the War").

Notes to Chapter IV

1. Goldstein, *Political Repression in Modern America*, p. 105.

2. *Ibid.*, p. 143.

3. *In re Debs* 158 U.S. 564 (1895).

4. *Youngstown Sheet & Tube Co. v. Sawyer*, 343 U.S. 579, 688 (Vinson, J., dissenting). See also Paul, *Conservative Crisis and the Rule of Law: Attitudes of Bar and Bench, 1887-1895*, pp. 130-158.

5. Paul, *Ibid.*, pp. 130-158.

6. *United States v. Debs*, 64 Fed. 714 (N.D. Ill., 1894).

7. *Farmer's Loan and Trust Co. v. Northern Pacific R.R. Co.*, 60 Fed. 803 (E.D. Wisc., 1893).

8. *Congressional Record*, 53d Cong., 2d sess. 26 (March 1-6, 1894).

9. United States Constitution, Article IV, Section 4.

10. Letter from Elihu Root to Hon. John Sparks, Governor, December 14, 1907, as reprinted in Kittrie and Wedlock, *Tree of Liberty*, p. 270.

11. After the war, President Harding dispatched federal troops against miners in West Virginia in 1920 and 1921, under authority of Title 10, Section 331 of the U.S. Code.

12. In addition to their use against labor, federal troops were used to put down the Dorr Rebellion (1842) and the Kansas Territory Disturbances (1854-58). In more recent times, troops were used to quell riots in Michigan (1967), and Washington, D.C., Baltimore and Chicago (1968). See infra at pp. 122-123.

13. 212 U.S. 78 (1909).

14. *Moyer v. Peabody*, 212 U.S. at 85.

15. *State ex rel. Mays v. Brown*, 71 W. Va. 519, 77 S.E. 243 (1912).

16. See infra, pp. 48-50.

17. Murphy, *World War I and the Origin of Civil Liberties in the United States*, p. 87.

18. *Ibid.*, p. 116.

19. *Ibid.*, pp. 89, 117.

20. Goldstein, *Political Repression in Modern America*, p. 129.

21. Murphy, *World War I and the Origin of Civil Liberties in the United States*, p. 90.

22. As quoted in Gunns, *Civil Liberties in Crisis*, p. 14.

23. Goldstein, *Political Repression in Modern America*, p. 111.

24. As quoted in Murphy, *World War I and the Origin of Civil Liberties in the United States*, p. 95.

25. Gunns, *Civil Liberties in Crisis*, p. 15.

26. Murphy, *World War I and the Origin of Civil Liberties in the United States*, p. 126.

27. Goldstein, *Political Repression in Modern America*, p. 112.

28. Murphy, *World War I and the Origin of Civil Liberties in the United States*, pp. 222-223.

29. *New York World*, September 6, 1918, p. 8, as quoted in Murphy, *ibid.*, p. 126.

30. 4 Wallace 2 (1866), see supra, p. 29.

31. Murphy, *World War I and the Origin of Civil Liberties in the United States,* p. 225.

32. *Ibid.,* p. 194.

33. *United States v. Ves Hall,* 248 Fed. 150 (1918); Murphy, *World War I and the Origin of Civil Liberties in the United States,* pp. 199-203.

34. Murphy, *ibid.,* p. 192.

35. *Ibid.,* p. 194.

36. Lawrence, "Eclipse of Liberty: Civil Liberties in the United States during the First World War," 21 *Wayne Law Review* 35, 75 (1974).

37. *Ibid.,* at 58.

38. *Ibid.,* at 59.

39. *Ibid.,* at 58.

40. Murphy, *World War I and the Origin of Civil Liberties in the United States,* pp. 128-132.

41. Boyer and Morais, *Labor's Untold Story,* p. 197.

42. Churchill and Vander Wall, *Agents of Repression,* p. 19, quoting Archer, Jules, *Strikes, Bombs and Bullets: Big Bill Haywood and the IWW,* Julian Messner, New York, 1972, p. 169.

43. Kittrie and Wedlock, *The Tree of Liberty,* pp. 290-291.

44. *Ibid.,* p. 292.

45. Volkman and Baggett, *Secret Intelligence: The Inside Story of America's Espionage Empire,* p. 15.

46. Kohn, *Jailed for Peace,* pp. 28-29.

47. *Political Prisoners in Federal Military Prisons,* pp. 4-5.

48. *Ibid.,* p. 13.

49. *Ibid.,* erratum insert before p. 3.

50. Summers, *Wartime Censorship of Press and Radio,* p. 67.

51. *Ibid.,* p. 79.

52. Chafee, *Free Speech in the United States,* p. 37.

53. 40 Stat. 217 (1917).

54. 40 Stat. 555 (1918).

55. Chafee, *Free Speech in the United States,* p. 40. See infra, p. 73.

56. *Ibid.,* p. 41. Passage of the Espionage Act did indeed follow two lynchings, several tar-and-featherings and the deportation of over IWW miners from their homes in Bisbee, Arizona.

57. *Ibid.,* p. 56. Wallace went insane and died in jail.

58. *Ibid.*

59. Two years later her conviction was set aside by the Circuit Court of Appeals, *United States v. Rose Pastor Stokes,* 264 Fed. 18 (8th Cir., 1920). The absurdity of these prosecutions can be gleaned from the fact that her statement was considered dangerous enough to warrant a ten year term, yet was printed for millions to see in the news accounts of the trial.

60. Murphy, *World War I and the Origin of Civil Liberties in the United States,* p. 130.

61. Churchill and Vander Wall, *Agents of Repression,* p. 20.

62. Murphy, *World War I and the Origin of Civil Liberties in the United States,* p. 132.

63. Chafee, *Free Speech in the United States*, p. 52. See, also Biddle, *The Fear of Freedom*, p. 58; Summers, *Wartime Censorship of Press and Radio*, p. 79.
64. Goldstein, *Political Repression in Modern America*, p. 113.
65. Chafee, *Free Speech in the United States*, pp. 387-394.
66. *Ibid.*, p. 51.
67. Chafee, "Freedom of Speech in War Time," 32 *Harvard Law Review* 932 (1919).
68. See, Irons, " 'Fighting Fair': Zechariah Chafee, Jr., the Department of Justice, and the 'Trial at the Harvard Club,' " 94 *Harvard Law Review* 1205 (1981).
69. See infra, pp. 99-101, 121ff.
70. During the Spanish-American War, General Greeley got the cooperation of Western Union to allow government censors to monitor telegraph transmissions in Tampa, Miami and Jacksonville, Florida. At the same time, the Secretary of War directed General Otis, commanding general of U.S. forces in the Philippines, to censor all press dispatches originating from that war zone.
When U.S. marines landed in Veracruz, Mexico in 1914, similar restrictions were enacted to prevent any unpleasant news from being reported. See Mock, *Censorship, 1917,* as reprinted in Summers, *Wartime Censorship of Press and Radio*, pp. 57-59.
71. *Ibid.*, p. 65.
72. *Ibid.*, p. 66.
73. *Masses Pub. Co. v. Patten*, 245 Fed. 102 (2d Cir., 1917); *Masses Pub. Co. v. Patten*, 246 Fed. 24 (2d Cir., 1917).
74. *United States ex rel. Milwaukee Social Democratic Publishing Co. v. Burleson, Postmaster General of the United States*, 255 U.S. 407 (1921).
75. Summers, *Wartime Censorship of Press and Radio*, p. 83.
76. See infra, pp. 48-50.
77. Chafee, *Free Speech in the United States*, p. 99; Summers, *Wartime Censorship of Press and Radio*, pp. 83-85.
78. Goldstein, *Political Repression in Modern America*, pp. 116-117.
79. *Ibid.*, p. 109.
80. Summers, *Wartime Censorship of Press and Radio*, p. 85.
81. Creel, "The Plight of the Last Censor," reprinted in Summers, *Wartime Censorship of Press and Radio*, p. 75. See also Biddle, *The Fear of Freedom*, p. 68; Mock, *Words that Won the War*, p. 28.
82. 40 Stat.411 (1917).
83. Mock, *Words that Won the War*, pp. 44-45.
84. 258 Fed. 908 (9th Cir., 1919).
85. Mock, *Words that Won the War*, p. 147. See *ibid.*, pp. 147-151 for other examples of war-time censorship, suppression and delay of films.
86. *Ibid.*, pp. 6-7.
87. *Ibid.*, p. 113.
88. *Ibid.*, p. 120.
89. *Ibid.*, p. 116.
90. *Ibid.*, p. 125.
91. *Ibid.*, p. 129.
92. U.S. Comm. on Public Information, *The Red, White and Blue Series: War Cyclopedia* (1918), as quoted in Lawrence, "Eclipse of Liberty," at 47.

Notes 217

93. Lawrence, "Eclipse of Liberty," at 86.
94. Creel, "The Plight of the Last Censor," reprinted in Summers, *Wartime Censorship of Press and Radio,* p. 70.
95. *Ibid.,* p. 71.
96. *Ibid.,* p. 70.
97. 249 U.S. 47 (1919).
98. Cover, "The Left, The Right and the First Amendment: 1918-1920," 40 *Maryland Law Review* 372 (1981).
99. *Frowerk v. United States,* 249 U.S. 204 (1919).
100. *Debs v. United States,* 249 U.S. 212 (1919).
101. 249 U.S. at 208.
102. See supra, p. 44.
103. 249 U.S. at 213.
104. See supra, p. 18.
105. See, e.g., William Safire, "On Language," *New York Times Magazine,* March 12, 1989, p. 24.
106. 250 U.S. 616 (1919).
107. 250 U.S. at 626.
108. 251 U.S. 466 (1920).
109. 251 U.S. at 479-80.
110. 251 U.S. at 476.
111. 252 U.S. 239 (1920).
112. 252 U.S. at 246.
113. See Brandeis-Frankfurter Conversations, Brandeis Papers, as quoted in Cover, "The Left, The Right and the First Amendment: 1918-1920," at 374.
114. As quoted in Chenery, *Freedom of the Press,* pp. 198-199.
115. *United States v. Steene,* 263 F. 130 (D.C.N.Y. 1920).
116. 254 U.S. 325 (1920).
117. 254 U.S. at 333.
118. Quoted in Chafee, *Free Speech in the United States,* p. 79.
119. *Near v. Minnesota,* 283 U.S. 697, 706, 709-710 (1931).
120. *State ex rel. Olson v. Guilford* 219 N.W. 770, 772 (1928).
121. 283 U.S. 697 (1931).
122. See Jeffries, "Rethinking Prior Restraint," 92 *Yale Law Journal* 409 (1983) ("In truth, *Near* involved nothing more or less than a repackaged version of the law of seditious libel.", as quoted in Lockhart, Kamisar, *et al., Constitutional Law,* p. 808).
123. 283 U.S. at 715-716. For a more recent affirmation, see *New York Times Co. v. United States,* 403 U.S. 713 (1971). (Prior judicial restraint is tolerated "when the Nation 'is at war'," Brennan, J., concurrence, quoting *Schenck.*)
124. See *United States v. Progressive,* 467 F.Supp. 990 (1979), infra, pp. 159-162.
125. Goldstein, *Political Repression in Modern America,* p. 106.
126. Gabriel Kolko, "Decline of American Radicalism in the Twentieth Century," as quoted in Goldstein, *ibid.,* p. 132.
127. See supra p. 46.
128. This account is taken mainly from Chafee, *Free Speech in the United States,* pp. 247-252.

218 FREEDOM UNDER FIRE

129. Berger was tried, convicted and sentenced to twenty years imprisonment before the U.S. Supreme Court reversed his conviction.

130. By contrast, even during the Civil War, "disloyalty was not a bar to an elected member of Congress...unless it was evidenced by actual aid to the enemy or words of acute virulence" (Chafee, *Free Speech in the United States*, p. 263).

131. *Ibid.*, pp. 269-282.

132. At the time, the Socialist Party was a duly recognized party under the election laws of the State of New York.

133. Biddle, *The Fear of Freedom*, pp. 67-68.

134. *New York Times* editorial, April 2, 1920, p. 14.

135. Statement of Mr. Ralph W.S. Hill, Assistant Solicitor, Department of State, *Trading with the Enemy Act: Hearing before the Committee on Interstate and Foreign Commerce of the House of Representatives.*

136. Statement of Mr. Lucien H. Boggs, Special Assistant to the Attorney General, *Trading with the Enemy Act*, p. 21

137. *Ibid.*, p. 7.

138. Statement of Mr. H.E. Ahern, Managing Director, Alien Property Custodian's Office, *Trading with the Enemy Act*, pp. 32-49.

139. *Stoehr v. Wallace*, 255 U.S. 239 (1921) ("That Congress in time of war may authorize and provide for the seizure and sequestration...of property believed to be enemy-owned, if adequate provision be made for a return in case of mistake, is not debatable." Van Devanter, J.).

140. *Youngstown Sheet & Tube Co. v. Sawyer*, 343 U.S. 579, 620 (Frankfurter, J. concurring, Appendix II).

141. *Dakota Coal Co. v. Fraser*, 283 Fed. 415, 417 (D.N.D.), *vacated as moot*, 267 Fed. 130 (8th Cir., 1920).

142. The two most notable exceptions were Roger Williams who was banished from the colony of Massachusetts and went on to found Rhode Island, and Clement Vallandigham who was expelled from the Union during the Civil War. See supra, pp. 10, 28.

143. *Turner v. Williams*, 194 U.S. 279 (1904). ("Deportation of an alien who is found to be here in violation of law is not a deprivation of liberty without due process of law, and that the provisions of the Constitution securing the right of trial by jury have no application.")

144. Chafee, *Free Speech in the United States*, pp. 197-198

145. Churchill and Vander Wall, *Agents of Repression*, p. 22.

146. Kittrie and Wedlock, *The Tree of Liberty*, p. 300.

147. Goldstein, *Political Repression in Modern America*, p. 157.

148. *Colyer v. Skeffington*, 265 Fed. 17, 43 (D. Mass., 1920).

149. *Ibid.*, at 41-45. Although the Government appealed numerous issues in this case, including Judge Anderson's finding that "[t]here is no evidence that the Communist Party is an organization advocating the overthrow of the government of the United States by force or violence," (*ibid.* at 79), there was no appeal from the Judge's findings of fact.

150. Biddle, *The Fear of Freedom*, p. 65.

151. *Ibid.*

152. Goldstein, *Political Repression in Modern America*, p. 157.

153. *Ibid.*, p. 156.

154. *Ibid.,* p. 162.
155. Churchill and Vander Wall, *Agents of Repression,* pp. 22-23.
156. Neier, "Surveillance as Censorship," in Rips, *The Campaign Against the Underground Press,* p. 10.
157. Churchill and Vander Wall, *Agents of Repression,* p. 11.
158. O'Reilly, *Hoover and the Un-Americans,* pp. 13-36; Donner, *The Age of Surveillance,* p. 147n.
159. Volkman and Baggett, *Secret Intelligence,* p. 17.
160. *Ibid.,* p. 18.
161. Churchill and Vander Wall, *Agents of Repression,* pp. 24-25.
162. *The Nation-Wide Spy System Centering in the Dept. of Justice,* pp. 11-12.
163. Chafee, *Free Speech in the United States,* p. 211.
164. *Ibid.,* p. 219.
165. Kittrie and Wedlock, *The Tree of Liberty,* p. 292.
166. Kahn, *The Codebreakers,* pp. 364-367.
167. Goodell, *Political Prisoners in America,* p. 67.
168. Murphy, *World War I and the Origin of Civil Liberties in the United States,* p. 106.
169. Goldstein, *Political Repression in Modern America,* p. 125.
170. See, Gunns, *Civil Liberties in Crisis,* pp. 74-75.
171. *State v. Hillstrom,* 46 Utah 341, 150 P. 935 (1915).
172. *Ex parte Jackson,* 263 Fed. 110, 111-112 (D. Mont. 1920).
173. Boyer and Morais, *Labor's Untold Story,* p. 198.
174. Goodell, *Political Prisoners in America,* pp. 71, 73.
175. Chafee, *Free Speech in the United States,* p. 166.
176. *State Political Prisoners,* pp. 5-6; Chafee, *ibid.,* p. 327.
177. 274 U.S. 357 (1927).
178. 274 U.S. 357, 375-76 (1927).
179. Goodell, *Political Prisoners in America,* p. 73.
180. *Ibid.,* p. 72.
181. Similar procedures were used by police agents in the 1960s. See infra, pp. 136, 140.
182. *Ex parte Jackson,* 263 Fed. 110, 113-14 (D. Mont. 1920).
183. *State Political Prisoners,* p. 2.
184. *Ibid.* Judge J.P. McCormick of Los Angeles offered to release the twenty-seven Wobblies who had been convicted in his court on the condition that there be no "industrial unionism in Los Angeles County."
185. Chafee, *Free Speech in the United States,* p. 159, 575-597. States with red flag statutes (and the penalty imposed) included: Alabama ($500-$5,000 fine); Arizona (6 months); Arkansas (6 months); California (6 months-5 years); Colorado (1-10 years); Connecticut (6 months); Delaware (15 years); Idaho (1-10 years); Illinois (1-10 years); Indiana (5 years); Iowa (6 months); Kansas (18 months-3 years); Kentucky (21 years); Massachusetts (6 months); Michigan (4 years); Minnesota (1-7 years); Montana (6 months-5 years); Nebraska (3 years); New Jersey (15 years); New Mexico (6 months); New York (1 year); North Dakota (30 days); Ohio ($100); Oklahoma (10 years); Oregon (10 years); Pennsylvania (3 months); Rhode Island (3 months); South Dakota (30 days); Utah (1-10 years); Vermont (6 months); Washington (10 years); West Virginia (1-5 years); Wisconsin

($10-$100). The laws of all but four states were still in effect at the start of World War II.

186. *Stromberg v. California*, 283 U.S. 359. The Court ruled that the California statute was void because of vagueness. Four years later, California re-enacted its red flag statute, making it unlawful to display a "red flag...or any flag...of any color or form whatever in any public place...*as a sign, symbol, or emblem of forceful or violent opposition to organized government* or as an invitation or stimulus to anarchistic actions or as aid to propaganda that advocates by force or violence the overthrow of government." (Mil. & Vet. Code, Sec. 616 (1935). The italicized words were added to overcome the objections of *Stromberg v. California*.

187. Biddle, *The Fear of Freedom*, p. 20.

188. *Ibid.*, p. 26.

189. *The State of Civil Liberties, 1923*. Out of this incident grew the Southern California affiliate of the American Civil Liberties Union.

190. New York Penal Code 1881, Sec. 468, chapter 371.

191. 268 U.S. 652, 666 (1925).

192. See, *e.g., Prudential Ins. Co. of Am. v. Cheek*, 259 U.S. 530, 538 (1922). ("The Constitution of the United States imposes upon the States no obligation to confer upon those within their jurisdiction either the right of free speech or the right of silence.")

193. *Gitlow v. New York*, 268 U.S. 652, 666 (1925) ("For present purposes we may and do assume that freedom of speech and of the press...are among the fundamental personal rights and liberties protected by the due process clause of the Fourteenth Amendment from impairment by the States.").

194. *Gitlow v. New York*, 268 U.S. 652 (1925).

195. Goodell, *Political Prisoners in America*, p. 85.

196. *The Police and the Radical.*

197. Cf. Justice Holmes speaking for the court in *Davis v. Massachusetts*, 162 Mass. 510, 511 (1895): "For the legislature absolutely or conditionally to forbid public speaking in a highway or public park is no more an infringement of rights of a member of the public than for the owner of a private house to forbid it in the house."

198. Chafee, *Free Speech in the United States*, p. 166.

199. *The Police and the Radical*, p. 11.

200. The president of Harvard University, A. Lawrence Lowell, however, encountered no trouble when he publicly urged Governor Fuller of Massachusetts not to give clemency to Sacco and Vanzetti. See Christenson, *Political Trials*, p. 6.

201. Chafee, *Free Speech in the United States*, p. 17.

202. *Ibid.*, p. 19.

203. Annual Report of the American Civil Liberties Union, 1927, as quoted in Gunns, *Civil Liberties in Crisis*, p. 83.

204. *Stromberg v. California*, 283 U.S. 359 (1931).

205. *Sterling v. Constantin*, 187 U.S. 378 (1932) (which held that the state of Texas' declaration of martial law to control oil and gas producers was unwarranted). It is interesting to note that when martial law has been declared to control labor organizing, the courts upheld the imposition of martial law. When a state declared martial law to control the oil companies—the largest economic interests in the state—the Court overturned the imposition of martial law.

206. *DeJonge v. Oregon*, 299 U.S. 353 (1937).
207. *United States ex rel. Weinberg v. Scholtfeldt*, 26 F. Supp. 283 (N.D. Ill., 1938). ("Under conditions as they now exist, it would be cruel and inhuman punishment to deport this petitioner to Czechoslovakia.")

Notes to Chapter V

1. Perret, *Days of Sadness, Years of Triumph*, pp. 357-358, as quoted in Goldstein, *Political Repression in Modern America*, p. 284.
2. Goldstein, *Political Repression in Modern America*, p. 284.
3. Gottschalk, " 'Consistent with Security'...A History of American Military Press Censorship," 5 *Communications & Law* at 39.
4. "Censorship of the News: Effect on Press and Reader," *U.S. News*, Feb. 6, 1942, as reprinted in Summers, *Wartime Censorship*.
5. "Censor's Office Works Smoothly on War News," *Editor & Publisher*, 75:9, Feb. 21, 1942, as reprinted in Summers, *Wartime Censorship*, p. 134.
6. Note, "The First Amendment and National Security," 17 *NYU Journal of International Law and Policy* at 377.
7. Nothing was allowed to be reported during an air raid, except "the fact that a raid has begun." "After the raid a general description [of the raid could be published] provided such accounts do not (1) play up horror or sensationalism; [or] (2) deal with or refer to unconfirmed versions or reports [of the raid]."
8. 7 Fed. Reg. 1499-1501 (Feb. 20, 1942).
9. The Assistant Director of Censorship rejected broadcasters' proposals for 'open-mike' interviews on a rigidly controlled basis, stating, "There is too much at stake both for the country and for the broadcasting industry to run even the slightest risk." J. Harold Ryan, Assistant Director of the Office of Censorship, as reprinted in Summers, *Wartime Censorship*, p. 145.
10. "Censors Clip LA Times at Post Office," *Editor and Publisher*, 75:6, Feb. 21, 1942, as reprinted in Summers, *Wartime Censorship*, pp. 184-185.
11. "Censorship Bans News of Race Riot," *Broadcasting*, 22:48, Apr. 13, 1942, as reprinted in Summers, *Wartime Censorship*, p. 185.
12. Editorial, *Editor and Publisher*, 75:18, Apr. 4, 1942, as reprinted in Summers, *Wartime Censorship*, p. 185.
13. Summers, *Wartime Censorship*, p. 164.
14. Goldstein, *Political Repression in Modern America*, p. 268.
15. "United States Steel Issues First 'Censored' Annual Report," *Advertising Age*, 13:25, Mar. 23, 1942, as reprinted in Summers, *Wartime Censorship*, p. 149.
16. Gottschalk, " 'Consistent with Security'...A History of American Military Press Censorship," 5 *Communications and Law* at 40.
17. *Ibid.* at 42-43.
18. See supra, p. 47.
19. *United States v. Krepper*, 159 F.2d 958 (3d Cir. 1946), *cert denied*, 330 U.S. 824 (1947).
20. Note, "The First Amendment and National Security," 17 *NYU Journal of International Law and Policy* at 379.

21. Robert C. Miller, writing in the *Nieman Reports*, as quoted by Gottschalk, " 'Consistent with Security'...A History of American Military Press Censorship," 5 *Communications and Law* at 47.
22. 52 Stat. 631 (1938).
23. See supra, pp. 43-47.
24. See, "Note: Government Exclusion of Foreign Political Propaganda," 68 *Harvard Law Review* 1393 (1955).
25. 381 U.S. 301 (1965).
26. See infra, pp. 107-111.
27. Margaret Truman, ed., *Where the Buck Stops: The Personal and Private Writings of Harry S. Truman*, as reprinted in "He Didn't Like Ike," *New York Times Magazine*, Sept. 17, 1989, p. 52.
28. See, Gottschalk, " 'Consistent with Security'...A History of American Military Press Censorship," 5 *Communications and Law* at 47.
29. Chafee, *Free Speech in the United States*, p. 441.
30. See supra, pp. 65-66.
31. Chafee, *Free Speech in the United States*, p. 442, fn. 3.
32. *Civil Liberties and National Defense*, 1941, p. 13.
33. *In the Shadow of War: The Story of Civil Liberty, 1939-1940*, p. 13.
34. *Ibid.*; see also, Biddle, *Civil Liberties and the War*, pp. 8-9.
35. Chafee, *Free Speech in the United States*, p. 444.
36. *Dunne v. United States*, 138 F.2d 137 (8th Cir., 1943), *cert denied*, 320 U.S. 790 (1943).
37. 138 F 2d, at 140.
38. 138 F 2d, at 141. ("An armed force which lacks loyalty, morale or discipline...is far worse than no armed force at all and is positively an active menace to constitutional government and to the liberties of the people. Therefore, the question here is whether...this Act goes so far beyond what is necessary or proper to effectuate its obviously necessary and proper purpose as to infringe upon protected individual rights.")
39. 341 U.S. 494 (1951).
40. Cf. *United States v. Carroll Towing Co.*, 159 F. 2d 169 (2d Cir., 1947). ("If the probability be called P; the injury, L; and the burden, B, liability depends upon whether...B [is less than] PL.")
41. 341 U.S. at 510.
42. Chafee, *The Blessings of Liberty*, p. 85.
43. *Nebraska Press Association v. Stuart*, 427 U.S. 539, 562 (1976).
44. *Digest of the Public Record of Communism in the United States*, pp. 194-205. *See also*, Belknap, *Cold War Political Justice*, pp. 152-176.
45. Belknap, *Cold War Political Justice*, p. 159.
46. As quoted in Belknap, *Cold War Political Justice*, p. 159.
47. *Yates v. United States*, 354 U.S. 298 (1957) (upholding the Smith Act, but distinguishing the advocacy of an abstract doctrine of revolution from a call to action; but cf. Black's dissent, "the statutory provisions on which these prosecutions are based abridge freedom of speech, press, and assembly in violation of the First Amendment").
48. *Scales v. United States*, 367 U.S. 203 (1961) (reaffirming *Dennis* that such advocacy is not protected speech, but upholding Smith Act prosecutions only "when

the statute is found to reach only 'active' members having also a guilty knowledge and intent").

49. Tom Clark, "Civil Rights: The Boundless Responsibility of Lawyers," 32 *American Bar Association Journal* 453 (1946), as quoted in Kutler, *The American Inquisition,* p. 154.

50. Tom Clark, "Why the Reds Won't Scare Us Any More," *Look,* August 30, 1949, p. 50.

51. The ABA resolution stated, in part:

> "Resolved... 1. That it is not inappropriate, with world conditions as they are, that any American citizen be required to attest to his loyalty to our form of government by anti-communist oath, and that it is especially appropriate that all licensed to practice law in the United States of America be required to do so;
>
> "2....each member of the Bar [be required] within a reasonable time and periodically thereafter, to file an affidavit stating whether he is or ever has been a member of the Communist Party or affiliated therewith...and in the event such affidavit reveals that he is or ever has been a member of said Communist Party...that the appropriate authority promptly and thoroughly investigate the activities and conduct of such member of the Bar to determine his fitness for continuance as an attorney."

52. Chafee, *The Blessings of Liberty,* pp. 157-159.

53. See Kutler, *The American Inquisition,* pp. 152-182.

54. *Sacher et al. v. United States,* 343 U.S. 1 (1952).

55. Kutler, *The American Inquisition,* p. 164.

56. *Association of the Bar of the City of New York v. Sacher,* 347 U.S. 388 (1954) (overturning disbarment of Sacher); *Isserman v. Ethics Committee of the Essex County Bar Association,* 345 U.S. 927 (1953) (upholding disbarment of Isserman); *In re Isserman,* 348 U.S. 1 (1954) (overturning disbarment of Isserman).

57. See *Digest of the Public Record of Communism in the United States,* pp. 420-426.

58. As quoted in Chafee, *The Blessings of Liberty,* p. 137.

59. Constitution of the United States, Art. I, Sec. 9, Cl. 2.

60. The Emergency Detention Act of 1950, 64 Stat. 1019, Sec. 103 (a).

61. One of these concentration camps, Tule Lake, had been used to intern Japanese-Americans during World War II. See infra, p. 97.

62. Chafee, "Investigations of Radicalism and Laws Against Subversion," in Wilcox, ed., *Civil Liberties Under Attack,* p. 70.

63. *Knauf v. Shaughnessy,* 338 U.S. 537 (1950) ("Whatever the procedure authorized by Congress is, it is due process as far as an alien denied entry is concerned.")

64. *Shaughnessy v. United States ex rel. Mezei,* 345 U.S. 206 (1953).

65. Caute, *The Great Fear,* p. 229.

66. Attorney General Tom Clark, in an address to the Cathedral Club of Brooklyn, January 13, 1948, as quoted in Caute, *The Great Fear,* p. 233.

67. U.S. Code Sec. 786(d)(6), amending Sec. 7(d) of McCarran Act, as quoted in Chafee, *The Blessings of Liberty,* p. 139.

68. 53 Stat. 1147 (1939).

69. Kittrie and Wedlock, *The Tree of Liberty,* p. 355.

70. *Ibid.,* p. 397.

71. An Act to Amend the National Labor Relations Act, 61 Stat. 136 (1947).

72. Taft-Hartley Act, Section 9(h).

73. 68 Stat. 775 (Aug. 24, 1954).

74. 68 Stat. 1146 (Sept. 3, 1954).

75. Between 1945 and 1953, 47,011 people were expatriated for violations of various penal laws. No one was expatriated for treason or conspiracy to overthrow the government. See "The Expatriation Act of 1954," 64 *Yale Law Journal* 1164, 1165 fn. 9 (1955).

76. *Ibid.* at 1169.

77. See, *Afroyim v. Rusk,* 381 U.S. 253 (1967).

78. The Labor Management Reporting and Disclosure Act, 73 Stat. 519 (1959), Sec. 504(a).

79. Churchill and Vander Wall, *Agents of Repression,* p. 36.

80. 42 U.S.C. Sec. 2000(e)-2000(e)(17).

81. Title VII, Sec. 703(f): *Members of Communist Party or Communist-Action or Communist-Front Organizations.*

As used in this subchapter, the phrase "unlawful employment practice" shall not be deemed to include any action or measure taken by an employer, labor organization, joint labor-management committee, or employment agency with respect to an individual who is a member of the Communist Party of the United States or of any other organization required to register as a Communist-action or Communist-front organization by final order of the Subversive Activities Control Board pursuant to the Subversive Activities Control Act of 1950.

82. Exec. Order No. 9835 (March 25, 1947).

83. Kittrie and Wedlock, *The Tree of Liberty,* p. 445

84. Chafee, "Statement in Opposition to a Bill...Entitled 'To Protect the U.S. against Un-American and Subversive Activities, 1950,' " p. 46.

85. Goldstein, *Political Repression in Modern America,* p. 303; Rogin, *Ronald Reagan, The Movie,* p. 70.

86. Goldstein, *Political Repression in Modern America,* pp. 302-303.

87. Adam Yarmolinsky, "Shades of McCarthyism," *New York Times,* Mar. 5, 1989, p. E23.

88. *Bailey v. Richardson,* 182 F.2d 46 (D.C. Cir., 1950) (Edgerton, J., dissenting), *aff'd by an equally divided Court,* 341 U.S. 918 (1951).

89. *Bailey v. Richardson,* 341 U.S. 918 (1951).

90. Alan Barth, *Loyalty,* p. 135, as quoted in Goldstein, *Political Repression in Modern America,* p. 304.

91. "An Act to Protect the National Security of the United States," 64 Stat. 476 (1950).

92. Exec. Order No. 10450 (Apr. 27, 1953).

93. Kittrie and Wedlock, *The Tree of Liberty*, p. 423.

94. See e.g., *Cole v. Richardson*, 405 U.S. 676 (1972) (upholding the constitutionality of an oath to uphold and defend the Constitution of the United
States).

95. "New Laws Take Effect Around U.S.," *New York Times*, Jun. 30, 1987, p.
A24.

96. As quoted in Donner, *The Un-Americans*, cover.

97. *Ibid.*, pp. 295-296.

98. *Ibid.*, p. i.

99. *Ibid.*, p. 9.

100. Caute, *The Great Fear*, p. 96.

101. *Ibid.*, pp. 96-97.

102. As quoted in Donner, *The Un-Americans*, p. 21.

103. *Ibid.*, p. 35.

104. As quoted in *ibid.*, p. 30.

105. Letter from Lillian Hellman to Rep. John S. Wood, chair of HUAC, May
19, 1952, as quoted in Hellman, *Scoundrel Time*, p. 93.

106. As quoted in Donner, *The Un-Americans*, p. 41.

107. Donner, *The Un-Americans*, pp. 142-143.

108. *Ibid.*, pp. 145-146.

109. Goldstein, *Political Repression in Modern America*, p. 347.

110. *Ibid.*

111. Donner, *The Un-Americans*, p. 113.

112. As quoted in Caute, *The Great Fear*, p. 97.

113. To give an idea of the effect of the blacklist, the following lists the number
of credits in U.S. films of the Hollywood Ten, both before and after the HUAC
hearings:

Alvah Bessie	5 credits, 1943-1948;	then none
Herbert Biberman	7 credits, 1935-1947;	then none until 1968
Lester Cole	36 credits, 1932-1948;	then none until 1970
Ring Lardner, Jr.	10 credits, 1939-1948;	then none until 1965
John Howard Lawson	16 credits, 1929-1947;	then none
Albert Maltz	7 credits, 1932-1948;	then none until 1969
Samuel Ornitz	26 credits, 1929-1945;	then none
Adrian Scott	11 credits, 1940-1947;	then none
Dalton Trumbo	27 credits, 1936-1945;	then none until 1959

See Caute, *The Great Fear*, pp. 557-60.

114. It is perhaps ironic that Ring Lardner, Jr. was sentenced to prison in
Danbury, Connecticut where he ran across former HUAC Chairman J. Parnell
Thomas who had been sentenced to prison for defrauding the government.

115. Caute, *The Great Fear*, pp. 491-498, 515.

116. *Ibid.*, p. 530.

117. As quoted in *ibid.*, p. 528.

118. Goldstein, *Political Repression in Modern America*, p. 361.

119. *Ibid.*

120. *Ibid.*, p. 362.

121. Donner, *The Un-Americans*, p. 98.

122. *Ibid.*, pp. 264-265.

123. Executive Order 10935 (Apr. 25, 1961), as quoted in Donner, *The Un-Americans,* p. 271.

124. Caute, *The Great Fear,* p. 104.

125. Condemnation was a less severe sanction than the censure that had been recommended by the Watkins Committee which had examined McCarthy's record.

126. Caute, *The Great Fear,* pp. 106-108.

127. *Duncan v. Kahanamoku* 327 U.S. 304 (1946).

128. *Ibid.*

129. 327 U.S. 304 (1946) (imposition of martial law, "while intended to authorize the military to act vigorously for the maintenance of an orderly civil government and for the defense of the island against actual or threatened rebellion or invasion", was not intended to authorize the supplanting of courts by military tribunals").

130. 55 Stat. 1700 (1941).

131. Kittrie and Wedlock, *The Tree of Liberty,* p. 357. These detentions should be distinguished from the subsequent evacuation and internment of Japanese-Americans which provided for no individual determination of loyalty.

132. President Roosevelt's Executive Order 9066, 3 C.F.R. 1092 (Feb. 19, 1942).

133. Constitution of the United States, Art. I, Sec. 9, and Art. III, Sec. 2.

134. *Korematsu v. United States.,* 323 U.S. 214, 243 (1944) (Jackson, J.).

135. Statement of Senator Spark Matsunaga, Hearing before the Sen. Comm. on Governmental Affairs on S.1647, 96th Cong. 2d Sess (Mar. 18, 1980).

136. Drinnon, *Keeper of Concentration Camps,* p. 4.

137. tenBroek, *et al., Prejudice, War and the Constitution,* p. 124.

138. Goldstein, *Political Repression in Modern America,* pp. 267-268.

139. Drinnon, *Keeper of Concentration Camps,* p. 43.

140. *Ibid.,* pp. 142-143.

141. *Ibid.,* p. 145.

142. *Ibid.,* p. 53.

143. Rostow, "The Japanese-American Cases—A Disaster," 54 *Yale Law Journal* 489, 501.

144. *Ibid.,* at fn. 2.

145. Josh Getlin, "Funds for WWII Internees Caught in Budget Squeeze," *Los Angeles Times,* May 7, 1989, p. 1.

146. 56 Stat. 173 (1942).

147. 320 U.S. 81 (1943).

148. George Hirabayashi, "On the Brink of Justice: The Continuing Battle over the Wartime Internment of Japanese Americans," speech at Harvard Law School, Dec. 8, 1987.

149. 320 U.S. 81 at 100-101.

150. 323 U.S. 213 (1944).

151. 323 U.S. at 216.

152. 323 U.S. 283 (1944).

153. Chief Justice Warren later commented:

[Hirabayashi and Korematsu] demonstrate dramatically that there are some circumstances in which the Court will, in effect, conclude that it is simply not in a position to reject descriptions by the Executive of the degree of military necessity...In such a situation, where time is of the essence, if the Court is to deny the asserted right of the military authorities, it must be on the theory that the claimed justification, though factually unassailable, is insufficient. [S]uch cases would be extraordinary indeed. [To] put it another way, the fact that the Court rules in a case like Hirabayashi that a given program is constitutional does not necessarily answer the question whether, in a broader sense, it actually is." Warren, C.J., *The Bill of Rights and the Military*, 37 *NYU Law Review* 181, 192-93 (1962), as quoted in Lockhart, *et al.*, *Constitutional Law*, p. 1153, fn. b.

154. See, *Hirabayashi v. United States of America* 828 F.2d 591 (9th Cir., 1987); see also *Korematsu v. United States*, 584 F.Supp. 1406 (N.D. Cal. 1984).

155. *Korematsu v. United States*, 323 U.S. 214, 241 (Justice Murphy, dissenting).

156. See Rostow, "The Japanese American Cases—A Disaster," 54 *Yale Law Journal* 489, 521.

157. As quoted in Drinnon, *Keeper of Concentration Camps*, p. 31.

158. *Ibid.*, p. 32.

159. Irons, *Justice at War*, p. 353.

160. Commission on Wartime Relocation, *Personal Justice Denied*, p. 18, as quoted in Irons, *Justice at War*, p. 362.

161. See, e.g., "Internee Payment Bill Gets Final OK," *Los Angeles Times*, Aug. 5, 1988, p. 1.

162. See, e.g., National Public Radio, "Morning Edition," August 5, 1988.

163. See, "Internee Payment Bill Gets Final OK," *Los Angeles Times*, Aug. 5, 1988, p. 1.

164. *Cramer v. United States* 325 U.S. 1 (1945).

165. *New York Herald Tribune*, February 14, 1946.

166. See Christenson, *Political Trials*, pp. 86-87, for the view that these insanity hearings were used to protect Ezra Pound.

167. see supra, pp. 43-47.

168. *Hartzel v. United States*, 322 U.S. 680 (1944).

169. Goldstein, *Political Repression in Modern America*, p. 268.

170. *United States v. Pelley*, 132 F.2d 170 (1942), *cert denied* 318 U.S. 764 (1942); *United States v. Bell*, 438 F.Supp. 986 (D.C.S.D. Calif., 1943), 159 F.2d 247 (9th Cir., 1946); *Fiedler v. Shuttleworth*, 57 F.Supp. 591 (D.C.W.D. Pa. 1944); *United States v. Gordon*, 138 F.2d 174 (7th Cir., 1943); *Butler v. United States*, 138 F.2d 977 (7th Cir., 1943); *Couchois v. United States*, 142 F.2d 1 (5th Cir., 1944); *United States v. Guido*, 161 F.2d 492 (3rd Cir., 1947).

171. Kutler, *The American Inquisition*, pp. 215-246.

172. *United States v. Powell*, 156 F.Supp. 526 (1957); *United States v. Powell et al.* 171 F.Supp. 202 (1959).

173. Volkman and Baggett, *Secret Intelligence: The Inside Story of America's Espionage Empire*, p. 32.

174. *Ibid.*, p. 75.

228   FREEDOM UNDER FIRE

175. Churchill and Vander Wall, *Agents of Repression*, p. 29.
176. *Ibid.*, pp. 30-31.
177. Donner, *The Age of Surveillance*, pp. 144-5.
178. *Ibid.*, pp. 163-167.
179. See, Waltzer, Kenneth, "The FBI, Congressman Vito Marcantonio, and the American Labor Party," in Theoharis, ed., *Beyond the Hiss Case*, pp. 176-214.
180. Theoharis, ed., *Beyond the Hiss Case*, p. 7.
181. O'Reilly, *Hoover and the Un-Americans*, p. 232 [footnotes omitted].
182. As quoted in Volkman and Baggett, *Secret Intelligence: The Inside Story of America's Espionage Empire*, p. 93.
183. Demac, *Liberty Denied*, p. 79; Mitgang, *Dangerous Dossiers: Exposing the Secret War Against America's Greatest Authors*, pp. 31-33.
184. Volkman and Baggett, *Secret Intelligence: The Inside Story of America's Espionage Empire*, p. xvii.
185. *Ibid.*, p. 33.
186. Mitgang, *Dangerous Dossiers: Exposing the Secret War Against America's Greatest Authors;* see also, Volkman and Baggett, *Secret Intelligence: The Inside Story of America's Espionage Empire*, p. 34; Demac, *Liberty Denied*, p. 75.
187. Churchill and Vander Wall, *Agents of Repression*, p. 36.
188. Volkman and Baggett, *Secret Intelligence: The Inside Story of America's Espionage Empire*, p. 93.
189. See Bailey, "The Case of the National Lawyers Guild, 1939-1958," in Theoharis, ed., *Beyond the Hiss Case*, pp. 129-175.
190. Diamond, "The Arrangement: The FBI and Harvard University in the McCarthy Period," in Theoharis, ed., *Beyond the Hiss Case*, pp. 341-371.
191. O'Reilly, *Hoover and the Un-Americans*, p. 208.
192. Donner, *The Age of Surveillance*, p. 156.
193. See, *Youngstown Sheet and Tube Co. v. Sawyer*, 343 U.S. 579, 649, n. 17 (Jackson, J. concurring).
194. *Youngstown Sheet & Tube Co. v. Sawyer*, 343 U.S. 579, 621 (Frankfurter, J. concurring, Appendix II).
195. See, e.g., *United States v. Pewee Coal Co., Inc.* 341 U.S. 114 (1951).
196. The seizure was upheld in *United States v. Montgomery Ward & Co.*, 150 F.2d 369 (7th Cir., 1945).
197. See *Youngstown Sheet & Tube Co. v. Sawyer*, 343 U.S. 579, 622-6 (Frankfurter, J. concurring, Appendix II); also 343 U.S. at 694-699 (Vinson, J., dissenting).
198. *Youngstown Sheet & Tube Co. v. Sawyer*, 343 U.S. 579, 626-627 (Frankfurter, J. concurring, Appendix II).
199. *Youngstown Sheet & Tube Co. v. Sawyer*, 343 U.S. 579, 628 (Frankfurter, J. concurring, Appendix II).
200. *Youngstown Sheet & Tube Co. v. Sawyer*, 343 U.S. 579 (1952).
201. *Youngstown Sheet & Tube Co. v. Sawyer*, 343 U.S. at 588.
202. *Youngstown Sheet & Tube Co. v. Sawyer*, 343 U.S. at 597-598.
203. Irons, *Justice at War*, p. 348.
204. *Ibid.;* Girdner and Loftis, *The Great Betrayal*, p. 436.
205. Girdner and Loftis, *The Great Betrayal*, p. 436.
206. See, in general, Brief for Petitioner, *Haig v. Agee*, 453 U.S. 280 (1981).

207. Brief for Respondent, *Haig v. Agee,* 453 U.S. 280 (1981).

208. See Reply Brief for Respondent, *Haig v. Agee,* 453. U.S. 280 (1981), p. 4. ("The revocation of respondent's passport is consistent with two hundred years of unequivocal and unbroken administrative practice.")

209. Brief for Petitioner, *Haig v. Agee,* fn. 30.

210. Caute, *The Great Fear,* pp. 247-251, 507-508.

211. *Ibid.*

212. *Ibid.*

213. See, Brief of Petitioner, *Haig v. Agee,* p. 38; See also Caute, *The Great Fear,* pp. 247-251.

214. Judge William Clark, Third Circuit Court. See Brief for Petitioner, *Kent v. Dulles,* p. 44, 357 U.S. 116. He was finally granted a passport after suing the government. *Clark v. Dulles,* 129 F. Supp. 950 (1955).

215. See, e.g., Caute, *The Great Fear,* pp. 247-251; *see also* "Human Rights in Time of War," *Envio,* Vol. 5, No. 60.

216. Jaffe, "The Right to Travel: The Passport Problem," 35 *Foreign Affairs* 17, 26-27 (Oct. 1956).

217. *Kent v. Dulles,* 248 F.2d 600 (1957).

218. Letter to Rockwell Kent from Francis G. Knight, Director, Passport Office, June 29, 1955.

219. *Ibid.*. Also see Brief for Petitioner, *Kent v. Dulles,* 357 U.S. 116 (1958), pp. 7-8.

220. *Kent v. Dulles,* 357 U.S. 116 (1958).

221. 54 Stat. 1201 (1940).

222. As quoted in Caute, *The Great Fear,* pp. 251-261.

223. *Ibid.*

224. *Ibid.,* pp. 517-518.

225. *Ibid.*

226. Paul Hoffman, "The Man who Loves only Numbers," *Atlantic,* Nov. 1987, pp. 62-63.

227. Chafee, *Free Speech in the United States,* pp. 572-597.

228. *The States and Subversion,* pp. 3-4.

229. Ordinances 97018, 97019, 97020, as quoted in *Digest of the Public Record of Communism in the United States,* pp. 461-471.

230. Ordinance BB-465 (1950). As quoted in *Digest of the Public Record of Communism in the United States,* pp. 458-459.

231. See, *Digest of the Public Record of Communism in the United States,* pp. 459-460.

232. Ordinance 81315. As quoted in *Digest of the Public Record of Communism in the United States,* p. 487.

233. *Garner v. Los Angeles Board,* 341 U.S. 716 (1951).

234. The resolution stated in part, "No person whose commitments or obligations to any organization, Communist or other, prejudice impartial scholarship and the free pursuit of truth will be employed by the University. Proved members of the Communist Party, by reason of such commitments to that party, are not acceptable as members of the faculty." Resolution of the Northern Section of the Academic Senate, University of California, approved 724-203, Mar. 7, 1950 (as

quoted in Baxter, "Freedom in Education," in Wilcox, *Civil Liberties Under Attack*, p. 141).

235. *Ibid.*, p. 143.

236. *Adler v. Board of Education*, 342 U.S. 485 (1952) ("[F]rom time immemorial, one's reputation has been determined in part by the company he keeps...we know of no rule...that prevents the state...from considering the organizations and persons with whom [teachers] associate;") but cf. *Wieman v. Updegraff*, 344 U.S. 183 (1952) (person must be aware of the "activities and purposes" of the proscribed organization; unknowing membership is not enough for dismissal).

237. *Slochower v. Board of Higher Education*, 350 U.S. 561 (1956) ("summary dismissal [of city employee who invokes Fifth Amendment] violates due process of law").

238. *Beilan v. Board of Public Education*, 357 U.S. 399 (1958) ("refusal to answer the employing board's relevant questions [is merely] statutory 'incompetency'").

239. *Nelson v. Los Angeles*, 362 U.S. 1 (1960).

240. Nelson, "Censors and Their Tactics," in Lyons, *Reporting the News*, pp. 366-375.

241. The Supreme Court dealt with the exclusion from the bar based on a person's political beliefs on at least three occasions. *In re Summers*, 325 U.S. 561 (1945) upheld the denial for admission to the Illinois Bar to a conscientious objector; *Schware v. Board of Bar Examiners*, 353 U.S. 237 (1957) overturned on due process grounds New Mexico's denial of entrance to the bar based on past Communist Party membership; *Konigsberg v. State Bar of California (II)*, 366 U.S. 36 (1961) upheld a California bar regulation asking questions about political affiliations.

242. Georgia Code Anno. Sec. 32-1022.

243. See generally, U.S. Senate Committee on the Judiciary, *Internal Security and Subversion: Principal State Laws and Cases*, Appendix A, Tables 1-36, pp. 439-451.

244. Code of Alabama, Title 52, Sec 433 (6a), as quoted in U.S. Senate Committee on the Judiciary, *Internal Security and Subversion*, p. 8.

245. New York Educ. Law Sec. 704, as quoted in U.S. Senate Committee on the Judiciary, *Internal Security and Subversion*, p. 309.

246. Illinois S.H. Anno., ch 67 1/2, Sec. 25, as quoted in U.S. Senate Committee on the Judiciary, *Internal Security and Subversion*, p. 139.

247. Michigan Stat. Anno. Sec. 4.448(1), as quoted in U.S. Senate Committee on the Judiciary, *Internal Security and Subversion*, p. 223.

248. California Constitution, Art 20, Sec. 19; West's Anno. Tax & Rev. Code Sec. 32 as quoted in U.S. Senate Committee on the Judiciary, *Internal Security and Subversion*, pp. 57-58. But note, *Speiser v. Randall*, 357 U.S. 513 (1958) held that it was unconstitutional to require the individual to prove that he or she did not advocate subversion ("When the constitutional right to speak is sought to be deterred by a State's general taxing program due process demands that the speech be unencumbered until the State comes forward with sufficient proof to justify its inhibition"). See also *First Unitarian Church v. Los Angeles* 357 U.S. 545 (1958).

249. New Jersey Stat. Anno. Sec. 26:8-40.5 as quoted in U.S. Senate Committee on the Judiciary, *Internal Security and Subversion*, p. 292.

250. Ohio Rev. Code Sec. 4123.037 (Supp. 1963) as quoted in U.S. Senate Committee on the Judiciary, *Internal Security and Subversion*, p. 325.

251. Ohio Rev. Code Sec. 4141.28(A) (Supp. 1963) as quoted in U.S. Senate Committee on the Judiciary, *Internal Security and Subversion*, p. 325.

252. Pennsylvania Stat. Sec 2509 (Supp. 1963) as quoted in U.S. Senate Committee on the Judiciary, *Internal Security and Subversion*, p. 365.

253. New York Judiciary Law, Sec. 655-a (Supp. 1963) as quoted in U.S. Senate Committee on the Judiciary, *Internal Security and Subversion*, p. 310.

254. Texas Anno Civ. Stat. Art. 4542a Sec. 9, as quoted in U.S. Senate Committee on the Judiciary, *Internal Security and Subversion*, p. 403.

255. North Carolina Gen. Stat. Sec. 116-199 (Supp. 1963) as quoted in U.S. Senate Committee on the Judiciary, *Internal Security and Subversion*, p. 313.

256. South Carolina Code of Laws, 1962 Sec. 21-420 as quoted in U.S. Senate Committee on the Judiciary, *Internal Security and Subversion*, p. 373.

257. *Baggett v. Bullitt*, 377 U.S. 360, 379-80 (1964).

258. *Baggett v. Bullitt*, 377 U.S. 360 (1964).

259. *Elfbrandt v. Russell*, 384 U.S. 11 (1966).

260. *Keyishian v. Board of Regents*, 385 U.S. 589 (1967).

261. *Communist Party of the United States v. United States*, 384 F.2d 957 (D.C. Cir., 1967). Regarding the registration of individual members of the Communist Party, the Supreme Court held in 1961 that such registration did not violate the First Amendment, *Communist Party of the United States v. Subversive Activities Control Board*, 367 U.S. 1 (1961). Four years later, the Court ruled that such registration violated the Fifth Amendment. *Albertson v. Subversive Activities Control Board*, 382 U.S. 70 (1965).

262. *United States v. Robel*, 389 U.S. 258 (1967).

Notes to Chapter VI

1. President Johnson Address to Demonstrators at the White House, August 3, 1965, reprinted in Kittrie and Wedlock, *Tree of Liberty*, p. 495.

2. *Mapp v. Ohio*, 367 U.S. 643 (1961).

3. *Malloy v. Hogan*, 378 U.S. 1 (1964).

4. *Benton v. Maryland*, 395 U.S. 784 (1969).

5. *Klopfer v. North Carolina*, 386 U.S. 213 (1967).

6. *Duncan v. Louisiana*, 391 U.S. 145 (1968).

7. *Gideon v. Wainwright*, 372 U.S. 335 (1963).

8. *Pointer v. Texas*, 380 U.S. 400 (1965).

9. *Washington v. Texas*, 388 U.S. 14 (1967).

10. *Robinson v. California*, 370 U.S. 660 (1962).

11. *Amnesty International Annual Report: 1975-1976*, p. 11.

12. Caute, David, *The Year of the Barricades: A Journey through 1968*, pp. 127, 130.

13. *Ibid.*, p. 129.

14. du Plessix Gray, "The Ultra Resistance," reprinted in Noam Chomsky, *et al.*, *Trials of the Resistance*, p. 125.

15. Among the more prominent were:

- The Baltimore Four: 600 draft cards destroyed with blood;
- The Catonsville Nine: 378 draft cards destroyed by napalm while the defendants prayed;
- The Boston Two: several hundred draft cards destroyed with black paint;
- The Milwaukee Fourteen: 10,000 draft cards destroyed with napalm;
- The Pasadena Three: 300 draft cards burned;
- The Silver Spring Three: several hundred records splattered with black paint and blood;
- The Chicago Fifteen: 40,000 draft cards burned;
- The New York Eight: 75,000 draft records mutilated;
- The Beaver Fifty-Five: the records of forty-four draft boards shredded;
- The Boston Eight: files of eight draft boards destroyed;
- Women Against Daddy Warbucks: several thousand draft records mutilated by an all-female contingent of protestors.

16. Houston, "Johnson Dines with Friends Here as Police Curb Protest," *Los Angeles Times*, Jun. 24, 1967, p. 1.

17. Halsted, *Out Now,* pp. 308-309.

18. Trimborn, "Los Angeles Counts Up Profits and Losses of President's Visit," *Los Angeles Times,* Jun. 25, 1967, p. 1.

19. Hayden, *Reunion,* p. 299.

20. *Ibid.,* p. 382.

21. Caute, *The Year of the Barricades: A Journey Through 1968,* p. 316.

22. Peck, *Uncovering the Sixties: The Life and Times of the Underground Press,* pp. 115-116.

23. Hayden, *Reunion,* p. 322.

24. As quoted in Caute, *The Year of the Barricades: A Journey Through 1968,* p. 320

25. *Ibid.,* p. 322; Hayden, *Reunion,* p. 320.

26. Caute, *The Year of the Barricades: A Journey Through 1968,* pp. 322-323.

27. As quoted in Hayden, *Reunion,* p. 393.

28. *Ibid.,* p. 369.

29. Peck, *Uncovering the Sixties: The Life and Times of the Underground Press,* p. 196.

30. See, in general, Hayden, *Reunion,* pp. 327-413; Peck, *Uncovering the Sixties: The Life and Times of the Underground Press,* pp. 192-194.

31. Peck, *Uncovering the Sixties: The Life and Times of the Underground Press,* p. 194.

32. Hayden, *Reunion,* p. 417.

33. Goldstein, *Political Repression in Modern America,* p. 430.

34. Peck, *Uncovering the Sixties: The Life and Times of the Underground Press,* p. 236.

35. Halsted, *Out Now,* pp. 538-546.

36. *Ibid.*, p. 581.
37. Peck, *Uncovering the Sixties: The Life and Times of the Underground Press*, p. 239.
38. *Ibid.*, p. 240.
39. James T. Wooten, "Activism Arrives at U. of Alabama," *New York Times*, May 24, 1970, p. 52.
40. Halsted, *Out Now*, pp. 557-558.
41. Caute, David, *The Year of the Barricades: A Journey Through 1968*, p. 418.
42. As quoted in Goldstein, *Political Repression in Modern America*, p. 513.
43. Halsted, *Out Now*, pp. 618-620.
44. As quoted in Halsted, *Out Now*, p. 621.
45. *Ibid.*, p. 623
46. See Hayden, *Reunion*, p. 505.
47. See *e.g.*, Bell, *Race, Racism and American Law*, p. 300, fn. 1, citing *Ware v. Nichols*, 266 F. Supp 564 (N.D. Miss. 1967) (criminal syndicalism), *People v. Epton*, 281 N.Y.S.2d 9, 227 N.E. 2d 829 (1967) (criminal anarchy), *State v. Cade*, 153 So. 2d 382 (1963) (insurrection).
48. Garrow, *The FBI and Martin Luther King, Jr.*, p. 115.
49. Volkman and Baggett, *Secret Intelligence: The Inside Story of America's Espionage Empire*, p. 164.
50. Churchill and Vander Wall, *Agents of Repression*, pp. 54-57; Donner, *The Age of Surveillance*, p. 216.
51. Caute, *The Year of the Barricades: A Journey Through 1968*, p. 146.
52. Peck, *Uncovering the Sixties: The Life and Times of the Underground Press*, p. 64.
53. Caute, *The Year of the Barricades: A Journey Through 1968*, p. 145.
54. *Time Magazine*, Jan. 11, 1988, p. 23. See also, Halsted, *Out Now*, p. 386.
55. Hayden, *Reunion*, p. 269; see supra, pp. 117-119.
56. Peck, *Uncovering the Sixties: The Life and Times of the Underground Press*, p. 150.
57. Testimony of Major General Winston P. Wilson, Chief, National Guard Bureau, before the President's Commission on Campus Unrest, as quoted in *The National Guard and the Constitution: An ACLU Legal Study*, p. 1.
58. Prior to the 1964 riots, general curfews had been imposed only twice. See *The National Guard and the Constitution: An ACLU Legal Study*, p. 56.
59. Although it did uphold a curfew against Japanese-Americans during World War II, *Hirabayashi v. United States*, 320 U.S. 81 (1943); see supra, p. 95.
60. See *The National Guard and the Constitution: An ACLU Legal Study*, pp. 61-64.
61. *Commonwealth v. Stotland*, 251 A. 2d 701 (1969); see *The National Guard and the Constitution: An ACLU Legal Study*, pp. 70-71.
62. As quoted in Churchill and Vander Wall, *Agents of Repression*, p. 58.
63. Donner, *The Age of Surveillance*, pp. 221-227.
64. See infra, pp. 134-139.
65. Rips, *The Campaign Against the Underground Press*, p. 125.
66. Churchill and Vander Wall, *Agents of Repression*, p. 42.
67. *Ibid.*, p. 65.

68. *Ibid.,* pp. 67-68.
69. As quoted in Goldstein, *Political Repression in Modern America,* p. 528.
70. As quoted in Hayden, *Reunion,* p. 380.
71. Churchill and Vander Wall, *Agents of Repression,* pp. 69-77.
72. Donner, *The Age of Surveillance,* p. 231.
73. Goodell, *Political Prisoners in America,* p. 114.
74. Goldstein, *Political Repression in Modern America,* p. 527.
75. Goodell, *Political Prisoners in America,* pp. 114-115; Christenson, *Political Trials,* p. 185.
76. Kiener, "Ex-Black Panther in Prison Cites Concealed Evidence," *New York Times,* April 3, 1989, p. B1.
77. Caute, *The Year of the Barricades: A Journey Through 1968,* p. 159.
78. As quoted in Christenson, *Political Trials,* p. 189.
79. As quoted in Rips, *The Campaign Against the Underground Press,* pp. 64-66.
80. As quoted in Churchill and Vander Wall, *Agents of Repression,* pp. 44-47.
81. Donner, *The Age of Surveillance,* p. 237.
82. See, e.g., Johansson and Maestas, *Wasi'chu, the Continuing Indian Wars.*
83. See, Churchill and Vander Wall, *Agents of Repression;* Glick, *War at Home: Covert Action Against U.S. Activists and What We Can Do About It;* Katsiaficas, *Imagination of the New Left:A Global Analysis of 1968;* and Muñoz, *Youth, Identity, Power: The Chicano Movement.*
84. *Amnesty International Annual Report: 1966-1967.*
85. *Amnesty International Annual Report: 1966-1967* through 1979.
86. *Amnesty International Annual Report: 1975-1976,* p. 111.
87. *Ibid.,* p. 112.
88. *Amnesty International Annual Report: 1977,* p. 162.
89. *Amnesty International Annual Report: 1979,* p. 74.
90. 39 Opp. Attorney General 348 (1939).
91. 40 Stat. 415, Sec. 5 (b) (1917).
92. 41 Stat. 1072, Sec. 16 (1920).
93. 40 Stat. 531 (1918).
94. 40 Stat. 219, Sec. 6 (1917).
95. 62 Stat. 736-38 (1948).
96. 62 Stat. 794 (a).
97. 62 Stat. 794 (b).
98. Proc. No. 2914, 15 Fed. Reg. 9029 (1950).
99. President Truman relied, in part, on the state of emergency to justify his seizure of the steel mills in face of a potential strike by steelworkers. The Supreme Court rejected this exercise of executive power as unconstitutional. *Youngstown Sheet and Tube v. Sawyer,* 343 U.S. 479 (1952).
100. In both *United States v. Achtenberg,* 459 F.2d 91 (8th Cir., 1972) *cert denied* 409 U.S. 932 (1972), and *United States v. Eisenberg,* 469 F.2d 156 (8th Cir., (1972), the state of emergency was used to justify a prosecution for the destruction of war premises, *i.e.,* a campus ROTC building, during times of national emergency. See also, *Sardino v. Federal Reserve Bank of New York,* 361 F.2d 106 (2nd Cir., 1966).
101. 67 Stat. 133 (1953).

102. As quoted in Shattuck, "The Constitution in Crisis: Covert Action and the National Security Act of 1974," p. 6. Comparing the Canadian and U.S. approaches to national security emergencies, the Canadian Attorney General, John Turner, commented, "...it is a credit to the civil liberties of a country that it has to invoke extraordinary powers to cope with a real emergency. Some countries have these powers at their disposal all the time." *Ibid.*

103. "Interim Report by the Special Committee on National Emergencies and Delegated Emergency Powers," Senate Report No. 93-1170, Sept. 24, 1974, p. 1.

104. *Ibid.*

105. *Ibid.*, p. 2.

106. 90 Stat. 1255 (September 14, 1976).

107. Volkman and Baggett, *Secret Intelligence: The Inside Story of America's Espionage Empire*, p. 165.

108. *Laird v. Tatum*, 408 U.S. 1, 26-27 (1972) (Douglas, J., dissent).

109. Halperin, *The Lawless State*, p. 165.

110. *Ibid.*, p. 166.

111. *Ibid.*, p. 155.

112. *Laird v. Tatum*, 408 U.S. 1, 15 (1972).

113. 408 U.S. at 28.

114. Volkman and Baggett, *Secret Intelligence: The Inside Story of America's Espionage Empire*, pp. 180-181.

115. *Ibid.*, p. 183; Halperin, *The Lawless State*, pp. 175-177.

116. Halperin, *The Lawless State*, p. 175.

117. *Halkin v. Helms*, 598 F.2d 1 (D.C. Cir., 1978). In another case, the NSA admitted interception of messages without obtaining a warrant, but the constitutionality of such action was not resolved. See *Jabara v. Webster*, 691 F.2d 272 (6th Cir., 1982).

118. Caute, *Year of the Barricades*, p. 41.

119. Commision on CIA Activities within the United States, *1975 Report to the President*, (Washington D.C., U.S. Government Printing Office, 1975).

120. In one case, *Lamont v. United States*, Slip Opinion, 77-C-975, 77-C-919, 77-C-1029, (E.D.N.Y., Feb. 17, 1978), Federal District Judge Jack B. Weinstein awarded the plaintiff $2,000 and required the CIA to send a "suitable letter of regret" for having opened and photocopied 155 letters the plaintiff had mailed to various people in the Soviet Union. Two of the letters opened by the CIA were love letters Lamont wrote to his wife. The Judge termed the CIA actions "despicable."

121. Halperin, *The Lawless State*, pp. 135-136; Mackenzie, "Sabotaging the Dissident Press," in Rips, *The Campaign Against the Underground Press*, p. 162.

122. Halperin, *The Lawless State*, p. 145.

123. *Ibid.*, pp. 146-148.

124. Volkman and Baggett, *Secret Intelligence: The Inside Story of America's Espionage Empire*, p. 166.

125. Demac, *Liberty Denied: The Current Rise of Censorship in America*, p. 132.

126. *Ibid.*, p. 154.

127. *Hobson v. Wilson*, 737 F.2d 1 (D.C. Cir., 1984).

128. Rips, *The Campaign Against the Underground Press*, p. 59.

129. Churchill and Vander Wall, *Agents of Repression*, pp. 37-62.

130. Volkman and Baggett, *Secret Intelligence: The Inside Story of America's Espionage Empire*, p. 161.

131. O'Reilly, *Hoover and the Un-Americans*, p. 194.

132. Donner, *The Age of Surveillance*, p. 137.

133. O'Reilly, *Hoover and the Un-Americans*, p. 232.

134. Donner, *The Age of Surveillance*, p. 131.

135. Churchill and Vander Wall, *Agents of Repression*, p. 47.

136. Berman, *et al.*, *Controlling the FBI: ACLU Testimony on Charter Legislation before the Senate Judiciary Committee*, April 25, 1978, p. 37.

137. O'Reilly, *Hoover and the Un-Americans*, p. 207.

138. Halperin, *The Lawless State*, p. 114.

139. *Ibid.*

140. *Ibid.*, p. 125.

141. *Ibid.*, p. 126. The FBI agent provocateur who led the Camden Nine in a draft board raid stated, "I taught them everything they knew...how to cut glass and open windows without making any noise...How to open file cabinets without a key...I began to feel like the Pied Piper."

142. *Ibid.*, p. 130.

143. Volkman and Baggett, *Secret Intelligence: The Inside Story of America's Espionage Empire*, p. 162; Rogin, *Ronald Reagan, The Movie*, p. 72.

144. Ginsberg, "Smoking Typewriters," in Rips, *The Campaign Against the Underground Press*, pp. 33-34.

145. Rips, *The Campaign Against the Underground Press*, pp. 55-56.

146. Donner, *The Age of Surveillance*, p. 127.

147. As quoted in Rips, *The Campaign Against the Underground Press*, pp. 61-63.

148. O'Reilly, *Hoover and the Un-Americans*, p. 200.

149. *Ibid.*, p. 236.

150. Hersh, "F.B.I. Informer is Linked to Bombings and Protests by Weathermen Groups," *New York Times*, May 20, 1973, p. 50.

151. Berman, *et al.*, *Controlling the FBI: ACLU Testimony on Charter Legislation before the Senate Judiciary Committee*, April 25, 1978, pp. 14, 36-37, iv, fn. 18.

152. O'Reilly, *Hoover and the Un-Americans*, p. 286.

153. Hayden, *Reunion*, p. 296.

154. Churchill and Vander Wall, *Agents of Repression*, p. 4.

155. Neier, "Surveillance as Censorship," in Rips, *The Campaign Against the Underground Press*, pp. 14-15; Churchill and Vander Wall, *Agents of Repression*, p. 6.

156. "FBI Files Reveal Wide Probe of Foes of US Latin Policy," *Boston Globe*, Jan. 27, 1988, p. 9.

157. Chevigny, "Politics and Law in the Control of Local Surveillance," 69 *Cornell Law Review* 735, 749, quoting deposition of John Valkenburg, patrol officer with the Intelligence Division of the Chicago Police Department.

158. See, *Alliance to End Repression v. Rochford*, 75 F.R.D. 438 (N.D. Ill. 1976).

159. See, *Coalition Against Police Abuse v. Board of Police Commissioners*, No. 243-458 (L.A. County Superior Ct., Feb. 22, 1984); see also, Chevigny, "Politics and Law in the Control of Local Surveillance," 69 *Cornell Law Review* 735, 770-771.

160. See, Chevigny, "Politics and Law in the Control of Local Surveillance," 69 *Cornell Law Review* 735.

161. Rosenbaum, "Run, Tommy, Run!" *Esquire*, July 1971, p. 55.

162. See, Rosenbaum, "Run, Tommy, Run!," *Esquire*, July 1971; "'Tommy the Traveler' Gets Suspension in Deputy Job," *New York Times*, July 2, 1970, p. 40; "Bail Posted for Jailed Police Agent," *New York Times*, July 25, 1970, p. 26.

163. See, Rosenbaum, "Run, Tommy, Run!," *Esquire*, July 1971, p. 137.

164. See, *e.g.*, "Hobart Goes on Trial over Campus Disorders," *New York Times*, Feb. 3, 1971, p. 32.

165. See, "Justice for the Campus," *New York Times*, Feb. 25, 1971, p. 36; "Ex-Spy for Sheriff on Hobart Campus Seeks Police Work," *New York Times*, Sept. 26, 1970, p. 31; "People," *New York Times*, July 27, 1971, p. 40.

166. "So far as the Associated Press is concerned, our correspondents are prepared to submit air base copy to formal censorship if the United States Army installs it. But correspondents should be free to see and cover all aspects of the war as was done in World War II." Wes Gallagher, general manager, AP, as quoted in Hallin, *The "Uncensored War*," p. 127.

167. As quoted in Hallin, *The "Uncensored War*," p. 213.

168. Gottschalk, " 'Consistent with Security'...A History of American Military Press Censorship," 5 *Communications & Law* at 49; Hallin, *The "Uncensored War*," pp. 127-128.

169. Chomsky and Herman, *Manufacturing Consent*, p. 172.

170. Hallin, *The "Uncensored War*," p. 148-149.

171. Memo from Carl Rowan, then Deputy Assistant Secretary of State for Public Affairs, as quoted in Karnow, "The Newsmen's War in Vietnam," Dec. 1963, in Lyons, *Reporting the News*, pp. 363-364.

172. Karnow, "The Newsmen's War in Vietnam," in Lyons, *Reporting the News*, p. 365.

173. Sheehan, "Vietnam Archive: Pentagon Study Traces 3 Decades of Growing U.S. Involvement," *New York Times*, June 13, 1971, p. 1.

174. Telegram from Attorney General John N. Mitchell to Arthur Schulzburger, President and Publisher, *New York Times*, June 14, 1971.

175. "Supreme Court, 6-3, Upholds Newspapers on Publication of the Pentagon Report; Times Resumes its Series, Halted 15 Days," *New York Times*, July 1, 1971, p. 1.

176. William B. Macomber, Under Secretary of State, as quoted in Lewis, "United States v. North," *New York Times*, Feb. 16, 1989, p. A35.

177. Oral Argument of Erwin Griswald, Solicitor General of the United States, *New York Times Co. v. United States*, 403 U.S. 713 (1971).

178. *New York Times v. United States*, 403 U.S. 713 (1971).

179. "Pentagon Papers Lawyer Raps 'Overclassification'," *Boston Globe*, Feb. 16, 1989, p. 16.; Griswald, "Secrets Not Worth Keeping," *Boston Globe*, Feb. 21, 1989, p. 11.

180. Chomsky and Herman, *Manufacturing Consent*, p. 191.

181. See, in general, Chomsky and Herman, *Manufacturing Consent*.

182. *Ibid.*, pp. 200-201.

183. *Ibid.*; Stoler, *The War Against the Press*, p. 66.

184. Stoler, *The War Against the Press*, p. 67.

185. In 1987, on the twentieth anniversary of the censorship and cancellation of their show, Tom Smothers stated that if they tried to do political satire about Nicaragua, and applied their Nixon jokes to Reagan, "we'd still get censored." See, "Smothering Satire," *Boston Globe,* Oct. 26, 1987, p. 2.

186. As quoted in Hallin, *The "Uncensored War,"* p. 117.

187. Caute, *The Year of the Barricades: A Journey Through 1968,* p. 449.

188. See, Leamer, *The Paper Revolutionaries,* p. 14 ("200 papers"); Salpukas, "Underground Papers are Thriving on Campuses and in Cities Across Nation," *New York Times,* April 5, 1970, p. 58 ("200 to 250 papers"); Rips, *The Campaign Against the Underground Press,* p. 61 ("over 400 underground papers"); Peck, *Uncovering the Sixties: The Life and Times of the Underground Press,* p. xv ("at least 500 underground papers").

189. Peck, *Uncovering the Sixties: The Life and Times of the Underground Press,* p. 86.

190. *Ibid.,* pp. 65-66, 183; Leamer, *The Paper Revolutionaries,* pp. 27-28, 51.

191. Salpukas, "Underground Papers are Thriving on Campuses and in Cities Across Nation," *New York Times,* April 5, 1970, p. 58.

192. Rips, *The Campaign Against the Underground Press,* p. 51.

193. Peck, *Uncovering the Sixties: The Life and Times of the Underground Press,* pp. 21, 187; Leamer, *The Paper Revolutionaries,* pp. 27-28.

194. Peck, *Uncovering the Sixties: The Life and Times of the Underground Press,* p. 270.

195. Leamer, *The Paper Revolutionaries,* pp. 125-126.

196. *Ibid.,* pp. 125-130; Peck, *Uncovering the Sixties: The Life and Times of the Underground Press,* pp. 190-191.

197. Peck, *Uncovering the Sixties: The Life and Times of the Underground Press,* pp. 229-230.

198. Leamer, *The Paper Revolutionaries,* p. 132.

199. Peck, *Uncovering the Sixties: The Life and Times of the Underground Press,* p. 231.

200. Salpukas, "Underground Papers are Thriving on Campuses and in Cities Across Nation," *New York Times,* April 5, 1970, p. 58.

201. Rips, *The Campaign Against the Underground Press,* pp. 130-133.

202. Peck, *Uncovering the Sixties: The Life and Times of the Underground Press,* pp. 126-127.

203. Leamer, *The Paper Revolutionaries,* pp. 141-145; Rips, *The Campaign Against the Underground Press,* p. 112.

204. Leamer, *The Paper Revolutionaries,* p. 135.

205. Rips, *The Campaign Against the Underground Press,* p. 102.

206. Salpukas, "Underground Papers are Thriving on Campuses and in Cities Across Nation," *New York Times,* April 5, 1970, p. 58.

207. Salpukas, "Underground Papers are Thriving on Campuses and in Cities Across Nation," *New York Times,* April 5, 1970, p. 58.

208. Rips, *The Campaign Against the Underground Press,* pp. 84-85.

209. Peck, *Uncovering the Sixties: The Life and Times of the Underground Press,* p. 143.

210. Mackenzie, Angus, "Sabotaging the Dissident Press," in Rips, *The Campaign Against the Underground Press,* pp. 160-161.

211. Rips, *The Campaign Against the Underground Press*, p. 75.
212. Peck, *Uncovering the Sixties: The Life and Times of the Underground Press*, p. 176.
213. Mackenzie, "Sabotaging the Dissident Press," in Rips, *The Campaign Against the Underground Press*, p. 165.
214. *Ibid.*, p. 166.
215. Leamer, *The Paper Revolutionaries*, p. 131; see also Rips, *The Campaign Against the Underground Press*, pp. 97-98.
216. Rips, *The Campaign Against the Underground Press*, p. 99.
217. *Ibid.*, p. 97.
218. *Ibid.*, p. 84.
219. *Ibid.*, pp. 82-83.
220. *Ibid.*, p. 125.
221. *Ibid.*, p. 57.
222. *Ibid.*, p. 51.
223. Mackenzie, "Sabotaging the Dissident Press," in Rips, *The Campaign Against the Underground Press*, p. 160.
224. Peck, *Uncovering the Sixties: The Life and Times of the Underground Press*, pp. 141-142.
225. *Ibid.*, p. 142.
226. Mackenzie, "Sabotaging the Dissident Press," in Rips, *The Campaign Against the Underground Press*, pp. 167-168; Peck, *Uncovering the Sixties: The LIfe and Times of the Underground Press*, pp. 142, 194.
227. As quoted in Peck, *Uncovering the Sixties: The Life and Times of the Underground Press*, pp. 140-141.
228. Rips, *The Campaign Against the Underground Press*, p. 81.
229. See supra, pp. 54-55.
230. *Bond v. Floyd*, 385 U.S. 116 (1966).
231. *Shuttlesworth v. Birmingham*, 394 U.S. 147 (1969).
232. *Walker v. Birmingham*, 388 U.S. 307 (1967)("no person may disregard or violate [a court order] with immunity from a charge of contempt of court").
233. *United States v. O'Brien*, 391 U.S. 367 (1968). The same year, however, the Court did rule that local draft boards could not deny a person a draft exemption for turning in his draft card; see *Oestereich v. Selective Service System*, 393 U.S. 233 (1968). Two years later the Court ruled that the draft board could not speed up a person's induction as a penalty for participating in anti-war demonstrations; see *Gutknecht v. United States*, 396 U.S. 295 (1970).
234. 82 Stat. 75 (1968).
235. One year later, the Supreme Court, overturning 40 years of precedent, threw out the 'clear and present danger' talisman for a more expansive reading of the First amendment. See, *Brandenburg v. Ohio*, 395 U.S. 444 (1969).
236. See supra, pp. 117-119.
237. Two of the originators of the petition, Noam Chomsky and Dwight Macdonald, were not indicted.
238. Christenson, *Political Trials*, p. 133.
239. *Massachusetts v. Laird*, 400 U.S. 886 (1970).
240. *Tinker v. Des Moines School District*, 393 U.S. 503 (1969).
241. *Cohen v. California*, 403 U.S. 15 (1971).

242. *Smith v. Goguen,* 415 U.S. 566 (1974) ("[f]lag contempt statutes [are] void for lack of notice on the theory that '[w]hat is contemptuous to one man may be a work of art to another' ".)

243. *Aptheker v. Secretary of State,* 378 U.S. 500 (1964)("travel abroad, like travel within the country [is] basic in our scheme of values").

244. *Aptheker v. Secretary of State,* 378 U.S. at 520 ("War may be occasion for serious curtailment of liberty. Absent war, I see no way to keep a citizen from traveling within or without the country...").

245. *Zemel v. Rusk,* 381 U.S. 1 (1965) ("th[is travel] restriction...is supported by the weightiest considerations of national security").

246. *Kleindienst v. Mandel,* 408 U.S. 753 (1972).

247. *Hortensia de Allende v. George P. Schultz, Secretary of State,* No. 87-1469, (1st Cir., April 13, 1988). See "Court Says Visas Can't be Denied for Political Beliefs or Affiliations," *Boston Globe,* April 17, 1988, p. 47.

Notes to Chapter VII

1. In general, see Klare and Kornbluh, *Low-Intensity Warfare.*

2. Neil C. Livingstone, "Fighting Terrorism and 'Dirty Little Wars'," as quoted in Klare and Kornbluh, *Low-Intensity Warfare,* p. 4.

3. Barnet, Richard J., "The Costs and Perils of Intervention," in Klare and Kornbluh, *Low-Intensity Warfare,* p. 210.

4. It should be remembered that these "low-intensity" conflicts are of low-intensity only from a U.S. perspective. The death toll and destruction in the countries against whom we deploy our military might is anything but "low."

5. Pincus, "Press Access to Military Operations: Grenada and the Need for a New Analytical Framework," 135 *University of Pennsylvania Law Review* 813 (1987); Note, "The First Amendment and National Security: 17 *NYU Journal of International Law and Politics* at 382-383.

6. Pincus, "Press Access to Military Operations: Grenada and the Need for a New Analytical Framework," 135 University of Pennsylvania Law Review at 814, fn 8.

7. See Stanley W. Cloud, "How Reporters Missed the War," *Time,* January 8, 1990, p. 61.

8. *United States v. Progressive,* 467 F.Supp 990 (W.D. Wis.), *dismissed mem.* 610 F.2d 619 (7th Cir. 1979).

9. supra, pp. 53-54.

10. 467 F.Supp at 996.

11. See "National Security: The Ultimate Threat to the First Amendment," 66 *Minnesota Law Review* at 161, 162.

12. See *United States v. Marchetti,* 466 F.2d 1309 (4th Cir. 1972).

13. See Koffler and Gershman, "The New Seditious Libel," 69 *Cornell Law Review* at 816, n. 139.

14. *Snepp v. United States,* 444 U.S. 507 (1980) ("the Government has a compelling interest in protecting both the secrecy of information important to our national security and the appearance of confidentiality so essential to the effective operation of our foreign intelligence service").

15. See Anthony Lewis "The Least Tolerable," *New York Times,* June 23, 1987; Dershowitz, *The Best Defense,* pp. 233-234.

16. *Knopf v. Colby,* 509 F.2d 925, Appellants Petition for Writ of Certiorari to the United States Court of Appeals for the Fourth Circuit, March 14, 1975, p. 21.

17. 444 U.S. 507 (1980).

18. Demac, Donna A., *Liberty Denied,* pp. 101-102.

19. *Regan v. Wald,* 468 U.S. 222 (1984), ("[these restrictions] are justified by weighty concerns of foreign policy.")

20. Demac, *Liberty Denied,* p. 139.

21. *Ibid.,* p. 141.

22. See supra, p. 160.

23. *Haig v. Agee,* 453 U.S. 280, 286 (1981).

24. *Agee v. Vance,* 483 F.Supp. 729 (D.D.C.), *aff'd sub nom. Agee v. Muskie,* 629 F.2d 80 (D.C. Cir., 1980).

25. 453 U.S. 280 (1981).

26. See supra, pp. 53-54.

27. See supra, p. 159.

28. *Haig v. Agee,* 453 U.S. at 308 (quoting *Near v. Minnesota,* 283 U.S. 697, 716 (1931)).

29. *Near v. Minnesota,* 283 U.S. 697, 715-16 (1931).

30. "Nicaraguan Officials Barred from U.S. Entry by Reagan," *New York Times,* October 26, 1988, p. A14; "Reagan Bars Visas for Many Nicaraguan Officials," *Boston Globe,* October 26, 1988, p. 3.

31. Miles Corwin, "2,500 Prisoners of U.S. Face No Charges," *Los Angeles Times,* Aug. 27, 1989, p. 1.

32. U.S. District Court Judge Marvin Shoob, as quoted in *ibid.*

33. *Ibid.*

34. Christenson, *Political Trials,* p. 105.

35. Woodward, *Veil: The Secret Wars of the CIA 1981-1987,* pp. 185, 204, 257.

36. "FBI Files Reveal Wide Probe of Foes of US Latin Policy," *Boston Globe,* Jan. 27, 1988, p. 9.

37. See, e.g., "Churches in Sanctuary Movement Win Suit Against US Over Spying," *Boston Globe,* March 16, 1989, p. 19.

38. Kohn, *Jailed for Peace,* p. 104.

39. *Wayte v. United States,* 470 U.S. 598 (1985).

40. See Alfonso Chardy, "Reagan Aides and the 'Secret' Government," *The Miami Herald,* July 5, 1987, p. 1A.

41. Charles Law Howe, "The Disaster Dossier: The Federal Government Has a Secret Plan for the Military to Take Over User's Computers in Case of National Emergency," *Datamation,* October 15, 1984.

42. *Ibid.*

43. In 1970, when FEMA director Giuffrida was attending the Army War College in Carlisle, Pennsylvania, he wrote a paper advocating the imposition of martial law in the event of an uprising by black militants. The paper urged the incarceration in relocation camps of at least 21 million "American Negroes." See, Alfonso Chardy, "Reagan Aides and the 'Secret' Government," *The Miami Herald,* July 5, 1987, p. 15A. This scenario was "tested" in a series of war games during

1968-72 called Operation Cable Splicer (I, II, III). See George Katsiaficas *Imagination of the New Left: A Global Analysis of 1968*, pp. 259-65.

44. As quoted in Sklar, *Washington's War on Nicaragua*, pp. 357-358:

> The *Miami Herald* article, discussing FEMA's plans to suspend the constitution was then alluded to. The following questioning then took place:
>
> Sen. Boren: ...did you participate in or advocate any such plan to suspend the Constitution...?
> North: Absolutely not.
> Sen. Boren: To your knowledge, has the government of the United States adopted any such plan, or does it have in place—in being, any such plan?
> North: No sir. None.
>
> There was no further questioning or discussion on this issue.

Notes to Chapter VIII

1. Justice William Brennan, "The Quest to Develop a Jurisprudence of Civil Liberties in Times of Security Crises," p. 12.

2. "Fifty-two percent of Americans consider freedom of the press more important than government censorship to protect national security, compared with 38% four years ago." Similar majorities now believe that the First Amendment protects the public good, rather than the special interests of news organizations. See Thomas Rosentiel, "Public Confidence in Press Dips Sharply, Surveys Find," *Los Angeles Times*, p. A1, November 16, 1989.

Notes to Appendix

1. "Congress shall make no law respecting an establishment of religion, nor prohibiting the free exercise thereof; or abridging the freedom of speech, or of the press, or of the right of the people peaceably to assemble and petition their government for a redress of grievances," Constitution of the United States, Amendment I.

2. Nicaraguan Constitution, Title IV, Chapter I, Article 30.

3. Nicaraguan Constitution, Title IV, Chapter III, Article 66.

4. Nicaraguan Constitution, Title IV, Chapter III, Article 67.

5. Nicaraguan Constitution, Title IV, Chapter III, Article 68.

6. "All persons have the right to freedom of conscience, thought and religion, including the right not to profess a religion. No one shall be the object of coercive measures which diminish these rights, or be obligated to declare his or her creed, ideology or beliefs." Nicaraguan Constitution, Title IV, Chapter I, Article 29.

"Citizens have the right, individually or collectively, to petition, denounce irregularities and make constructive criticisms to the branches of government or to any authority, and to obtain a quick resolution or response and to have the result made known. The respective laws shall regulate these time periods." Nicaraguan Constitution, Title IV, Chapter II, Article 52.

"The right to peaceful gathering is recognized; the exercise of this right does not require prior permission." Nicaraguan Constitution, Title IV, Chapter II, Article 53.

"The right to assemble, demonstrate and mobilize publicly in conformity with the law is recognized." Nicaraguan Constitution, Title IV, Chapter II, Article 55.

7. Nicaraguan Constitution, Title X, Chapter I, Article 186.

8. The Chamorro family has been closely tied with the Nicaraguan Conservative Party; four Chamorros have been President of Nicaragua. (See, *Right to Survive: Human Rights in Nicaragua,* p. 81; also *"La Prensa:* Post-Mortem on a Suicide," *Envio,* Vol. 5, No. 62, p. 31.)

9. Under the Somoza dictatorship, the editor of *La Prensa* was, at various times, imprisoned, prohibited from travel, internally exiled and finally assassinated. *La Prensa* was subject to continuous censorship by Somoza, as well as being required to print articles favorable to him. During the last few months of the revolution against Somoza, the *La Prensa* office was bombed, machine-gunned and finally burnt to the ground by Somoza's forces. It re-opened after the Sandinista victory. (See, *Human Rights in Nicaragua, Reagan, Rhetoric and Reality,* p. 30, fn. 21.)

10. Nichols, "The Media," in Walker, ed., *Nicaragua, The First Five Years,* Praeger Publishers, 1985.

11. *"La Prensa:* Post-Mortem on a Suicide," *Envio,* Vol. 5, No. 62, p. 32. Among "The Group of Twelve" were:

> Sergio Ramirez (currently Vice-President of Nicaragua),
> Miguel D'Escoto (currently Foreign Minister),
> Ernesto Cardenal (currently Director of the Institute of Culture),
> Carlos Tunnerman (Nicaragua's Ambassador to the United States and the OAS), and
> Roberto Argüello Hurtado (the first President of the Supreme Court of Nicaragua).

The only two members of "The Group of Twelve" who no longer support the government are:

> Arturo Cruz, former president of the Inter-American Development Bank and, after the Revolution, Nicaragua's Ambassador to the United States. Cruz left the government to join the contras in 1981. He has now disassociated himself from the contras, considering his affiliation with them "the biggest mistake I have ever made in my life" (*Harvard Law Bulletin,* Spring 1988, p. 25), and
> Alfonso Robelo, a millionaire industrialist who was a member of the original five-member governing junta immediately following the revolution, but resigned less than one year later and is now one of the leaders of the contras.

12. At the time of the split, the Sandinista government neither nationalized the paper nor declared it a workers' cooperative. Either of these actions would have allowed the editor and the pro-Sandinista majority of the workers to continue running *La Prensa*. See, *Boletin #7*, p. 15.

13. All parties in the current dispute can currently claim the allegiance of the Chamorro family. Xavier Chamorro is editor of *El Nuevo Diario*, a non-governmental but pro-revolution paper. His brother Jaime Chamorro was editor of *La Prensa* when it was closed in August 1986. Carlos Chamorro, son of Pedro Joaquín, is editor of *Barricada*, the official Sandinista daily. Another son, Pedro Joaquín, Jr., lives in Costa Rica and supports the contras. A daughter, Claudia, is the Nicaraguan Ambassador to Costa Rica.

14. *"La Prensa:* Post-Mortem on a Suicide," *Envio,* Vol. 5, No. 62, p. 34.

15. *Ibid.,* pp. 36-43.

16. *Ibid.,* p. 34.

17. *Human Rights in Nicaragua, Reagan, Rhetoric and Reality,* p. 62.

18. See, *"La Prensa* Returns to Nicaragua's Streets—Unrepentant, and Just as Unconstructive," mimeograph.

19. Woodward, *Veil: The Secret Wars of the CIA 1981-1987,* p. 111.

20. *Human Rights in Nicaragua: 1986,* pp. 116-117. *Human Rights in Nicaragua: Reagan, Rhetoric and Reality,* p. 33.

21. "We never received any money from the United States...not anything. We are an independent paper and are not subsidized by anyone. We did not receive any money [from the National Endowment for Democracy]." (Interview with Violeta de Chamorro, Jan. 25, 1988, Managua, Nicaragua.)

22. Robert Pear, "U.S. Allots $2 Million to Aid Anti-Sandinistas," *New York Times,* April 25, 1989, p. A8; "Nicaragua Bans Opposition From Getting U.S. Aid," *New York Times,* November 17, 1988, p. A11 ("In the past, American money has been openly sent to the opposition paper *La Prensa* and to a variety of other anti-Sandinista institutions."); Steven Kinzer, "La Prensa: Gadfly of the Sandinista State," *New York Times,* March 7, 1988, p. A6 (quoting Jaime Chamorro Cardenal, principal editor of *La Prensa,* that the newspaper has been receiving $7,000 per month from NED).

23. *"La Prensa:* Post-Mortem on a Suicide," *Envio,* Vol. 5, No. 62, p. 36; see also *Boletin #7,* p. 19.

24. Charges that American embassy officials attended *La Prensa* editorial meetings were termed by Violeta de Chamorro to be pure "propaganda." (Interview with Violeta de Chamorro, Jan. 25, 1988, Managua, Nicaragua.)

25. "Ley para Regular las Informaciones sobre Seguridad Interna y Defensa Nacional," Decree 511 (Sept. 10, 1980); "Ley para Regular Informaciones de Contenido Economico," Decree 512 (Sept. 10, 1980).

26. *Right to Survive: Human Rights in Nicaragua,* p. 82.

27. See, *Sandinista Elections in Nicaragua,* United States Department of State, 1984; *Freedom of Expression and Assembly in Nicaragua during the Election Period,* 1984.

28. *Right to Survive: Human Rights in Nicaragua,* p. 83-84. But see, *Boletin #7,* p. 16 (disputing these figures and noting that *La Prensa* "has a practice of withdrawing entire articles where only a word or sentence has been altered by the censor").

29. *Right to Survive: Human Rights in Nicaragua,* p. 83.

30. *Human Rights in Nicaragua 1985-1986,* p. 47.

31. *"La Prensa:* Post-Mortem on a Suicide," *Envio,* Vol. 5, No. 62, p. 33.

32. *Ibid.*

33. "[A]lthough criteria used in deletion of news items are ostensibly related to matters of national security, the nature of items deleted has been wide-ranging," Amnesty International Background Briefing on Nicaragua, Dec. 1982, as quoted in *Nicaragua: Comments on the Nicaraguan Government's Report to the U.N. Human Rights Committee,* p. 25.

34. *Right to Survive: Human Rights in Nicaragua,* p. 84.

35. *"La Prensa:* Post-Mortem on a Suicide," *Envio,* Vol. 5, No. 62, p. 28.

36. *Human Rights in Nicaragua: 1986,* p. 116.

37. *"La Prensa:* Post-Mortem on a Suicide," pp. 29-30.

38. *See., e.g.* "Levantada la Censura," *Barricada Internacional,* No. 254, October 8, 1987, p. 6.

39. *La Prensa,* October 1, 1987, p. 1.

40. Interview with Violeta de Chamorro, Managua, Nicaragua, January 25, 1988.

41. *Human Rights in Nicaragua: August 1987 to August 1988,* pp. 13-15. On Dec. 7, 1988, five months after the demonstration, the last of those arrested and convicted after Nandaime were released from jail. Thirty-eight people, including the leaders of several opposition parties, were arrested in the demonstration; in November, 25 of them were absolved of all charges. Kinzer, "Nicaragua Releases Last of the July Protesters," *New York Times,* December 8, 1988, p. A6.

42. *Human Rights in Nicaragua: August 1987 to August 1988,* p. 34.

43. see infra, pp. 180-181.

44. *Right to Survive: Human Rights in Nicaragua,* p. 87. See also, *Iglesia: Informativo Catolico,* Vol. 1, No. 1, October 12, 1985.

45. *Boletin #7,* p. 18.

46. Interview with Dr. Rodolfo Robelo Herrera, former Justice of the Nicaraguan Supreme Court, and leader of the Partido Liberal Independiente (PLI), January 20, 1988.

47. As with so much in Nicaraguan life, there are two competing, and opposed, human rights organizations. The Comisión Permanente de Derechos Humanos de Nicaragua (CPDH)—which has received funding from the United States government—is anti-government, while the Comisión Nacional de Promoción y Protección de los Derechos Humanos (CNPPDH) receives government funding and is pro-Sandinista. In November 1985, the government announced that it would require the CPDH to submit its publications for prior approval. However, after protest by various international human rights organizations, the government announced that there would be no prior censorship of the CPDH bulletins, but that a copy of the bulletin should be delivered to the government simultaneously with public distribution. See, *Human Rights in Nicaragua, 1986,* pp. 118-119; *Human Rights in Nicaragua, 1985-1986,* pp. 56-58.

48. "Situación de los Derechos Humanos," p. 20 (author's translation).

49. These publications are generally available at the largest hotels and at dollar stores—stores that carry American imports, but where items can only be purchased using American dollars, not Nicaraguan cordobas. Any Nicaraguan can

246 FREEDOM UNDER FIRE

legally own dollars, and it is not unusual to see middle- and upper-class Nicaraguans purchasing goods at the dollar stores.

50. *Nicaragua, Comment,* p. 27.

51. The books distributed were *Contra Toda Esperanza: 22 Años en el 'Gulag de Las Americas'* by Armando Valladares, and *Nicaragua: Revolución en la Familia* by Shirley Christian.

52. *Barricada,* July 21, 1987, p. 1.

53. *"La Prensa:* Post-Mortem on a Suicide," *Envio,* Vol. 5, No. 62, p. 37. *Barricada,* the official Sandinista daily, had a circulation of approximately 105,000, followed closely by *El Nuevo Diario.* However, all such statistics should be viewed with skepticism. For instance, see Fisher, "The Sandinista Record: Toward Totalitarianism or Participatory Democracy?," p. 17, who states that, with a circulation of 60-70,000, *La Prensa* was the largest daily in Nicaragua.

54. *"La Prensa:* Post-Mortem on a Suicide," *Envio,* Vol. 5, No. 62, p. 37.

55. Gastil, *Freedom in the World: Political Rights and Civil Liberties, 1983-1984,* p. 405.

56. *Boletin #7,* p. 18.

57. *Human Rights in Nicaragua, 1986,* pp. 119-120.

58. The daily talk show Contacto 6-20 thus has an audience almost ten times the size of *La Prensa.*

59. "Radio Contacto 6-20—A Hot-Line for Criticism," *Envio,* Vol. 5, Number 66, Dec. 1986, pp. 21-34.

60. *Right to Survive: Human Rights in Nicaragua,* p. 88.

61. *Boletin #7,* p. 18.

62. "Levantada la Censura," *Barricada Internacional,* No. 254, October 8, 1987, p. 6.

63. *Human Rights in Nicaragua: August 1987 to August 1988,* p. 36.

64. *Ibid.,* pp. 23, 32, 34, 36.

65. *Ibid.,* p. 40.

66. *Ibid.,* p. 39.

67. Howard H. Frederick, "Electric Penetration," in Walker, *Reagan Versus the Sandinistas,* pp. 127-134.

68. *Boletin #7,* p. 118.

69. *Human Rights in Nicaragua: Reagan, Rhetoric and Reality,* p. 6. See also, *A Political Opening in Nicaragua: Report on the Nicaraguan Elections of November 4, 1984.*

70. See also, *Human Rights in Nicaragua: Reagan, Rhetoric and Reality,* p. 3 ("debate on major social and political questions is robust, outspoken, even often strident").

71. "Nicaraguans have the right to travel and to establish their residence in any part of the national territory and to freely enter and exit the country." Constitution of the Republic of Nicaragua, Title IV, Chapter I, Article 31.

72. Constitution of the Republic of Nicaragua, Title IV, Chapter I, Article 185 and 186.

73. See, e.g., Taubman, "Nicaragua Said to Get Soviet Attack Copters," *New York Times,* November 7, 1984, p. 1 ("Administration officials said they were concerned about a Soviet freighter apparently headed for Nicaragua that intelligence reports indicated was carrying crates that could contain MiG fighter

aircraft."); Taubman, "U.S. Warns Soviet it Won't Tolerate MiG's in Nicaragua," *New York Times,* November 8, 1984, p. 1. ("The United States [is] concerned that a Soviet freighter that has reached Nicaragua might be carrying advanced fighter aircraft.")

74. See, e.g., Kinzer, "Nicaragua Says No Jet Fighters Are Being Sent," *New York Times,* November 8, 1984, p. 1.

75. See, e.g., Taubman, "Officials Doubt Soviet Freighter Contains MiGs," *New York Times,* November 10, 1984, p. 1. ("The Reagan Administration is almost certain that no advanced jet fighter planes were aboard a Soviet freighter that reached Nicaragua this week.")

76. *Right to Survive: Human Rights in Nicaragua,* p. 97.

77. "Derechos Humanos en Tiempos de Guerra," *Envio,* Vol. 5 No. 60, June 1986, p. 6b.

78. A special permit is needed for foreigners to visit the Atlantic Coast region. The permit takes 2-3 days to obtain and costs approximately $7; it seems to be granted pro-forma to anyone who applies. There are also restrictions upon entering the war zone, ostensibly for the protection of the visitors. Foreign press routinely has access to the war zone.

79. *Human Rights in Nicaragua: August 1987 to August 1988,* p. 31.

80. See infra, p. 199.

81. *Nicaragua: The Human Rights Record,* p. 21; *Human Rights in Nicaragua: Reagan, Rhetoric and Reality,* p. 15.

82. See, "Church-State Relations: A Chronology—Part I," *Envio,* Volume 6, Number 77, November 1987, p. 39.

83. As quoted in *Ibid.,* p. 39.

84. *Ibid.,* pp. 40-41.

85. *Ibid.,* p. 40.

86. In the fall and winter of 1986-1987, a dialogue had resumed between the Sandinista government and the Catholic church, in an attempt to reach a *modus vivendi.* While most of the church hierarchy was supporting these talks, Bishop Vega, still in exile, broadcast a radio message on the contra radio station from El Salvador, in which he compared the dialogue to "those homosexual marriages they're talking about these days...What is a marriage between homosexuals? It is simply a sterile masturbation, with no true hope of achieving a communion that will generate new life. In the same way, a dialogue with people who are totalitarian Marxists is nothing more than a marriage—which can't even be called a marriage—between homosexuals. It's sterile, it doesn't lead to anything..." ("Church-State Relations: A Chronology—Part II," *Envio,* Volume 6, Number 78, December 1987, p. 40.

87. *Human Rights in Nicaragua: August 1987 to August 1988,* p. 48; "Church-State Relations: A Chronology—Part II," *Envio,* Volume 6, Number 78, December 1987, p. 47.

88. "The right of the people to be secure in their persons, houses, papers, and effects, against unreasonable searches and seizures, shall not be violated, and no Warrants shall issue, but upon probable cause..." Constitution of the United States, Amendment IV.

89. "No person shall be held to answer for a capital, or otherwise infamous crime, unless on a presentment or indictment of a Grand Jury...nor shall any

person be subject for the same offence to be twice put in jeopardy of life or limb; nor shall be compelled in any criminal case to be a witness against himself, nor be deprived of life, liberty or property, without due process of law..." Constitution of the United States, Amendment V.

90. "In all criminal prosecutions, the accused shall enjoy the right to a speedy and public trial, by an impartial jury...and to be informed of the nature and cause of the accusation; to be confronted by witnesses against him; to have compulsory process for obtaining witnesses in his favor, and to have the Assistance of Counsel for his defense." Constitution of the United States, Amendment VI.

91. "Excessive bail shall not be required, nor excessive fines imposed, nor cruel and unusual punishments inflicted." Constitution of the United States, Amendment VIII.

92. "...nor shall any State deprive any person of life, liberty, or property, without due process of law; nor deny to any person within its jurisdiction the equal protection of the laws." Constitution of the United States, Amendment XIV.

93. "The privilege of the Writ of *habeas corpus* shall not be suspended, unless when in Cases of Rebellion or Invasion the public Safety may require it." Constitution of the United States, Article I, Section 9, Clause 2.

94. "No Bill of Attainder or *ex post facto* Law shall be passed." Constitution of the United States, Article I, Section 9, Clause 3.

95. Title IV lists the "Rights, Duties and Guarantees of the Nicaraguan People."

96. "All persons have the right to: 1) their private life and that of their family; 2) the inviolability of their home, correspondence and communication...

"A private home may be searched only with a written order from a competent judge...

"Illegally seized letters, documents and other private papers shall have no legal weight in a trial or elsewhere." Constitution of the Republic of Nicaragua, Title IV, Chapter I, Article 26.

97. "All those awaiting trial...shall be tried without undue delay by a court of competent jurisdiction established by law." Constitution of the Republic of Nicaragua, Title IV, Chapter I, Article 34.

98. "All those awaiting trial...are innocent until proven guilty according to the law." Constitution of the Republic of Nicaragua, Title IV, Chapter I, Article 34.

99. "All those awaiting trial...

4) ...shall be guaranteed the right to defense and to intervention on their own behalf from the outset of the proceedings, together with adequate time and means to prepare that defense.

5) ...a public defender shall be named when legal counsel has not been designated by the time of the first hearing...The accused shall have the right to communicate freely and in private with their legal counsel." Constitution of the Republic of Nicaragua, Title IV, Chapter I, Article 34.

100. "All those awaiting trial...shall not be obligated to testify against themselves or against a spouse or a partner in a stable de facto union, or a family member...or to admit their own guilt." Constitution of the Republic of Nicaragua, Title IV, Chapter I, Article 34.

101. "Persons whose constitutional rights have been violated or are in danger of violation shall have recourse to *habeas corpus* or protection (*mandamus*)." Constitution of the Republic of Nicaragua, Title IV, Chapter I, Article 45.

102. "[A]ll those sentenced for any crime shall have the right to review by a superior court; and not to be tried in the future for any crime for which they have been finally convicted or acquitted." Constitution of the Republic of Nicaragua, Title IV, Chapter I, Article 34.

103. "[No one] may be brought to trial or sentenced for acts or omissions which at the time committed had not been unequivocally established by law as a punishable crime..." Constitution of the Republic of Nicaragua, Title IV, Chapter I, Article 34.

104. "The right to life is inviolable and inherent to all persons. In Nicaragua there is no death penalty." Constitution of the Republic of Nicaragua, Title IV, Chapter I, Article 23.

105. "No one may be arbitrarily detained or imprisoned, or be deprived of liberty except in cases established by law and in accordance with legal procedures: Therefore;

1. An individual may be detained only by a written order from a competent Judge...

2. All detained persons have the right to be:

2.1 Informed in detail of the causes of their detainment and the accusations against them, without delay...

2.2 To be brought before the official expressly authorized by law within 72 hours..."

Constitution of the Republic of Nicaragua, Title IV, Chapter I, Article 33.

106. "All persons shall have the right to physical, psychological and moral integrity. No one shall be subjected to torture nor inhumane, cruel or degrading punishment..." Constitution of the Republic of Nicaragua, Title IV, Chapter I, Article 36.

107. "All persons...shall enjoy the protection and recognition by the state of the rights inherent to human beings...and the full exercise of the rights set forth in the Universal Declaration of Human Rights; the American Declaration of the Rights of Man; the International Pact of Economic, Social and Cultural Rights and the International Pact of Civil and Political Rights of the United Nations; and the American Convention of Human Rights of the Organization of American States." Constitution of the Republic of Nicaragua, Title IV, Chapter I, Article 45.

108. "The President of the Republic may suspend...the rights and guarantees consecrated in this Constitution in case of war or when demanded by the security of the nation, economic conditions or a national catastrophe.

"This suspension decree shall put the State of Emergency into effect for a specific and reasonable period." Constitution of the Republic of Nicaragua, Title X, Chapter I, Article 185.

109. Constitution of the Republic of Nicaragua, Title X, Chapter I, Article 186.

110. The U.S. State Department reports on Nicaragua contend that Nicaragua has a policy of blatant disregard for fundamental human rights. Human rights organizations have termed these reports "deceptive," "misleading," "irresponsible," and employing "misrepresentations" and "pervasive" misuse of data. (*Human Rights in Nicaragua: Reagan, Rhetoric and Reality*, pp. 3, 21, 22, 26, 27).

For example, the Reagan Administration has stated unequivocally that "[i]n the American continent, there is no regime more barbaric and bloody, no regime that violates human rights in a manner more constant and permanent, than the Sandinista regime." ("The Challenge to Democracy in Central America," a joint U.S. State Department-Defense Department publication, p. 28, 1986). As Americas Watch retorted, "this is nonsense." *Human Rights in Nicaragua, 1986,* p. 140. A high-level official in the American Embassy in Managua admitted to this author that the State Department's characterization of the Sandinista regime was clearly false.

111. The term "disappearance" refers to a systematic policy whereby political opponents are secretly kidnapped and executed. To all intents and purposes, the missing person simply 'disappears', not to be seen again. Thus "disappearance" is a euphemism for secret political murder, although, since bodies are often not found, proof is hard to come by.

There is no such policy of disappearances in Nicaragua. The United States has redefined the term, however, in order to give the impression of human rights violations by Nicaragua. If a Nicaraguan is arrested, and his family is not notified, or if the person is moved to a new jail without immediate notification of the family, the United States State Department claims that the person has "disappeared." In virtually all such cases in Nicaragua, however, the arrestee has been located unharmed a short while later. Many times these temporary "disappearances" are the result of poor communications in remote areas of the country. By creatively redefining the term, the United States has been able to imply that disappearances are a systematic policy of the Sandinista government.

The U.S. State Department's use of the term 'disappearances' in this situation has been condemned by human rights organizations.

See, e.g. *Human Rights in Nicaragua: Reagan, Rhetoric and Reality,* pp. 24-28.

112. *Amnesty International Report: 1981,* p. 175.

113. *Human Rights in Nicaragua: November 1982 Update,* 1982, p. 6 ("Human rights are afforded far greater respect in Nicaragua than in the nearby states of El Salvador and Guatemala...[or than was afforded] under the regime of Anastasio Somoza Debayle").

114. *Human Rights in Nicaragua: 1986,* p. 13.

115. *Violations of the Laws of War by Both Sides in Nicaragua: 1981-1985,* p. 58.

116. See *Amnesty International Report: 1984,* p. 182; also *Nicaragua: The Human Rights Record,* 1986, p. 26.

117. *The Miskitos in Nicaragua: 1981-1984,* p. 8.

118. *Human Rights in Nicaragua: Reagan, Rhetoric and Reality,* p. 22.

119. *Nicaragua: The Human Rights Record,* p. 30.

120. *Human Rights in Nicaragua: 1986,* pp. 5-19, p. 63; *Nicaragua: Violations of the Laws of War by Both Sides, First Supplement, January-March, 1986,* p. 7.

121. *Human Rights in Nicaragua: Reagan, Rhetoric and Reality,* p. 23; *The Miskitos in Nicaragua: 1981-1984,* p. 9.

122. *Human Rights in Nicaragua: Reagan, Rhetoric and Reality,* p. 23.

123. *Human Rights in Nicaragua: August 1987 to August 1988,* p. 2.

124. See *The Testimony of Sofonias Cisneros Leiva.*

125. See, *Human Rights in Nicaragua under the Sandinistas: From Revolution to Repression.*

126. This account is taken from *The Testimony of Sofonias Cisneros Leiva,* pp. 1-6.

127. *Ibid.,* pp. 3-4.

128. Laverty, "Report on Interview with Mr. Sofonias Cisneros Leiva."

129. *Ibid.,* pp. 3-4.

130. *Ibid.,* pp. 5-7.

131. *Ibid.,* p. 7.

132. *Critique: Review of the Department of State's Country Reports on Human Rights Practices for 1984,* p. 77.

133. *Human Rights in Nicaragua: 1986,* America's Watch Report, pp. 70-84; *Nicaragua, the Human Rights Record,* 1986, pp. 19-20.

134. *Critique: A Review of the Department of State's Country Reports on Human Rights Practices for 1986,* p. 100.

135. *On Human Rights in Nicaragua,* May 1982, p. 15.

136. *Nicaragua: Revolutionary Justice, A Report on Human Rights and the Judicial System,* pp. 122-3.

137. *Amnesty International Report, 1980,* p. 153-154. See also, *Right to Survive: Human Rights in Nicaragua,* pp. 29-31; *Nicaragua: Revolutionary Justice, A Report on Human Rights and the Judicial System,* p. 13.

138. *Amnesty International Report: 1980,* pp. 153-154; see also *Right to Survive: Human Rights in Nicaragua,* pp. 29-31.

139. When the Sandinistas took power, there was only $3 million dollars left in the National Treasury; the rest had been looted by the fleeing Somozas.

140. Estatuto Fundamental, July 20, 1979; Estatuto Sobre Derechos y Garantias de los Nicaragüenses, August 21, 1979.

141. *Amnesty International Report: 1980,* p. 156. See also, *Right to Survive, Human Rights in Nicaragua,* p. 47.

142. *Right to Survive: Human Rights in Nicaragua,* p. 48. By comparison, "[a]t the end of WWII, the French Government charged 4,598 people with espionage or treason, of whom 756 were condemned to death."

143. *Right to Survive: Human Rights in Nicaragua,* p. 48. See also *Nicaragua, Revolutionary Justice, A Report on Human Rights and the Judicial System,* pp. 33-40.

144. *Right to Survive: Human Rights in Nicaragua,* p. 48.

145. Sometimes the prosecution claimed that the victim was the "Nicaraguan people."

146. *Amnesty International Report: 1981,* p. 171.

147. *Right to Survive: Human Rights in Nicaragua,* p. 48.

148. Interview with Dr. Rodolfo Robelo, former justice of the Supreme Court of Nicaragua, and leader of the Partido Liberal Independiente, January 20, 1988, Managua, Nicaragua.

149. *Human Rights in Nicaragua, 1987,* p. 9.

150. *Right to Survive: Human Rights in Nicaragua,* p. 49; *Amnesty International Report: 1983,* p. 162.

151. Comisión Nacional de Promoción y Protección de los Derechos Humanos—the National Commission for the Promotion and Protection of Human Rights.

152. Ley de Gracia (Clemency Law), Decree #854 (October 24, 1981).

153. The government also established labor courts and agrarian reform courts. Both currently operate under the normal judicial structure, although the Supreme Court did not originally have appellate jurisdiction over these courts.

154. Constitution of the Republic of Nicaragua, Title VIII, Chapter V, Article 163.

155. At the time of the promulgation of the Constitution, three of the Supreme Court Justices (Orlando Corrales Mejia, Mariano Barahona Portocarrero and Ernesto Somarriba Garcia) were members of the FSLN, two (Hernaldo Zúniga Montenegro and Santiago Rivas Haslam) were from the Conservative Party, one (Rodolfo Robelo Herrera) was from the PLI, and the President of the Court (Alejandro Serrano Caldera) was not a member of any party.

In Dec. 1987, under authority of the Constitution, the National Assembly appointed a new Court for a term of six years. The new Court consisted of five men and two women: Alejandro Serrano Caldera (President of the Court), Orlando Corrales Mejia (Vice-President), and Ernesto Somarriba Garcia, all three of whom had been members of the prior Court; Maria Haydee Flores Rivas, Rafael Chamorro Mora (the former Dean of the School of Law at the University of Central America), Ramon Romero Alonso, and Alba Luz Ramos Vanegas (the former Vice-Minister of Justice). At least two of the new justices are not members of the FSLN (Alejandro Serrano and Rafael Chamorro), although none of the Justices on the current Court are members of opposition parties.

156. The Court consists of seven Justices; between my two trips to Nicaragua, four of the Justices on the Court were replaced.

157. See, e.g., interview with Dr. Rodolfo Robelo, former Supreme Court Justice and member of the Partido Liberal Independiente, January 20, 1988, Managua, Nicaragua ("There are no political influences on our findings.")

158. Interview with Dr. Alejandro Serrano, Chief Justice of the Supreme Court of Nicaragua, by a delegation from the National Lawyer's Guild, January 26, 1988, Managua, Nicaragua.

159. *Ibid.*

160. Amparo is a cause of action by an individual against the government for allegedly illegal action on the part of a government official or office and includes our concept of *habeas corpus*.

161. Interview with Dr. Alejandro Serrano by a delegation from the National Lawyer's Guild, January 26, 1988, Managua, Nicaragua.

162. On February 14, 1982, the first articles about the covert war against Nicaragua appeared in the *Washington Post*. See, Woodward, *Veil: The Secret Wars of the CIA 1981-1987*, p. 185, 204.

163. Ley Sobre el Mantenimiento del Orden y Seguridad Publica, Decree 1074 (July 6, 1982), amending Ley Sobre el Mantenimiento del Orden y Seguridad Publica, Decree 5 (July 20, 1979).

164. Contras were being trained in Honduras, Costa Rica and Panama, and the U.S. was conducting anti-Nicaraguan activity in all six Central American countries. "[T]he plan was to split [Nicaragua] east-west by summer [1983], attack

from the north through Honduras and the south through Costa Rica, and be in Managua by Christmas." See, Woodward, *Veil: The Secret Wars of the CIA 1981-1987,* p. 257.

165. Ley de Tribunales Populares Anti-Somocistas, Decree 1233, (April 11, 1983).

166. During the revolution, block committees were established in each barrio to coordinate anti-Somoza activities. After the Sandinista victory in 1979, the FSLN expanded these committees, now known as Comites de Defensa Sandinista (CDS). Each neighborhood, and sometimes each block, has its own CDS. The committees were originally established as front-line civilian defense committees. They have been used as the organizing base for educational, literacy and health campaigns as well as serving as the political infrastructure for the FSLN.

167. *Nicaragua: Revolutionary Justice, A Report on Human Rights and the Judicial System,* p. 62-63.

168. See *Human Rights in Nicaragua, 1986,* pp. 91-92; also *Right to Survive, Human Rights in Nicaragua,* pp. 59-63. But compare this with an 79.9 percent conviction rate for criminal offenses in the United States District Courts in 1979, and a 78.2 percent conviction rate in 1980. (*Annual Report of the Director, 1980,* Administrative Office of the United States Courts, p. 97-98.

169. Americas Watch reported in 1986 that one TPA judge was a former government attorney; the president of the TPA was a former employee of the Ministry of Justice; one former TPA judge headed the criminal division of the Ministry of Justice; the previous president of the TPA was Director of Registry for the Ministry of Justice. *Human Rights in Nicaragua, 1986,* Americas Watch, pp. 93-94.

But this was defended by current Supreme Court Justice (and former Vice-Minister of the Ministry of Justice) Dra. Alba Luz Ramos by noting that there is a very small cadre of trained lawyers and judicial personnel in Nicaragua, and that the majority of them work for the Ministry of Justice. "The Ministry of Justice, since its formation in 1979, has been the creator of the juridical cadre; it is where new [legal] graduates from the University have been trained...Even in the United States, where there are many lawyers, functionaries come from the prosecutor's office and no one accuses them of a lack of autonomy." (Interview with Dra. Alba Luz Ramos, January 19, 1988, Managua, Nicaragua.)

170. But cf., comments of the CNPPDH, defending the use of lay judges in the TPA's by comparing them to jury selection techniques in the United States:

> The criticism of the lay element of the tribunals is the same that could be made of any jury court in the world. Suggestions that the TPAs are not trials by peers because the lay figures come from popular organizations is the same criticism that is often made of jury trials in the United States (names taken from voter registration lists, for example, skew the juries in favor of better-off and more stable elements of the society; the prosecution frequently uses FBI and other U.S. government dossiers on prospective jurors to disqualify those considered politically unreliable).

Boletin #7, CNPPDH, p. 15 (Parenthetical comments in original).

171. *Nicaragua: Revolutionary Justice, A Report on Human Rights and the Judicial System*, pp. 68-70.

172. "There is no pressure whatever against any of the students who work as public defenders for accused criminals before the TPAs," interview with Dr. Rafael Chamorro Mora, then Dean of the School of Law, University of Central America, Managua, July 15, 1987 (and currently Justice of the Supreme Court of Nicaragua).

"There is no pressure against the attorneys who represent the accused in the TPAs," interview with Dr. Nidia Barbosa, Director of the Bufete Popular (Defenders Office), School of Law, University of Central America, Managua, July 14, 1987.

173. *Nicaragua: Revolutionary Justice, A Report on Human Rights and the Judicial System*, p. 62. See also *Human Rights in Nicaragua: 1987*, p. 17.

174. "Defense attorneys do not have the resources to get from Managua to the remote regions to conduct an adequate defense," interview with Dr. Nidia Barbosa, Director of the Bufete Popular (Defenders Office), School of Law, University of Central America, Managua, Nicaragua, July 14, 1987.

175. *Nicaragua: Revolutionary Justice, A Report on Human Rights and the Judicial System*, p. 67.

176. "Since [public defenders] are working for nothing, often they would ask the family of the accused to pay a fee, and when the family couldn't or wouldn't, they would often just forget about the case. They would be given notice of [court] appearances, but they just wouldn't appear." Interview with Dra. Alba Luz Ramos, Supreme Court Justice, January 19, 1988, Managua, Nicaragua.

177. "In general, the system of public defenders doesn't work. The public defenders are overworked and not conscientious enough. This is true in both the regular court system and the TPAs." Interview with Dr. Nidia Barbosa, Director of the Bufete Popular (Defenders Office), School of Law, University of Central America, Managua, Nicaragua, July 14, 1987.

178. *Human Rights in Nicaragua, 1987*, pp. 15-18.

179. The state of emergency suspended the right to a speedy trial. Under Decree 1074, once the accused was arrested, the prosecution had unlimited time to investigate the case and prepare the prosecution. During this time, the arrestee remained in jail. The state of emergency was abolished in 1988.

180. see infra, pp. 205-206.

181. See, e.g., interview with Dr. Rodolfo Robelo, former Supreme Court Justice, January 20, 1988, Managua, Nicaragua.

182. "It is clear that there were probably some injustices under the TPAs." (Interview with Dr. Mariano Barahona, former Supreme Court Justice and current International Secretary, American Association of Democratic Jurists, January 28, 1988, Managua, Nicaragua.)

"I am absolutely sure that there are cases in which people have been convicted [in the TPAs] without proof...there are many cases that should be nullified...to undo the injustices that were committed." (Interview with Dr. Rodolfo Robelo, former Supreme Court Justice, January 20, 1988, Managua, Nicaragua.)

But cf., interview with Dra. Vilma Nuñez, former Supreme Court Justice and current Director of the CNPPDH (National Commission for the Promotion and Protection of Human Rights), July, 23, 1987, stating that such problems are no greater in the TPAs than in the regular system.

183. The establishment of the TPAs "was not desirable, but it was inevitable." Given the lack of resources available to the judicial branch when the TPAs were created in 1982, trying the contras "would have split the court system apart. Therefore [the creation of the TPAs] was necessary." (Interview with Dr. Alejandro Serrano, Chief Justice, Supreme Court of Nicaragua, January 27, 1988, Managua, Nicaragua.)

Only Dr. Rodolfo Robelo, former Supreme Court Justice, believed that the establishment of the TPAs "was not justified." He felt that, although the creation of the special tribunals in 1979 to try former Somocistas was justified, circumstances had changed by the time the TPAs were established in 1983 which would have permitted the regular court system to handle these cases. (Interview with Dr. Rodolfo Robelo, January 20, 1988, Managua, Nicaragua.)

184. "There shouldn't be TPAs. But one has to live in a state of war to understand the necessity for them.," interview with Dr. Rafael Chamorro Mora, then Dean of the Law School, University of Central America, and now Supreme Court Justice, July 15, 1987.

"The TPAs are legal, but they are not 100 percent just. Mistakes are made." interview with Dra. Nidia Barbosa, Director of the Bufete Popular (Defenders Office), School of Law, University of Central America, Managua, Nicaragua, July 14, 1987.

185. "The [Supreme Court] always pointed out that [the TPAs] had to be eliminated. We always maintained that position." (Interview with Dr. Alejandro Serrano, Chief Justice of the Supreme Court of Nicaragua, January 27, 1988, Managua, Nicaragua.)

186. Decree 296 (January 19, 1988) suspended the functioning of the TPAs; Decree 297 (January 19, 1988) lifted the State of Emergency. See, *Barricada,* January 19, 1988, p. 1.

187. Interview with Dr. Alejandro Serrano, Chief Justice of the Supreme Court of Nicaragua, January 27, 1988, Managua, Nicaragua.

188. *Amnesty International Report: 1988,* p. 127.

189. *Nicaragua: The Human Rights Record,* p. 25.

190. Since 30 years imprisonment is the maximum possible sentence under Nicaraguan law, this sentence is the equivalent of two consecutive life sentences in the United States: it guarantees that the defendant will serve the maximum permissible time behind bars.

191. *Nicaragua: The Human Rights Record,* p. 25.

192. *Human Rights in Nicaragua: Reagan, Rhetoric and Reality,* pp. 18-19; *Nicaragua: The Human Rights Record,* p. 25.

193. "Informe Estadistico del Trabajo de la Auditoría General de los FF.AA.SS. en el Primer Semestre del Año '87" ("Statistical Information on the Work of the Auditoría General of the Armed Forces in the First Half of 1987"), unpublished document, viewed by author at the Auditoría Militar, July 30, 1987.

194. 16 percent of officers convicted were sentenced to terms greater than 3 years; 9 percent of enlisted men convicted were sentenced to terms of greater than 3 years.

195. *Human Rights in Nicaragua: August 1987 to August 1988,* p. 99.

196. *Nicaragua: The Human Rights Record,* p. 24.

197. *Human Rights in Nicaragua: August 1987 to August 1988,* pp. 16-17.

198. Richard Boudreaux, "Managua Accuses 13 in Armed Forces of Murder," *Los Angeles Times*, August 25, 1989, p. 8.
199. See *Amnesty International, Country Reports*, for the years 1981 through 1986.
200. *Amnesty International Report: 1982*, p. 160.
201. *Ibid.*
202. Gilbert, Dennis, "The Bourgeoisie," in Walker, Thomas, ed., *Nicaragua: The First Five Years*, p. 175.
203. *Amnesty International Report: 1983*, p. 159.
204. Interview with Dr. Mariano Barahona, former Justice of the Supreme Court of Nicaragua, and currently International Secretary of the American Association of Democratic Jurists, Managua, Nicaragua, January 28, 1988.
205. *Nicaragua: The Human Rights Record*, p. 21.
206. *Amnesty International Report: 1988*, p. 126.
207. *Human Rights in Nicaragua: August 1987 to August 1988*, p. 79.
208. *Amnesty International Report: 1988*, pp. 125-126.
209. *Human Rights in Nicaragua: August 1987 to August 1988*, p. 80.
210. *Ibid.*, p. 11.
211. *Ibid.*, p. 9.
212. *Ibid.*, p. 11.
213. "Nicaragua Releases 1,894 Former National Guardsmen," *New York Times*, March 18, 1989, p. 1.
214. Constitution of the Republic of Nicaragua, Title IV, Chapter 1, Art. 45.
215. Constitution of the Republic of Nicaragua, Title X, Chapter 1, Articles 185 and 186.
216. See, e.g., European Convention on Human Rights, Art. 15; American Convention on Human Rights, Art. 4.
217. *Nicaragua: The Human Rights Record*, p. 18.
218. Interview with Dr. Alejandro Serrano, Chief Justice of the Supreme Court of Nicaragua, by the National Lawyers Guild, January 26, 1988, Managua, Nicaragua.
219. Interview with Justice Humberto Obregón, Criminal Court of Appeals for Managua, January 28, 1988, Managua, Nicaragua.
220. This author tends to doubt the figures presented by Justice Obregón. If these figures are correct, then the two justices on the criminal panel for the Managua Court of Appeals are processing 10 *habeas corpus* petitions daily—a quantity of work which, in addition to the regular work of the Appeals Court, would be virtually impossible. Moreover, 5,000 *habeas corpus* petitions in one year from a population (in Managua) of 1,000,000 means that 1 out of 200 residents of Managua had not only been arrested during the past year, but had actually filed a *habeas corpus* petition. Reporters and long-time residents of Managua with whom I spoke felt that these figures could not possibly be correct.
221. Decree 559 (October 28, 1980); Decree 1074 (July 6, 1982).
222. *Nicaragua: Revolutionary Justice*, p. 98.
223. Interview with Dr. Mariano Barahona, former Justice of the Supreme Court of Nicaragua, and currently International Secretary of the American Association of Democratic Jurists, Managua, Nicaragua, January 28, 1988.
224. *Nicaragua: Revolutionary Justice*, pp. 96-102.

225. Interview with Dr. Alejandro Serrano, Chief Justice of the Supreme Court, January 27, 1988, Managua Nicaragua.

226. *Violations of the Laws of War by Both Sides in Nicaragua, 1981-1985,* p. 85.

227. The Reagan Administration has accused the Sandinistas of "genocide" against the Miskito Indians. Then-United Nations Ambassador Jeanne Kirkpatrick stated that 250,000 Miskitos (this is several times the total Miskito population in Nicaragua) had been herded into concentration camps. In February, 1982, then-U.S. Secretary of State Alexander Haig exhibited a photograph showing what he claimed were Miskito bodies being burned after a 'massacre' by the Sandinista government, and accused the Nicaraguan government of "atrocious genocidal actions." It was later verified that the photograph was taken four years earlier, and showed Red Cross workers burning the bodies of victims massacred by Somoza during the uprising leading to the 1979 Revolution. See, "French Rightist Paper Admits Misuse of Picture," *New York Times,* March 3, 1982, p. 5; See also, *Report on the Relocation of Miskito Indians by the Nicaraguan Government in Light of International Laws and Standards,* pp. 21-22.

Although widely reported in the American press at the time, stories of "genocide" and "massacres" (with the exception of the Leimus incident, supra, pp. 186-188) have proven unfounded. The OAS Inter-American Commission on Human Rights could not substantiate the "loss of life during the [Miskito] relocation, with which the Government had been initially accused." "Report on the Situation of Human Rights of a Segment of the Nicaraguan Population of Miskito Origin," OAS Inter-American Commission on Human Rights, May 16, 1984, p. 129. Americas Watch reported "no evidence of widespread 'disappearances'...Miskitos interviewed at the settlements also denied any killings by the Sandinista forces." *The Miskitos in Nicaragua: 1981-1984,* pp. 17-18.

228. *Report on the Relocation of Miskito Indians by the Nicaraguan Government in Light of International Laws and Standards,* p. 28.

229. *On Human Rights in Nicaragua,* May 1982, pp. 59-60.

230. *Critique: Review of the Department of State's Country Reports on Human Rights Practices for 1984,* p. 80.

231. *The Miskitos in Nicaragua: 1981-1984,* p. 20.

232. *Human Rights in Nicaragua: August 1987 to August 1988,* pp. 95-97.

233. *Critique: Review of the Department of State's Country Reports on Human Rights Practices for 1984,* p. 80; *The Miskitos in Nicaragua: 1981-1984,* pp. 19, 22.

234. The relocation of the Miskito Indians compares quite favorably with the relocation of Vietnamese villagers under the "pacification program" during the Vietnam War; the relocation of Japanese-Americans on the West Coast of the United States during World War II, (See, infra, pp. 91-97); and the "Trail of Tears"—the relocation of Cherokee and other American Indian peoples under the Indian Removal Act of 1829, when 25,000 Native Americans died during a forced march from their homes in Georgia to reservations in Oklahoma.

235. UNHCR, *Refugees,* December 1988, p. 39.

236. For a general account of the Nicaraguan penal system and penalogical methods, see "Las Carceles y La Justicia en Nicaragua," *Envio* Vol. 5, No. 64, October 1986.

237. *Human Rights in Nicaragua: 1986,* p. 102.

238. *Ibid.*, p. 103.

239. *Ibid.*

240. *Right to Survive: Human Rights in Nicaragua*, pp. 64-65. See also *Envio*, Vol 5, No. 64, October 1986.

241. *Human Rights in Nicaragua: August 1987 to August 1988*, p. 51.

242. The existence of "chiquitas" was denied by Tomás Borge, Minister of Interior, in response to a question from the author during an interview in Matagalpa, July 17, 1987. Nonetheless, reports of their use in a prison in Esteli continued. This was brought to the attention of Borge by journalist Mark Cook in the Fall of 1987. Three weeks later, the head of the prison in Esteli was demoted, and the use of the 'chiquitas' apparently ended.

243. See supra, pp. 189-190.

244. *Amnesty International Report: 1988*, p. 126.

245. *Human Rights in Nicaragua: August 1987 to August 1988*, p. 51 (parenthesis in original).

246. *Ibid.*, pp. 58-59.

247. See e.g., *Boletin*, #7, p. 13, *Human Rights in Nicaragua: 1987*, p. 7; *Human Rights in Nicaragua*, 1986, pp. 112-113.

248. *Nicaragua en Cifras, 1985*, pp. 32-33.

249. "The First 3,000 Days: Revolution in Review," *Envio*, Volume 6, Number 73, July 1987, p. 36.

250. *Right to Survive: Human Rights in Nicaragua*, p. 31.

251. *Ibid.*

252. "The First 3,000 Days: Revolution in Review," *Envio*, Volume 6, Number 73, July 1987, p. 38.

253. *Ibid.*

254. "Gunmen Murder 3 in Nicaragua," *New York Times*, August 3, 1980, p. 6.

255. Bassing, Tom, "Slow Death in Nicaragua," *San Francisco Chronicle*, Nov. 21, 1988, p.A13.

256. "The First 3,000 Days: Revolution in Review," *Envio*, Volume 6, Number 73, July 1987, p. 25.

257. *See, e.g.*, Bennett, "Nicaragua's Crisis: Economy, Long in Decline, Now Seen Plunging Toward Paralysis," *The Boston Globe*, Feb 1, 1988, p. 1.

258. *Barricada*, July 20, 1987, p. 1.

259. At the unofficial rate of exchange, this would be less than $200,000.

260. *Barricada*, July 8, 1986.

261. Interview with Dr. Alejandro Serrano, Chief Justice of the Supreme Court of Nicaragua, January 22, 1988, Managua, Nicaragua.

262. "One U.S. resident in Nicaragua commented, 'If the police behaved here [in Managua] as they do in New York, we would be horrified.'" *Right to Survive*, p. 72.

Bibliography

A Political Opening in Nicaragua: Report on the Nicaraguan Elections of November 4, 1984, Washington Office on Latin America, Washington, D.C., December 11, 1984.

Abrams, Floyd, "Freedom of Press Revisited in its Historical Context," *New York Law Journal*, p. 19, Jan 25, 1982.

Abstract of the Laws of the American States, Now in Force, Relative to Debts Due to Loyalists, Subjects of Great Britain, London, 1789.

American Principles Sacrificed: U.S. Foreign Policy in Central America, Report of a Fact-Finding Mission to El Salvador and Nicaragua, Unitarian Universalist Service Committee, 1983.

Amnesty International Report: 1966-1967, Amnesty International, London, 1967.

Amnesty International Report: 1967-1968, Amnesty International, London, 1968.

Amnesty International Report: 1968-1969, Amnesty International, London, 1969.

Amnesty International Report: 1970-1971, Amnesty International, London, 1971.

Amnesty International Report: 1972-1973, Amnesty International, London, 1973.

Amnesty International Report: 1973-1974, Amnesty International, London, 1974.

Amnesty International Report: 1974-1975, Amnesty International, London, 1975.

Amnesty International Report: 1975-1976, Amnesty International, London, 1976.

Amnesty International Report: 1977, Amnesty International, London, 1978.

Amnesty International Report: 1978, Amnesty International, London, 1979.

Amnesty International Report: 1979, Amnesty International, London, 1980.

Amnesty International Report: 1980, Amnesty International, London, 1981.

Amnesty International Report: 1981, Amnesty International, London, 1982.

Amnesty International Report: 1982, Amnesty International, London, 1983.

Amnesty International Report: 1983, Amnesty International, London, 1984.

Amnesty International Report: 1984, Amnesty International, London, 1985.

Amnesty International Report: 1985, Amnesty International, London, 1986.

Amnesty International Report: 1986, Amnesty International, London, 1987.

Amnesty International Report: 1988, Amnesty International, London, 1988.

Annual Report of the Director, 1980, Administrative Office of the United States Courts, Washington, D.C., 1980.

Annual Report of the Inter-American Commission on Human Rights, 1985-1986, Organization of American States, Washington, D.C., 1986.

Babington, Anthony, *For the Sake of Example, Capital Courts-Martial, 1914-1920*, Secker & Warburg Ltd., London, 1983.

Background Paper: Nicaragua's Military Build-Up and Support for Central American Subversion, United States Department of State and Department of Defense, Washington, D.C., 1984.

Balbus, Isaac D., *The Dialectics of Legal Repression: Black Rebels before the American Criminal Courts*, Russell Sage Foundation, New York, 1973.

Belknap, Michael R., *Cold War Political Justice: The Smith Act, the Communist Party, and American Civil Liberties*, Greenwood Press, Westport, Connecticut, 1977.

Bell, Derrick, *And We Are Not Saved: The Elusive Quest for Racial Justice*, Basic Books, Inc., New York, 1987.

_____, *Race, Racism and American Law*, Little, Brown and Co., Boston, 1980.

Berman, Jerry J., Halperin, Morton H. and Shattuck, John H.F., *Controlling the FBI: American Civil Liberties Union Testimony on Charter Legislation before the Senate Judiciary Committee*, April 25, 1978, ACLU, New York.

Biddle, Francis, *Civil Liberties and the War*, address before the Junior Bar Conference, Philadelphia, Pennsylvania, broadcast over Mutual Broadcasting Co., September 10, 1940.

_____, *The Fear of Freedom*, Doubleday & Co., New York, 1951.

Boletin #7, Comisión Nacional de Promoción y Protección de los Derechos Humanos, mimeograph, Managua, Nicaragua, June 1986.

Boyer, Richard O. and Morais, Herbert M., *Labor's Untold Story*, United Electrical, Radio & Machine Workers of America, New York, 1955.

Bradley, A. G., *Colonial Americans in Exile: Founders of British Canada*, E.P. Dutton & Co., New York, 1932.

Brennan, William J. Jr., "The Quest to Develop a Jurisprudence of Civil Liberties in Times of Security Crises," speech given before the Law School of Hebrew University, Jerusalem, Israel, December 22, 1987.

Broken Promises: Sandinista Repression of Human Rights, United States Department of State, October, 1984.

Brownlie, Ian, ed., *Basic Documents on Human Rights*, Clarendon Press, Oxford, 1981.

_____, *International Law and the Use of Force by States*, Clarendon Press, Oxford, 1963.

Burns, E. Bradford, *At War in Nicaragua: The Reagan Doctrine and the Politics of Nostalgia*, Harper and Row, New York, 1987.

C.P.D.H. Report on the Situation of Human Rights in Nicaragua, Puebla Institute, New York, October 1987.

Calhoon, Robert McCluer, *The Loyalists in Revolutionary America, 1760-1781*, Harcourt Brace Jovanovich, New York, 1965.

Carroll, Thomas F., "Freedom of Speech and of the Press in the Federalist Period: The Sedition Act," 18 *Michigan Law Review* 615 (1920).

_____, "Freedom of Speech and of the Press in War Time: The Espionage Act," 17 *Michigan Law Review* 621 (1919).

Caute, David, *The Great Fear: The Anti-Communist Purge under Truman and Eisenhower*, Simon & Schuster, New York, 1978.

_____, *The Year of the Barricades: A Journey Through 1968*, Harper & Row, New York, 1988.

Censorship in Times of Crisis, Civil Liberties Committee of Massachusetts, 1941.

Censorship of Comic Books, American Civil Liberties Union, New York, 1955.

Chafee, Zechariah Jr., "Book Review: American Visa Policy and Foreign Scientists," 101 *University of Pennsylvania Law Review* 903 (1953).

_____, *Free Speech in the United States*, Athenaeum Press, New York, 1969.

_____, *Freedom of Speech*, Harcourt, Brace and Co., New York, 1920.

_____, "Statement in Opposition to a Bill...Entitled 'To Protect the U.S. Against Un-American and Subversive Activities'," 1950.

_____, *The Blessings of Liberty*, J.B. Lippincott Co., Philadelphia, 1956.

_____, *The Censorship in Boston*, Civil Liberties Committee of Massachusetts, Boston, 1930.

_____, "The Encroachments on Freedom," *Atlantic Monthly*, May, 1956.

Chenery, William Law, *Freedom of the Press*, Harcourt, Brace and Co., New York, 1955.

Chevigny, Paul G., "Politics and Law in the Control of Local Surveillance," 69 *Cornell Law Review* 735 (1984).

Childs, Marquis W., *The Erosion of Individual Liberties*, St. Louis Post Dispatch Reprint, 1961.

Chomsky, Noam, "Is Peace at Hand?," *Zeta* Magazine, January, 1988.

_____, *et al.*, *Trials of the Resistance*, New York Book Review, New York, 1970.

Christenson, Ron, *Political Trials: Gordian Knots in the Law*, Transaction Books, New Brunswick, New Jersey, 1986.

"Church-State Relations: A Chronology Part I," *Envio*, Volume 6, Number 77, Central American Historical Institute, Managua, Nicaragua, November 1987.

"Church-State Relations: A Chronology Part II," *Envio*, Volume 6, Number 78, Central American Historical Institute, Managua, Nicaragua, December 1987.

Churchill, Ward and Vander Wall, Jim, *Agents of Repression: The FBI's Secret War against the Black Panther Party and the American Indian Movement*, South End Press, Boston, 1988.

Civil Liberties and National Defense, American Civil Liberties Union, New York, 1941.

Clark, Grenville, *The Limits of Free Expression: A Lecture at the Association of the Bar of the City of New York*, May 23, 1939.

Country Reports on Human Rights Practices for 1986, United States Department of State, February 1987.

Cover, Robert M., "The Left, the Right and the First Amendment: 1918-1928," 40 *Maryland Law Review* 372 (1981).

Critique: Review of the Department of State's Country Reports on Human Rights Practices for 1984, Americas Watch, Helsinki Watch and Lawyers Committee for International Human Rights, New York, May 1985.

Critique: Review of the Department of State's Country Reports on Human Rights Practices for 1986, The Watch Committees and Lawyers Committee for Human Rights, New York, April 1987.

Daniels, Roger, *The Decision to Relocate the Japanese Americans*, J.B. Lippincott Co., Philadelphia, 1975.

Davis, William Watson, *Studies in History, Economics and Public Law, Vol. LII: The Civil War and Reconstruction in Florida*, Columbia University Press, New York, 1913.

Demac, Donna A., *Liberty Denied: The Current Rise of Censorship in America*, PEN American Center, New York, 1988.

Dershowitz, Alan, *The Best Defense*, Random House, New York, 1982.

Digest of the Public Record of Communism in the United States, Fund for the Republic, New York, 1955.

Donner, Frank J., *The Age of Surveillance: The Aims and Methods of America's Political Intelligence System,* Alfred A. Knopf, New York, 1980.

_____, *The Un-Americans,* Ballantine Books, New York, 1961.

Drinnon, Richard, *Keeper of Concentration Camps: Dillon S. Myer and American Racism,* University of California Press, Berkeley, 1987.

Dutcher, Mary, *Nicaragua, Violations of the Laws of War by Both Sides. First Supplement: January-March 1986,* Washington Office on Latin America, Washington, D.C., 1986.

Edgar, Harold and Schmidt, Benno C. Jr., "The Espionage Statutes," 73 *Columbia Law Review* 929 (1973).

Elias, Robert, *The Politics of Victimization: Victims, Victimology and Human Rights,* Oxford University Press, New York, 1986.

Emerson, Thomas I., "National Security and Civil Liberties," 9 *Yale Journal of World Public Order* 78 (April 1982).

Fisher, Steve, "The Sandinista Record: Toward Totalitarianism or Participatory Democracy?," mimeographed paper, presented at the 1985 Annual Meeting of the American Political Science Association, New Orleans, Louisiana, August 29-Sept. 1, 1985.

Fleming, Walter Law, *Documentary History of Reconstruction: Political, Military, Social, Religious & Industrial, 1865 to the Present Time,* Vol. I, Arthur C. Clark Co., Ohio, 1906.

Flick, Alexander Clarence, *Studies in History, Economics and Public Law,* Vol. XIV, No. 1: "Loyalism in New York during the American Revolution," Columbia University Press, New York, 1901.

Freedom of Expression and Assembly in Nicaragua During the Election Period, An Americas Watch Report, New York, December 1984.

"Freedom of Speech: How Does it Differ in Other Countries," news story, *Los Angeles Daily Journal,* p. 3, May 19, 1980.

Gastil, Raymond D., *Freedom in the World: Political Rights and Civil Liberties, 1983-1984,* Greenwood Press, Westport, Connecticut, 1984.

Girdner, Audrie and Loftis, Anne, *The Great Betrayal: The Evacuation of the Japanese-Americans During World War II,* The MacMillan Co., London, 1969.

Glick, Brian, *War at Home: Covert Action Against U.S. Activists and What We Can Do About It,* South End Press, Boston, 1989.

Goldstein, Robert Justin, *Political Repression in Modern America, from 1870 to the Present,* Schenkman Publishing Co., Cambridge, Massachusetts, 1978.

Goodell, Charles, *Political Prisoners in America,* Random House, New York, 1973.

Gottschalk, Jack A., " 'Consistent with Security'...A History of American Military Press Censorship," 5 *Communications & Law* 35 (Summer 1983).

Gunns, Albert F., *Civil Liberties in Crisis: The Pacific Northwest, 1917-1940,* Garland Publishing, Inc., New York, 1983.

Hallin, Daniel C., *The "Uncensored War": The Media and Vietnam,* Oxford University Press, New York, 1986.

Halperin, Morton H., *et al., The Lawless State: The Crimes of the U.S. Intelligence Agencies,* Penguin Books, New York, 1976.

Halstead, Fred, *Out Now: A Participant's Account of the American Movement Against the War in Vietnam,* Monad Press, New York, 1978.

Handbook of Existing Rules Pertaining to Human Rights in the Inter-American System, Inter-American Commission on Human Rights, Organization of American States, Washington, D.C., 1983.

Harriman, Edward A., "Confiscation of Enemy Private Property," 3 *Boston University Law Review,* 156 (1923).

Harris, Isaac Samuel, *Loyalism in Virginia,* Duke University Press, 1926.

Hartman, Joan F., "Derogation from Human Rights Treaties in Public Emergencies," 22 *Harvard International Law Journal* 1 (Winter 1981).

Hayden, Tom, *Reunion: A Memoir,* Random House, New York, 1988.

Hellman, Lillian, *Scoundrel Time,* Little, Brown, and Co., Boston, 1976.

Herman, Edward S., and Chomsky, Noam, *Manufacturing Consent: The Political Economy of the Mass Media,* Pantheon Books, New York, 1988.

Hoffman, Paul, "The Man Who Loves Only Numbers," *The Atlantic,* Volume 260, No. 5, November 1987.

Hough, Charles M., "Law in War Time 1917," 31 *Harvard Law Review* 692 (1917).

Human Rights: A Compilation of International Instruments, United Nations Publication, New York, 1983.

Human Rights in Nicaragua, An Americas Watch Report, New York, April 1984.

Human Rights in Nicaragua, November 1982 Update, An Americas Watch Report, New York, 1982.

Human Rights in Nicaragua: 1985-1986, An Americas Watch Report, New York, March 1986.

Human Rights in Nicaragua: 1986, An Americas Watch Report, Washington, D.C., February 1987.

Human Rights in Nicaragua: 1987, Lawyers Committee for Human Rights, November 1987.

Human Rights in Nicaragua: August 1987 to August 1988, An Americas Watch Report, New York, August 1988.

Human Rights in Nicaragua: Reagan, Rhetoric and Reality, An Americas Watch Report, New York, July 1985.

Human Rights in Nicaragua Under the Sandinistas: From Revolution to Repression, Department of State Publication 9467, Washington, D.C., December 1986.

"Human Rights in Times of War," *Envio,* Vol. 5, No. 60, Central American Historical Institute, Managua, Nicaragua, June, 1986.

"Human Rights: Nicaragua's Record," *Envio,* Volume 6, Number 76, Central American Historical Institute, Managua, Nicaragua, October 1987.

Hyman, Harold M., *To Try Men's Souls: Loyalty Tests in American History,* University of California Press, Berkeley and Los Angeles, 1959.

Iklé, Fred C. and Wohlstetter, Albert, "Discriminate Deterrence: Report of The Commission on Integrated Long-Term Strategy," Memorandum to the Secretary of Defense and the Assistant to the President for National Security Affairs, January 11, 1988.

In the Shadow of War: The Story of Civil Liberty, 1939-40, American Civil Liberties Union, New York, 1940.

In Time of Challenge: U.S. Liberties, 1946-47, American Civil Liberties Union, New York, 1947.

Informe de la Comisión Permanente de Derechos Humanos en Nicaragua, Nicaragua, 1982.

Irons, Peter, *Justice at War,* Oxford University Press, New York, 1983.

Irons, Peter H., " 'Fighting Fair': Zechariah Chafee, Jr., the Department of Justice, and the 'Trial at the Harvard Club'," 94 *Harvard Law Review* 1205 (1981).

Jaffe, Louis Law, "The Right to Travel: The Passport Problem," 35 *Foreign Affairs* 17 (October 1956).

Johansen, Bruce and Maestas, Roberto, *Wasi'chu: The Continuing Indian Wars,* Monthly Review Press, New York, 1979.

Kahn, David, *The Codebreakers: The Story of Secret Writing,* MacMillan Co., New York, 1967.

Kalven, Harry Jr., "The Supreme Court," 85 *Harvard Law Review* 3 (1971).

Katsiaficas, George, *The Imagination of the New Left: A Global Analysis of 1968,* South End Press, Boston, 1987.

Kittrie, Nicholas N. and Wedlock, Eldon D. Jr., *The Tree of Liberty: A Documentary History of Rebellion and Political Crime in America,* The Johns Hopkins University Press, Baltimore, 1986.

Klare, Michael T., and Kornbluh, Peter, eds., *Low-Intensity Warfare: Counterinsurgency, Proinsurgency and Anti-Terrorism in the Eighties,* Pantheon Books, New York, 1988.

Kleeger, James David, "The First Amendment, the Press and the U.S. Invasion of Grenada: Balancing the Constitutional Interests," 12 *Western State University Law Review* 217 (1984).

Knoll, Erwin, "National Security: The Ultimate Threat to the First Amendment," 66 *Minnesota Law Review* 161 (1981).

Koffler, Judith Schenck and Gershman, Bennett Law, "The New Seditious Libel," 69 *Cornell Law Review* 816 (1984).

Kohn, Stephen M., *Jailed for Peace: The History of American Draft Law Violators, 1658-1985,* Greenwood Press, Westport, Connecticut, 1986.

Kutler, Stanley I., *The American Inquisition: Justice and Injustice in the Cold War,* Hill and Wang, New York, 1982.

"La Prensa Returns to Nicaragua's Streets Unrepentant, and Just as Unconstructive," mimeograph, Managua, Nicaragua, November 1987.

Lahav, Pnina, ed., *Press Law in Modern Democracies: A Comparative Study,* Longman, New York, 1985.

"Las Carceles y la Justicia en Nicaragua," *Envio,* Vol. 5, No. 64, Instituto Historico Centroamericano, Managua, Nicaragua, October 1986.

Laverty, Paul, "Report on Interview with Mr. Sofonias Cisneros Leiva," unpublished manuscript, May 13, 1987.

Lawrence, Thomas A., "Eclipse of Liberty: Civil Liberties in the United States during the First World War," 21 *Wayne Law Review* 35 (1974).

Leamer, Laurence, *The Paper Revolutionaries: The Rise of the Underground Press,* Simon & Schuster, New York, 1972.

Levy, Leonard W., *Jefferson and Civil Liberties: The Darker Side,* Harvard University Press, Cambridge, Massachusetts, 1963.

_____, *Legacy of Suppression: Freedom of Speech and Press in Early American History,* Harvard University Press, Cambridge, Massachusetts, 1964.

Linde, Hans A., "Courts and Censorship," 66 *Minnesota Law Review* 171 (1981).

Linfield, Michael, Book Review, 1 *Harvard Human Rights Yearbook*, 349 (Spring 1988).

Lockhart, William B., Kamisar, Yale, Choper, Jesse H. and Shiffrin, Steven H., *Constitutional Law: Cases, Comments, Questions*, Sixth Edition, West Publishing Co., St. Paul, Minnesota, 1986.

Los Derechos Humanos en Nicaragua: Informe, Asociación pro Derechos Humanos de España, Madrid, May, 1984.

Lyons, Louis M., ed., *Reporting the News: Fifty-One Articles on the Practice & Problems of Journalism from the Magazine of the Nieman Fellows*, Harvard University Press, Cambridge, Massachusetts, 1965.

Massing, Michael, "Who Are the Sandinistas?," *The New York Review of Books*, Volume XXV, Number 8, May 12, 1988.

Memorandum on Restrictions of Press Freedom in the United States, Submitted to Senate Subcommittees on Constitutional Rights, Daily Worker, New York, mimeograph, November 21, 1955.

Menke, B. W., *Martial Law—Its Use in Case of Atomic Attack*, Industrial College of the Armed Forces, Washington, D.C., 1955-56.

Mestral, Armand de, *The Limitation of Human Rights in Comparative Constitutional Law*, Les Editions Yvon Blais Inc., Quebec, Canada, 1986.

Mitgang, Herbert, *Dangerous Dossiers: Exposing the Secret War Against America's Greatest Authors*, Donald I. Fine, Inc., New York, 1988.

Mock, James R., and Larson, Cedric, *Words that Won the War: The Story of The Committee on Public Information, 1917-1919*, Princeton University Press, Princeton, 1939.

Muñoz, Carlos, *Youth, Identity, Power: The Chicano Movement*, Verso, London, 1989.

Murphy, Paul L., *World War I and the Origin of Civil Liberties in the United States*, W.W. Norton & Co., New York, 1979.

Myrick, Rawson C., *State Papers of Vermont: Sequestration, Confiscation and Sale of Estates*, Vol. Six, State of Vermont, 1941.

Nelson, William H., *The American Tory*, Clarendon Press, Oxford, 1961.

Nicaragua: Comment, Catholic Institute for International Relations, London, 1987.

Nicaragua: Comments on the Nicaraguan Government's Report to the U.N. Human Rights Committee, Lawyers Committee for International Human Rights, New York, March 1983.

Nicaragua en Cifras, Instituto Nacional de Estadisticas y Censos, Managua, Nicaragua, July 1986.

Nicaragua: Revolutionary Justice, A Report on Human Rights and the Judicial System, Lawyers Committee for International Human Rights, New York, April 1985.

Nicaragua: The Human Rights Record, Amnesty International, London, March 1986.

"Note: The Expatriation Act of 1954," 64 *Yale Law Journal* 1164 (1955).

"Note, The First Amendment and National Security: The Constitutionality of Press Censorship and Access Denial in Military Operations," 17 *New York University Journal of International Law and Policy* 369.

"Note: Freedom of Speech and of the Press—Resolution of the Missouri Bar Association," 2 *Illinois Law Bulletin* 440 (Feb. 1920).

"Note: Government Exclusion of Foreign Political Propaganda," 68 *Harvard Law Review* 1393 (1955).

O'Reilly, Kenneth, *Hoover and the Un-Americans: The FBI, HUAC, and the Red Menace,* Temple University Press, Philadelphia, 1983.

On Human Rights in Nicaragua, An Americas Watch Report, New York, May 1982.

Paul, Arnold M., *Conservative Crisis and the Rule of Law: Attitudes of Bar and Bench, 1887-1895,* Cornell University Press, Ithaca, New York, 1960.

Peck, Abe, *Uncovering the Sixties: The Life and Times of the Underground Press,* Pantheon Books, New York, 1985.

Peck, C. F., *A Brief Statement Concerning Claims for Captured or Abandoned Property, with an Appendix containing Acts of Congress, Proclamations of the President, and the Decisions of the Supreme Court,* Judd & DeWeiler, Washington, D.C., 1873.

Peck, Epaphroditus, *Tercentenary Commission of the State of Connecticut, Vol XXX, I: The Loyalists of Connecticut,* Commission on Historical Publications, Yale University Press, New Haven, 1931.

Pincus, Roger W., "Press Access to Military Operations: Grenada and the Need for a New Analytical Framework," 135 *University of Pennsylvania Law Review* 813 (March 1987).

Political Prisoners in Federal Military Prisons, National Civil Liberties Bureau, New York, 1918.

Refugees, United Nations High Commissioner for Refugees, Geneva, Switzerland, December 1988.

Report on the Relocation of Miskito Indians by the Nicaraguan Government in Light of International Laws and Standards; The Role of the United States Government in Creating the Conditions which Required the Relocation, and Subsequent Developments on the Atlantic Coast, International Justice Fund, Los Angeles, 1985.

Resource Book: Sandinista Elections in Nicaragua, United States Department of State, Washington, D.C., 1984.

Revista Juridica por la Libertad con las Armas del Derecho y la Justicia, No. 1, La Barra de Abogados de Nicaragua, Managua, Nicaragua, July 1, 1987.

Right to Survive: Human Rights in Nicaragua, Catholic Institute for International Relations, London, 1987.

Rips, Geoffrey, *The Campaign Against the Underground Press,* PEN American Center Report, City Lights Books, San Francisco, 1981.

Rogin, Michael Paul, *Ronald Reagan, The Movie,* University of California Press, Berkeley, 1987.

Rostow, Eugene V., "The Japanese American Cases—A Disaster," 54 *Yale Law Journal* 489 (June 1945).

Schreuer, Christoph, "Derogation of Human Rights in Situations of Public Emergency: The Experience of the European Convention on Human Rights," 9 *Yale Journal of World Public Order* 113 (April, 1982).

Serrano Caldera, Alejandro, "Estado de Derecho," speech before the V Congreso Nicaragüense de Ciencias Sociales, mimeograph, Managua, Nicaragua, October 1986.

Shattuck, John, "The Constitution in Crisis: Covert Action and the National Security Act of 1947," speech given at Harvard Law School, April 26, 1988.

Situación de Los Derechos Humanos en Nicaragua, Comisión Permanente de Derechos Humanos de Nicaragua, mimeograph, Managua, Nicaragua, April 1987.

Sklar, Holly, *Washington's War on Nicaragua*, South End Press, Boston, 1988.

Smith, James Morton, *Freedom's Fetters: The Alien and Sedition Laws and American Civil Liberties*, Cornell University Press, Ithaca, New York, 1956.

Stammer, Neil, *Civil Liberties in Britain During the 2nd World War: A Political Study*, St. Martin's Press, New York, 1983.

State Political Prisoners, 1924, American Civil Liberties Union, New York, 1924.

Stern, Mark David, "A New Constitution for Nicaragua," *The National Law Journal*, January 19, 1987.

Stoler, Peter, *The War Against the Press: Politics, Pressure and Intimidation in the 80's*, Dodd, Mead & Co., New York, 1986.

Summers, Robert E., *Wartime Censorship of Press and Radio*, H.W. Wilson Co., New York, 1942.

tenBroek, Jacobus, Barnhart, Edward N., and Matson, Floyd W., *Prejudice, War and the Constitution*, University of California Press, Berkeley, 1968.

The Bill of Rights in War-Time, American Civil Liberties Union, New York, 1942.

"The First 3,000 Days: Revolution in Review," *Envio*, Volume 6, Number 73, Central American Historical Institute, Managua, Nicaragua, July 1987.

The McCarran Act, Civil Liberties Union of Massachusetts, Boston, October, 1951.

The Miskitos in Nicaragua: 1981-1984, An Americas Watch Report, New York, November 1984.

The Nation-Wide Spy System Centering in the Dept. of Justice, American Civil Liberties Union, New York, 1924.

The National Guard and the Constitution: An ACLU Legal Study, American Civil Liberties Union, New York, 1971.

The Police and the Radical, American Civil Liberties Union, New York, 1921.

The Post Office Ban on "Revolutionary Age," American Civil Liberties Union, New York, 1931.

The Smith Act and the Supreme Court, American Civil Liberties Union, New York, 1952.

The State of Civil Liberty in 1923, American Civil Liberties Union, New York, 1924.

The Testimony of Sofonias Cisneros Lieva, Comisión Permanente de Derechos Humanos, San José, Costa Rica, May 1985.

The States and Subversion, American Civil Liberties Union, New York, 1953.

The Virginia and Kentucky Resolutions of 1798 and '99, with Jefferson's Original Draught Thereof. And Madison's Report, Calhoun's Address, Resolutions of the Several States in Relation to State Rights. With Other Documents in Support of the Jeffersonian Doctrines of '98. Published by Jonathon Elliot, Washington, D.C., May 1832.

Theoharis, Athan G., ed., *Beyond the Hiss Case: The FBI, Congress, and the Cold War*, Temple University Press, Philadelphia, 1982.

Thurman, Judith, "A Reporter at Large: Dry Season," *The New Yorker*, March 14, 1988.

Trading With the Enemy Act: Hearing before the Committee on Interstate and Foreign Commerce of the House of Representatives, Government Printing Office, Washington, D.C., 1920.

"Triunfo de Nicaragua en la Haya," *Envio*, Vol. 5, No. 61, Instituto Historico Centroamericano, Managua, Nicaragua, July 1986.

U.S. Senate Committee on Government Operations, *National Emergencies Act Report to Accompany S. 3957*, Report 93-1136, U.S. Government Printing Office, Washington, D.C., 1974.

U.S. Senate Committee on the Judiciary, 89th Congress, 1st Session, *Internal Security and Subversion: Principal State Laws and Cases*, U.S. Government Printing Office, Washington, D.C., 1965, reprinted by Da Capo Press, New York, 1971.

U.S. Senate Special Committee on National Emergencies and Delegated Emergency Powers, *Interim Report*, U.S. Government Printing Office, Report 93-1170, Washington, D.C., September 24, 1974.

Van Tyne, Claude Halstead, *The Loyalists in the American Revolution*, Peter Smith, New York, 1929.

Vidal, Gore, *Burr*, Random House, New York, 1973.

_____, *Lincoln*, Ballantine Books, New York, 1984.

Violations of the Laws of War by Both Sides in Nicaragua, 1981-1985, An Americas Watch Report, New York, 1985

Volkman, Ernest, and Baggett, Blaine, *Secret Intelligence: The Inside Story of America's Espionage Empire*, Doubleday, New York, 1989.

Walker, Thomas W., ed., *Nicaragua: The First Five Years*, Praeger Publishers, New York, 1985.

_____, *Reagan versus the Sandinistas: the Undeclared War on Nicaragua*, Westview Press, Boulder, Colorado, 1987.

War and the Bill of Rights, 1942, American Civil Liberties Union, New York, 1942.

Wilcox, Clair, ed., *Civil Liberties Under Attack*, University of Pennsylvania Press, Philadelphia, 1951.

Woodward, Bob, *Veil: The Secret Wars of the CIA 1981-1987*, Pocket Books, New York, 1987.

Woodward, C. Vann, "Reconstruction: America's Unfinished Revolution, 1863-1877," *The New York Review of Books*, Volume XXV, Number 8, May 12, 1988.

Wormuth, Francis D. and Firmage, Edwin B., *To Chain the Dog of War: The War Power of Congress in History and Law*, Southern Methodist University Press, Dallas, Texas, 1986.

Yoshpe, Harry B., *Disposition of Loyalist Estates in Southern New York*, Columbia University Press, New York, 1939.

Case Index

Abrams v. United States, 51, 52, 54
Adler v. Board of Education, 108, 110
Afroyim v. Rusk, 83 at n. 77
Agee v. Vance, 161 at n. 24
Albertson v. Subversive Activities Control Board, 231 at n. 261
Alliance to End Repression v. Rochford, 139 at n. 158
Aptheker v. Secretary of State, 155
Association of the Bar of the City of New York v. Sacher, 78 at n. 56

Baggett v. Bullitt, 110 at n. 258
Bailey v. Richardson, 84, 85 at n. 89
Beilan v. Board of Public Education, 109 at n. 238
Benton v. Maryland, 113 at n. 4
Bond v. Floyd, 153 at n. 230
Brandenburg v. Ohio, 239 at n. 235
Butler v. United States, 98 at n. 170

Clark v. Dulles, 105 at n. 214
Coalition Against Police Abuse v. Board of Police Commissioners, 139 at n. 159
Cohen v. California, 155 at n. 241
Cole v. Richardson, 85 at n. 94
Colyer v. Skeffington, 57 at n. 148, 58 at n. 149
Commonwealth v. Stotland, 123 at n. 61
Communist Party of the United States v. Subversive Activities Control Board, 231 at n. 261
Communist Party of the United States v. United States, 110 at n. 261
Couchois v. United States, 98 at n. 170
Cramer v. United States, 97 at n. 164

Dakota Coal Co. v. Fraser, 56 at n. 141
Davis v. Massachusetts, 220 at n. 197
Debs v. United States, 51 at n. 102, 52
DeJonge v. Oregon, 67 at n. 206
Dennis v. United States, 77, 78
Duncan v. Kahanamoku, 92
Duncan v. Louisiana, 113 at n. 6
Dunne v. United States, 77 at n. 36

Elfbrandt v. Russell, 110 at n. 259
Ex parte Endo, 95
Ex parte Jackson, 64 at n. 182
Ex parte McCardle, 30 at n. 29

Index